BRICKS, BUILDINGS AND TRA

A history of Mark Gentry, the Hedingham red brick
road and rail transport

by

Adrian Corder-Birch

with photographs, photo restoration and illustrations by Christine Walker

MARK GENTRY (1851-1912)

An Essex Brickmaker and Builder

To Patrick,
With very best wishes
from
Adrian Corder-Birch
October 2013.

Published by Adrian Corder-Birch
Rustlings
Howe Drive
Halstead
Essex
CO9 2QL

Email: corder-birch@lineone.net

Printed by The Lavenham Press Limited
Arbons House
47 Water Street
Lavenham
Suffolk
CO10 9RN

ISBN 978-0-9567219-1-4

Further copies of this book are available from the Author/Publisher as above

Price £14.95 plus postage and packing

Cheques and postal orders in English pounds sterling, payable to Adrian Corder-Birch

CONTENTS

AUTHOR'S PREFACE

Following the success of my previous book, *'Our Ancestors Were Brickmakers and Potters, A history of the Corder and related families in the clayworking industries'*, published in 2010, I decided to write another book about local brickmakers, using more of the information and illustrations, which I have collected during the last forty five years.

This book is principally a history of Mark Gentry, a Stratford builder and contractor, who became a master brickmaker, owning two brickworks in Sible Hedingham. These were the Langthorne Brick Works at Wethersfield Road and the Highfields Brick Works near Purls Hill. He lived at Rookwoods and later at Grove House, both in Sible Hedingham. At Rookwoods he constructed a number of buildings, which are now listed and are excellent examples of ornamental brickwork.

On the national scene he was a member and later chairman of the Institute of Clayworkers. The Institute was established by Greville Montgomery, who also lived in Sible Hedingham during the early 1900s and later became Member of Parliament for Bridgwater. He founded The British Clayworker magazine and arranged the Building Trades Exhibitions in London at which Mark Gentry was one of many exhibitors. They were both active in the development of Sible Hedingham with Mark Gentry building two terraces of industrial houses in Wethersfield Road and Greville Montgomery owning the land, which was developed as Alexandra Road and a major part of Swan Street. Mark Gentry also built four houses in Nunnery Street, Castle Hedingham.

As a builder and later a brickmaker, Mark Gentry built and supplied bricks for many large buildings in and around London, particularly at Stratford, East and West Ham. He built the Guildhall School of Music on the Victoria Embankment and supplied the bricks for Claridge's Hotel and many churches and schools. He even exported 'Hedingham reds' to Ireland, Egypt and Africa. The majority of bricks were transported by rail along the Colne Valley and Halstead Railway. He supported the proposed construction of the Central Essex and other Light Railways but they were never built.

Mark Gentry married Jane Glover, whose nephew later lived at Hilton House in Sible Hedingham. This was previously the home of John Hilton and later his son Charles Augustus Hilton, who were both master brickmakers and farmers in the village. They were proprietors of brickworks at Southey Green and Alderford Farm respectively. Mark Gentry's Highfields Brick Works and the adjacent Hedingham Brick Company owned by Eli Cornish at Purls Hill were combined in 1919 to form The Sible Hedingham Red Brick Company Limited, which was principally controlled by members of the Ripper family, who also owned the extensive joinery works in the village. The Langthorne Brick Works closed in 1911 and in 2006 part of the site was the subject of an archaeological excavation, which is briefly described in this book.

Whilst a few of the brickworks, which the Cornish family were associated with have been referred to, I intend to write a book about this well known brickmaking family including the Hedingham Brick Company. This forthcoming book will also contain a detailed history of the Maiden Ley Brick Works at Castle Hedingham, which was owned by the Rayner family.

The craft of brickmaking by hand is briefly described on page 11 of *'Our Ancestors Were Brickmakers and Potters'* and therefore it is not repeated in this book. Although the use of abbreviations has been kept to a minimum a short list appears on page 172. Measurements are recorded in the imperial and not the metric system and similarly all amounts are pre-decimal. For a glossary of terms please see pages 147 to 149 of *'Our Ancestors Were Brickmakers and Potters'* but there is a short glossary of additional terms on page. There is also a detailed bibliography, sources, notes and references section, which corresponds with the numbered sequence in each chapter where the reference numbers are enclosed in brackets.

Whilst I have carried out extensive research to compile this book one important item has proved elusive. It is recorded that Mark Gentry published a number of catalogues to advertise his bricks, including one *"elaborate"* catalogue of 60 pages containing some 6,000 examples of brickwork and other catalogues in three parts but despite wide enquiries no copies of any of these catalogues have been traced. If any reader can inform me of the location of any of these catalogues or of any additional information or illustrations I should be most grateful.

Adrian Corder-Birch

Rustlings
Howe Drive
Halstead
Essex CO9 2QL

4th January 2013

ACKNOWLEDGEMENTS

In common with my earlier book, *'Our Ancestors Were Brickmakers and Potters, a history of the Corder and related families in the clay working industries'* much of the information for this book has been collected over many years. Therefore it is very sad to recall that several contributors have passed away since I commenced this work, namely:

Beatrice and Wilfred Birch (my late parents), Clive Boreham, Edith E. M. (May) Corder (of Sible Hedingham), (Herbert) Charles Corder (of Bocking), Percy and Edith E. Corder (of Sible Hedingham), Sarah Corder (my grandmother), Walter and Ethel Corder (of Castle Hedingham), William D. Corder (of Sible Hedingham), Margery Foster (nee Corder) and Bertram Hogarth (my father in law). Harry (Higgler) Broyd, John (Jack) Cornell, Tim Heffernan, Lewis Hamilton Joscelyne, M.B.E., Sir Ronald Long, Kt., David Possee, George H. Rayner (last owner of Maiden Ley Brick Works, Castle Hedingham) and Mary Rayner (his sister), William Raynham, Albert Redgewell, senior (burner at The Sible Hedingham Red Brick Company Limited) and his son Albert Redgewell, junior, Norman Ripper, Stephen Ripper, Ellen Ruffle, Dixon Smith, Alfred J. (Arkie) Spurgeon, Edgar J. (Ned) Spurgeon and Stanley Springett.

I have also received information and photographs from the following:

Paul Belton, Charles Bird, Enid M. Neville Bird, Cleone Branwhite, Ashley Cooper, Tony Crosby, Brian Day, Dr. Fiona Denny, J.P., David Drury, Peter Drury, Dr. Norman Edwards, M.B., Nick Ellis, Brian Fleming, John and Michael Glover, Robin A. Harding, William Heffernan, Alison and Steven Horne, Paul James, Malcolm Marjoram, M.A., Peter and Tony Minter (of Bulmer Brick Works), Norman Page, David Pannell, Frederick W. Pawsey, D.F.C., J.P., Keith Pilgrim, Major Michael Portway, T.D., Doreen Potts, Andrew Putnam, Shirley Radley, Frances Ripper, Peter and Sandra Robinson, Alf Ruffle, Arthur Ruffle, Jenny Ruffle, Richard Shackle (former Librarian), Robin Waywell and Angela Weatherley.

I am particularly grateful to my late friend, Andrew Leech, Executive Director of the National Home Improvement Council, for the history of the Montgomery Worldwide companies contained in appendix two.

The photographs used were copied by John Abbott, Kenneth Stanhope, Christine Walker, the late Harry Cole and the late Arthur Morgan, to all of whom I would like to express my appreciation.

I have carried out research in the Essex Record Office, Colchester Central Library, Newham Library at Stratford and the National Archive Office whose archivists, librarians and staff were always most helpful. The maps were copied from originals at the Essex Record Office, Colchester Central Library and the Map Room at the British Museum, later transferred to the British Library. Members of the Archaeology Section (as it then was) of Essex County Council have assisted, notably Shane Gould, Adam Garwood and Laura Belton.

I would particularly like to record my appreciation to Dave Osborne, Geoffrey Root and Liz Tolfts and other former staff at the 'Halstead Gazette' for allowing me to peruse back copies of this very informative newspaper. These are now in the care of Doreen Potts who has kindly continued to allow access to this valuable resource.

I also wish to record my thanks to current and former members of the British Brick Society and the Brick Section of the British Archaeological Association for information and support, particularly to Dr. Patrick Crouch, Michael Hammett, Dip. Arch., A.R.I.B.A., David H. Kennett, B.A., M.Sc., Ann Los, Graeme Perry, Pat Ryan, M.A., Terence Paul Smith and the late Bill Blowers and Martin Hammond.

The following have graciously given permission to reproduce illustrations; Malcolm Root, F.G.R.A., for his painting on the front cover and the photograph on page . Peter and Sandra Robinson for photographs of Rookwoods and Brian Day for the loan of other photographs. The late Stephen Ripper kindly gave permission to reproduce five family photographs from "Recollections of an old Woodpecker" and Kenneth Stanhope and Braintree District Museum for photographs in chapter 16. The Essex Record Office for various maps and documents, the British Museum, the British Library and Colchester Central Library for the remaining maps. I am also grateful to the British Library Board for permission to reproduce illustrations from the British Clayworker and the Brickbuilder held at the British Library Newspaper Library.

I should like to record my grateful thanks to my wife, Pam, for her support, encouragement and help, and to my sister, Christine Walker, for her expertise with photography, photo restoration and copying illustrations to enhance this book. Pam has also read the proofs and suggested many helpful improvements, which have been much appreciated.

Finally, I should like to thank Dr. James Bettley, for writing the splendid Foreword, and for using his specialist knowledge to make some valuable comments on the architectural aspects of this book.

ADRIAN CORDER-BIRCH

11th March 2013.

FOREWORD
by
Dr. James Bettley, Ph.D., F.S.A.,

Architectural historian who revised the Essex volume of The Buildings of England by Sir Nikolaus Pevsner in 2007 and is Chairman of the Chelmsford Diocesan Advisory Committee for the Care of Churches.

Driving into Sible Hedingham from the direction of Great Yeldham, just after passing Hedingham School, the motorist may spot, out of the corner of the eye, an intriguing-looking red brick building on the other side of the road. Closer inspection reveals a gable with a sort of urn finial, and some rather fancy brickwork, including panels depicting vases of flowers.

The size and style of the building clearly indicates that it is an entrance lodge, and anyone with a normal sense of curiosity will want to follow the fingerpost pointing towards 'Rookwoods' to find our more. He or she will be rewarded, not so much perhaps by the house itself, which is a nice enough Regency mansion of gault brick, but by the red brick buildings in its grounds that clearly belong to the same era as the lodge, because they too make much use of ornamental brick and other decorative features.

The explanation for this outbreak of architectural exuberance is that Rookwoods was, from 1885 to 1894, the home of Mark Gentry, master brickmaker and owner of two brickworks in Sible Hedingham. When adding new cottages and stables to his property he no doubt wanted to use the opportunity to advertise his firm's wares. As a result, these buildings - now listed as being nationally important and of special interest - are the most obvious visible reminders of Gentry's brickworks.

Now, however, thanks to Adrian Corder-Birch's meticulous research, we know a great deal more about Mark Gentry's life and career, and have a much fuller picture of his legacy. In particular, he emerges as a character of much more than purely local interest. He began as a builder in Stratford, briefly branching out - improbably, and unsuccessfully - into the manufacture of celluloid collars and cuffs. As a contractor he was involved in the construction of a number of important London buildings, including the City of London's Central Market and the Guildhall School of Music.

In 1884 he entered the brickmaking business, and it is for this that he will be principally remembered. His bricks are to be found in buildings not just in the immediate neighbourhood of Sible Hedingham, but as far afield as Egypt and Ireland. Three million of his bricks were used by the Great Central Railway in the construction of their stations and other buildings. The Blackwall Tunnel and Claridge's Hotel are faced with the finest products of Gentry's brickworks.

Adrian Corder-Birch's history of Mark Gentry's life and work is a significant contribution to the story of Essex's industrial past in general and brickmaking in particular, and will help to ensure that this important aspect of the county's heritage is better known and more widely celebrated.

James Bettley
March 2013

Descendants of Joseph Gentry

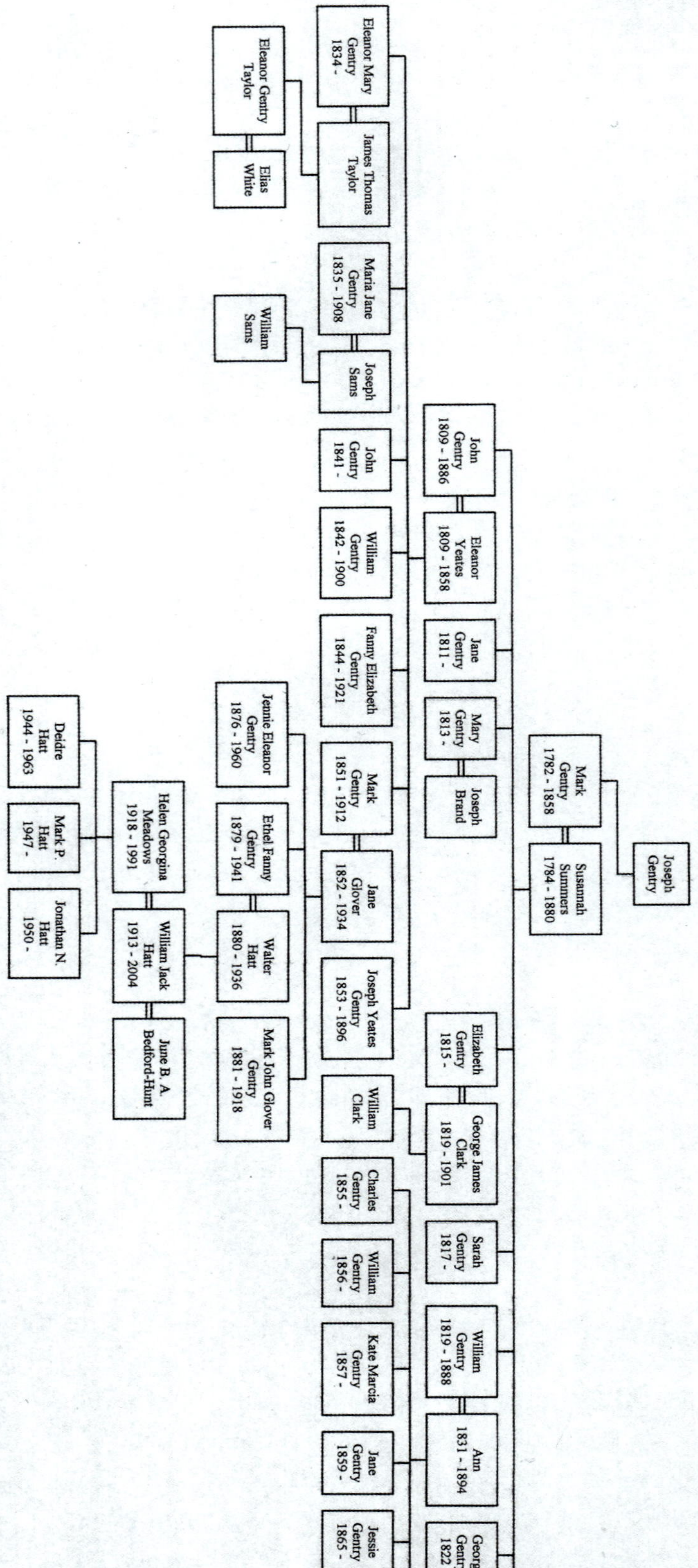

Chapter 1

THE GENTRY FAMILY

During the eighteenth century the Gentry family lived at Bocking where the first Mark Gentry (1782-1858) was born on 3rd November 1782. He was baptized on 30th November 1782 at Bocking Church and was the son of Joseph Gentry. (1)

Mark married Susannah Summers (c1784-1880) on 27th April 1808 at St. Laurence Church, Upminster, Essex. (2) They moved to Rainham, a south Essex village, where their children were born and baptized between 1809 and 1824 as follows:

John Gentry, born 1st February and baptized 26th February 1809
Jane Gentry, born 3rd January and baptized 3rd February 1811
Mary Gentry, baptized 4th April 1813
Elizabeth Gentry, baptized 14th May 1815
Sarah Gentry, baptized 11th May 1817
William Gentry, baptized 9th May 1819
George Gentry, baptized 9th June 1822
James Gentry, baptized 9th June 1822
Frances Gentry, baptized 31st October 1824 (3)

Mark was buried at Rainham on 6th May 1858 aged 75 years and his widow, Susannah, was also buried at Rainham on 22nd April 1880 aged 96 years. (4) She was one of the oldest inhabitants of Rainham when she died on 14th April 1880.

Several members of the Gentry family remained in Rainham throughout the nineteenth century where some of them were bakers. By 1851 Mark was a master baker employing three men. (5) Following the death of Mark in 1858, his son William (1819-1888) continued his father's business as a baker. When William died in 1888, his widow Ann Gentry continued the bakery, which ceased upon her death in 1894. Their son Charles Gentry, born 1855, was also a baker circa 1889.

Mark's eldest son John Gentry (1809-1886) who was born on 1st February 1809 at Rainham married Eleanor Yeates (1809-1858) on 6th March 1833 at St. Botolph's Without, Aldgate in the City of London. (6) John and Eleanor had the following children:

Eleanor Mary Gentry, born 1834, married James Thomas Taylor and their only daughter Eleanor Gentry Taylor married Elias White in June 1883.
Maria Jane Gentry (1835-1908) was baptized on 18th October 1835 at Rainham and married Joseph Sams. Their son William Sams, became a pawnbroker and was executor to Fanny Elizabeth Gentry who died in 1921.
John Gentry (1841-1901)
William Gentry (1842-1900)
Fanny Elizabeth Gentry (1844-1921)
Mark Gentry (1851-1912)
Joseph Yeates Gentry (1853-1896)

In 1835 John was recorded as a schoolmaster living at Rainham but he had been taught the trade of a baker by his father and by the late 1830s had become a master baker and also a corn dealer at Stratford. By the 1860s he was an Overseer for the Stratford Ward of West Ham Parish. His initial premises were at Stratford Broadway and by 1851 the business moved to The Grove also at Stratford. That year he employed two men, (7) which increased to six men and two boys by 1871 (8) including his second son William Gentry (1842-1900). However by 1886 William was a wine merchant at 50 Broadway, Stratford. The youngest son Joseph Yeates Gentry (1853-1896) became an ironmonger at 112 The Grove, Stratford. (9)

The younger sons, Mark and Joseph did not follow the family trade of becoming bakers and choose different careers. It is the middle son, Mark Gentry (1851-1912) who became a master builder, contractor, timber merchant, farmer and brickmaker who is the main subject of this book. He was born 2nd April 1851 at The Grove, Stratford and was only seven years old when his mother died. He married Jane Glover (1852-1934) on 11th March 1875 at St. Paul's Church, Stratford when he was 24 years of age, a bachelor and his occupation was a builder. Jane Glover was 23 years old, a spinster, living at The Grove, Stratford and was a daughter of Richard Glover, a coach proprietor. At the time of their marriage Mark was living at 14 Saxon Road, North Bow, London. (10)

They had three children, two daughters and a son. (For further information about their son, Mark John Glover Gentry (1881-1918), please see chapter 17)

The eldest daughter was Jennie Eleanor Gentry (1876-1960). She was born on 4th April and baptized on 3rd May 1876 at St. Paul's Church, Stratford, where her parents had married the previous year. At the time of Jennie's baptism her parents were still living at 14 Saxon Road, North Bow. (11) Jennie lived with her parents at Stratford and Sible Hedingham and later with her mother at Clacton on Sea and Reading. Jennie was for some years, dispenser to Dr. Henry Joseph Twamley, physician and surgeon of Sible Hedingham. She lived latterly at Cherry Tree Cottage, Park Lane, Langham, Essex. She died on 27th November 1960 aged 84 years and was buried in Sible Hedingham Churchyard on 1st December 1960. (12) Her executors were her nephew, William Jack Hatt, a company director and Hannah Frances Eileen Twamley, known as Eileen, the daughter of Dr. H. J. Twamley. The Gentry and Twamley families were friends for over sixty years.

The youngest daughter was Ethel Fanny Gentry (1879-1941) who was born on 9th October 1879. She was baptized on 31st October 1879 at St. John's Church, Stratford, by which time her parents had left 14 Saxon Road, North Bow and were living at 1 Buxton Villas, Leytonstone Road, Stratford. (13) Ethel married Walter Hatt (1880-1936) in 1911 at Paddington, London. Walter was employed by Messrs. Balls & Balls, Auctioneers and Land Agents at Castle Hedingham and by 1905 lodged with Mr. & Mrs. Charles Everitt in their newly built house in Alexandra Road, Sible Hedingham. (See Chapter 14) He later became a farmer at Bottom Farm, Chickendon, Oxfordshire. They had one son, William Jack Hatt (1913-2004) who was the only grandchild of Mark Gentry.

Chapter 2

MARK GENTRY. HIS LIFE AND PUBLIC POSITIONS

Upon completing his education, Mark Gentry entered the building trade in which he made good progress, becoming a foreman by the age of 20. In 1878 he established his own building business in Stratford, which he continued until 1892. (See chapter 4)

In 1884 he became interested as a promoter, shareholder and director in the London Impermeable Collar and Cuff Company Limited, which had its factory at Bower Road, Victoria Park, London E. The objects of this company were to make celluloid impermeable collars and cuffs and other articles for domestic use. Its registered office was at Langthorne House, West Ham Lane, Stratford until March 1885 when it was changed to 2 Wormwood Street, London EC, which was the address of Mark Gentry's London office and also that of the Hedingham Brick and Tile Works. The London Impermeable Collar and Cuff Company Limited was not a success, it made losses and was voluntarily wound up in 1887. (1)

In that year Mark Gentry became a shareholder in the West Ham Press Company Limited, steam printers and the publishers of the West Ham Guardian and East Ham Leader newspaper, which operated from The Grove, Stratford and from 524 Mile End Road, London E. The first directors were Mark Gentry, G. W. Courtney, Captain Thomas E. Jones, Major Wickens and Richard Wortley Maylin, a coffee merchant of West Ham who was the managing director and first chairman. Its registered office was at Langthorne Works, West Ham Lane, Stratford until 19th January 1888 when it was changed to 156 The Grove, Stratford. (2) The company was incorporated on 6th July 1887 and when it failed in 1888 Mark Gentry purchased the business and became the registered proprietor of the newspaper, the publication of which he continued until December 1890 when he sold the concern. (3)

Broadway, Stratford during the Edwardian era as Mark Gentry would have known it

Mark Gentry took a prominent part in the municipal life of West Ham, where he stood as a candidate in the Stratford Ward of the newly created Borough of West Ham in October 1886 to which he was successfully elected. He gave his address as Langthorne House, West Ham Lane, Stratford, (4) although he was actually living in Sible Hedingham. However in March 1889 he tendered his resignation after serving two and a half years of a three year term. The authority decided to impose a penalty of £25 against him as he had not completed his term. However his resignation left him free to tender for extensive drainage works, which were to be undertaken in West Ham. (5)

Upon moving to Sible Hedingham in 1885, Mark Gentry took a significant interest in everything appertaining to the welfare of the inhabitants of the two Hedinghams. He was of a generous nature, being ready and willing to assist any deserving object with his support and purse, especially on such occasions as Queen Victoria's Golden Jubilee Celebrations in 1887 and her Diamond Jubilee Celebrations in 1897. In May 1887 he joined the Committee to make arrangements for the Golden Jubilee. On Diamond Jubilee Day, 22nd June 1897, the members of the Constitutional Club sat down to a capital dinner in the Assembly Rooms at 12.30. The excellent spread was arranged by Mark Gentry who also provided a substantial meal for the children of his work people who came in afterwards. He also contributed prizes for winners in the sports competitions and supplied a large number of fireworks, which later in the evening made a magnificent display. In 1902 he was also active in connection with the Coronation celebrations for King Edward VII and Queen Alexandra. At the conclusion of the celebrations £24 remained in the funds and at a meeting held in July 1902 to consider the best means of disposing of this balance it was proposed by Mark Gentry that a piece of land containing 5½ acres should be procured as a Recreation Ground for the parish. This land was situate on the Alexandra Estate and owned by H. Greville Montgomery (See chapter 13) who was willing to sell it for £80. (6) Unfortunately the scheme did not proceed at that time, but 25 years later in 1927 the subsequent owner, Arthur Frank Gibson, conveyed the land to Sible Hedingham Parish Council for the Recreation Ground. (See chapter 14)

In 1887 Mark Gentry was one of the founders of the Joshua Nunn Lodge of Freemasons in Halstead of which he became Master and Provincial Grand Superintendent of Works for Essex. (7) In October 1888 he was installed as Worshipful Master of the Lodge. Interest in the proceedings was enhanced by the presence of The Rt. Hon. The Lord Brooke of Easton Lodge, Dunmow, the Right Worshipful Provincial Grand Master. At the ceremony Mark Gentry presented the Lodge with a handsome banner. (8) When The Colne Valley Chapter (attached to the Joshua Nunn Lodge) was founded, Mark Gentry was one of the founder members. The Chapter was consecrated on 23rd May 1891 when Companion Mark Gentry was elected as an Officer of the Chapter namely 2nd Assistant Sojourner. At the first regular meeting on 24th July 1891 he made a gift of a 'Set of Robes for Principals' and in 1899 was elected as First Principal of the Chapter for the year 1899-1900. In February 1908 he resigned from the Chapter, which was much regretted by the Companions. (9)

On 5th November 1888, being Guy Fawkes' day, he arranged a fireworks display at Rookwoods. This was on a very extensive scale and all the children from the neighbouring schools were invited to his grounds to watch. (10)

During 1888 Mark Gentry purchased the Assembly Rooms, (11) house and premises at Swan Street from Norval Dobson Hunt, who was landlord of the Bell Public House opposite. The Assembly Rooms were erected by Norval Hunt during 1886 for use by organisations and residents in the village. Mark Gentry continued the use of the Assembly Rooms for the community as a Public Hall and it was later used by the Constitutional Club, the Working Men's Club and as the Oddfellows Hall. He immediately enlarged it and made improvements including doubling the width of the entrance door and having the main hall match-boarded, stained and varnished. At the far end an elliptical archway was erected, which formed the front of a stage 12 feet deep, supplied with footlights, drop curtains, wings and scenery. From the stage a doorway led into two dressing rooms, one of which was opened as a reading room and library. The rooms were heated with hot water, the fittings for which were installed by Portway and Son of Halstead. The hall was lit by Wenham lights and the ventilation supplied by Tobin shafts and a lantern in the roof. (12) In c1910 ownership of the Assembly Rooms was transferred by Mark Gentry to the Loyal Webster Lodge of Oddfellows. (13)

In October 1888, Mark Gentry decided to stand at the first election to Essex County Council the following year. In his letter to electors he stated, inter alia, *".....my connection with the Corporation of West Ham and other public bodies has given me a fair insight into Local Government."* (14) A meeting in support of his candidature for the Hedingham Division was held in the Assembly Rooms, with a large and enthusiastic audience. Richard Glover of West Ham presided and spoke highly of Mark Gentry's suitability for the work of the County Council from experience of the excellent work done by him on the Town Council of West Ham. (15) In December 1888 a meeting took place at Earls Colne under the chairmanship of Reuben Hunt regarding the new County Councils, being established under the Local Government Act 1888. A special train was arranged for electors to travel from Hedingham Station to Ford Gate (later named Earls Colne) Station. Reuben Hunt introduced the three candidates for the Hedingham Division namely Vero Taylor, Harris Hills and Mark Gentry. Reuben was careful not to favour any one candidate and gave a balanced view of all three. He spoke highly of Vero Taylor having worked with him on the Board of Guardians and he thought Mark Gentry was very able and business-like though not so well known. Harris Hills he knew to be a careful, thoughtful and hardworking man who always tried to carry anything he undertook to a successful conclusion. (16)

At the election Mark Gentry was unsuccessful and the result was as follows:

Mark Gentry	269
Harris Hills	408
Vero William Taylor J.P.,	519

It must be remembered that Mark Gentry had only lived in Sible Hedingham for four years at the time of the election and his opponents were well known and had long standing connections in the area.

However in 1894 Mark Gentry was elected as one of the Sible Hedingham representatives on the Halstead Board of Guardians and Rural District Council on which he served for fifteen years until resigning in July 1909. At the March 1907 election he was top of the poll, the result being as follows:

Mark Gentry, brick manufacturer	154 elected

Eli Cornish, brick manufacturer	148 elected
E. P. Barnard, farmer	138 elected
Frederick George Bishop, junior, miller	135 not elected
William John Rayner, brick manufacturer	63 not elected (17)

Mark Gentry's election card when he stood for Halstead Rural District Council and Board of Guardians in 1907 and was elected at the top of the poll

He became a member of Sible Hedingham Parish Council when it was formed in 1894 and was Chairman from 1898 until 1907 having succeeded Vero William Taylor, J.P., who was the first Chairman from 1894 until 1898. For some years Mark Gentry was one of the five representatives from Sible Hedingham Parish Council on the Joint Fire Brigade Committee with Castle Hedingham Parish Council and was Chairman of this Committee from 1903 to 1905. In 1904 Walter Hatt, later his son in law, became Secretary of this Committee and Robert Balls was captain of the Fire Brigade. From 1904 until September 1909 Mark Gentry was the Parish Council's representative on the Sible Hedingham Primary School Managing Body. He was also an Overseer for Sible Hedingham and a Churchwarden at Sible Hedingham Church. At the Parish Council elections in 1896 a contemporary report stated: *"At Sible Hedingham, where there has been a considerable commotion Mark Gentry whose name figured conspicuously in connection with the election, was returned at the top of the poll."* (18) The results were as follows:

Mark Gentry, brick manufacturer	58
John Drury, innkeeper	44
John Coe, innkeeper	39
Vero William Taylor, maltster	38
Frederick George Bishop, miller	37
Joseph Scott Hale, farmer	33
Henry Joseph Twamley, surgeon	32
George Malcolm, retired army colonel	31
John Baldwin, farmer	26

The above were elected but in addition there were three unsuccessful candidates.

In April 1886 a meeting was held in the British Schoolroom at Castle Hedingham to discuss the desirability of forming a Working Men's Club. Vero Taylor presided, Henry Ranger (19) was secretary and a committee of twenty members was elected, to try and purchase a field of about six acres between Castle and Sible Hedingham upon which to erect a large hall to contain reading, smoking, refreshment rooms and a library, with the field to be laid out for cricket and other games. Mark Gentry promised to take 100 shares, to supply the bricks at cost price and to give his services as architect. (20) The project did not proceed but in 1889 the 'Hedingham Working Men's Club' was formed with the Rev. Henry Warburton as President. Mark Gentry provided the Assembly Rooms for use by the Working Men's Club. In January 1890 at the first annual dinner of the club held in the Assembly Rooms, Mark Gentry who was Chairman was elected as President in succession to the Rev. Warburton. (21) Mark Gentry stated that he hoped more working men would join and also farmers and agricultural labourers. One speaker said he was astounded at the transformation effected in the parish by Mark Gentry. He had done much to break down class feeling in the neighbourhood. The speaker thought the district owed a debt of deep gratitude to Mark Gentry for the notable work he had done and was doing. (22) When the Working Men's Club was later absorbed into the Loyal Webster Lodge of Oddfellows he became a member as did other master brickmakers including Harry Corder and Eli Cornish. (23)

In February 1889 Mark Gentry attended a meeting in Colchester in connection with the proposed amalgamation of the Essex and Suffolk Equitable Fire Insurance Society with Alliance Insurance, which was rejected. (24) In 1898 he became a shareholder of The

British Clayworkers' Mutual Insurance Corporation Limited (see appendix three) when he purchased 50 shares at £10 each. He retained these shares until his death when they were inherited by his family who continued to own them until the company was wound up in 1952. (25)

During the 1890s Mark Gentry allowed the Sible Hedingham Football Club the free use of a meadow in Wethersfield Road. The captain was Robert Lewis Webb, one of his employees. (See chapter 9) Mark Gentry was concerned for the welfare of all his employees for example on Easter Monday 1889 he provided dinner for 66 workmen at the White Horse Inn. At the conclusion his manager, Orbell Cornish, thanked Mr. Gentry and described him as a most generous employer. (26) At Christmas 1889 he supplied his *"work people"* with beef for their Christmas dinner. In January 1891 Mark Gentry generously distributed a large quantity of soup to all the families of the men employed by him and contemplated further distributions during the season. (27)

When the Halstead Bank Holiday Gala was held at Dynes Hall, Great Maplestead, the seat of Viscount Deerhurst, (28) in August 1903 the arrangements were made by Mark Gentry. At the conclusion, Charles Wing Gray, Member of Parliament for Saffron Walden, thanked Lord and Lady Deerhurst and Mark Gentry. He thanked one and all on behalf of Lord and Lady Deerhurst for having turned out in their thousands. He continued by saying that Mark Gentry who always did things on a large scale, would no doubt have him say millions. The success of the gathering had been mainly due to the enormous energy of Mark Gentry who they knew so well. *"Good old brick"* shouted someone in the crowd. *"Yes"* added his Lordship, taking up the point, *"bricks and mortar are strong stuff and they usually stand where other things fall"*. There is no doubt that Viscount Deerhurst said this with some knowledge. He had a most varied career and at one time his travels took him to America where his Lordship worked for a time as a bricklayer and claimed that he could lay 1,000 bricks a day. In 1926 his Lordship made use of this experience to protest with some authority against the Bricklayers' Union rule that no member should lay more than 350 bricks a day. (29)

In common with many other master brickmakers, Mark Gentry was a staunch Conservative and was President of the Sible Hedingham branch. In January 1891 he was chairman of a dinner for 350 people held at Halstead Town Hall in connection with the Conservative Working Men's Club. It was reported in 1898 that at the time of an earlier election he told his employees if the Conservatives did not win they need not come to work the following day. At a dinner held at Sible Hedingham in the Conservative interest in February 1898, Mark Gentry said that he had raised the wages in the district more than any man had ever done but he was often hauled over the coals for it by the farmers. (30) The Hedingham Constitutional Club was formed on 19th October 1895 and operated from the Assembly Rooms, owned by him. By 1899 the Club had one hundred members with Mark Gentry as President, Vero W. Taylor, J.P. Hon., President, Charles Wing Gray, M.P., Vice President, Dr. Henry Twamley, Treasurer, Mark Gentry, junior, Hon. Secretary and William Willett, Steward. (31)

Mark Gentry actively supported the candidature of Charles Wing Gray, the Conservative and Unionist candidate for the Saffron Walden Division. During one election campaign on 13th October 1900 a wagonette in which Charles Wing Gray and Mark Gentry were travelling was attacked upon entering Helions Bumpstead by about twenty men throwing stones. They attempted to stop the horses, cut the traces and took the wheels off the wagonette. Charles Wing Gray, Mark Gentry, their coachman and two other occupants were struck. The lamps were smashed, the wagonette and an accompanying carriage were damaged and the horses were cut. (32) Another account of this incident states that Mark Gentry was struck with stones three times and that H. Greville Montgomery, Charles Wing Gray junior and Dr. Henry Twamley were also present.

At the annual dinner of the Hedingham Constitutional Club held in the Assembly Rooms in December 1900, Mark Gentry presided. H. Greville Montgomery who was a Vice President of the Club stated that as a Liberal he had great pleasure in voting and working for Charles Wing Gray because he thought he was the best man. (33) By 1899 Charles Wing Gray was farming Hostage Farm, Sible Hedingham where he employed Thomas Pilgrim as his farm bailiff. (34)

In January 1910, Robert Balls, the Castle Hedingham estate agent, whilst speaking at a political meeting regarding Tariff Reform compared the condition of Sible Hedingham with what it was twenty years earlier when Mark Gentry was carrying on a flourishing business in the brickmaking trade. Every week a large amount of money was spent in wages and houses could not be obtained for the work people to live in. He stated that ought to be enough to make some of them support home industries by voting for Tariff Reform. At the January 1910 General Election, Col. Douglas James Proby, the Conservative candidate for the Saffron Walden constituency defeated the sitting Liberal member, Joseph Albert Pease with a majority of 272. When news of the Conservative victory reached Castle and Sible Hedingham, a number of supporters met Mark Gentry at the railway station on his return home. They gained possession of the carriage, which was waiting for him, they took out the horse and dragged the vehicle to his residence at Grove House a distance of just over one mile. (35)

When Ulick Burke owned Rookwoods there was a 'Rookwoods Cricket Club', which played in the grounds. When Mark Gentry purchased Rookwoods he was unable to allow the Club to use his grounds but offered £10 towards the preparation of another ground. The Club agreed that although they would no longer play at Rookwoods the name should be retained. A new ground was found on a meadow belonging to L. Smith, the Club Captain, at a rent of £3 3s 0d a year. In 1885 Rev. Henry Warburton succeeded Ulick Burke as President of the Club and in 1889 Mark Gentry succeeded the Rev. Warburton when it was reiterated that the name of Rookwoods Cricket Club remains.

Mark Gentry generously gave donations to many worthy causes and in particular to those in Sible Hedingham. For example in 1904 he gave a donation of 10s 6d to the Sible Hedingham Cottagers' Garden Show and the same year gave a donation of £1 1s 0d towards the Sible Hedingham Widows' Coal Fund. (36) He was associated with and supported a wide range of organisations including the Parish Council, the Church, Working Men's Club, Oddfellows, Constitutional Club, Football and Cricket Clubs. In addition he represented Sible Hedingham on the Halstead Board of Guardians and Halstead Rural District Council. He provided many of his employees with houses and the whole community with a public hall. He was undoubtedly a most generous benefactor to the village.

In London, Mark Gentry had the distinction of being a Freeman of the City to which he was admitted on 12th January 1884 and a Liveryman of the Worshipful Company of Shipwrights. (37)

Mark Gentry died at Grove House, Sible Hedingham on 1st June 1912 aged 61 years and was buried in Sible Hedingham Churchyard on 5th June 1912. In an obituary it was stated that *"quite a gloom was cast over the two Hedinghams when it became known that he had passed away. Although he had been in failing health for eighteen months prior to his death it was said that right up to the time of his decease he was keenly interested in the brickmaking industry, which he had tried so hard to develop."* (38)

His widow, Jane Gentry, left Grove House in 1914 and initially lived at Clacton on Sea before moving to Woodcote, near Reading. She died on 6th April 1934 at the age of 82 years and was buried with her husband at Sible Hedingham. Their only son, Mark John Glover Gentry and a daughter, Jennie Gentry were also buried in Sible Hedingham Churchyard.

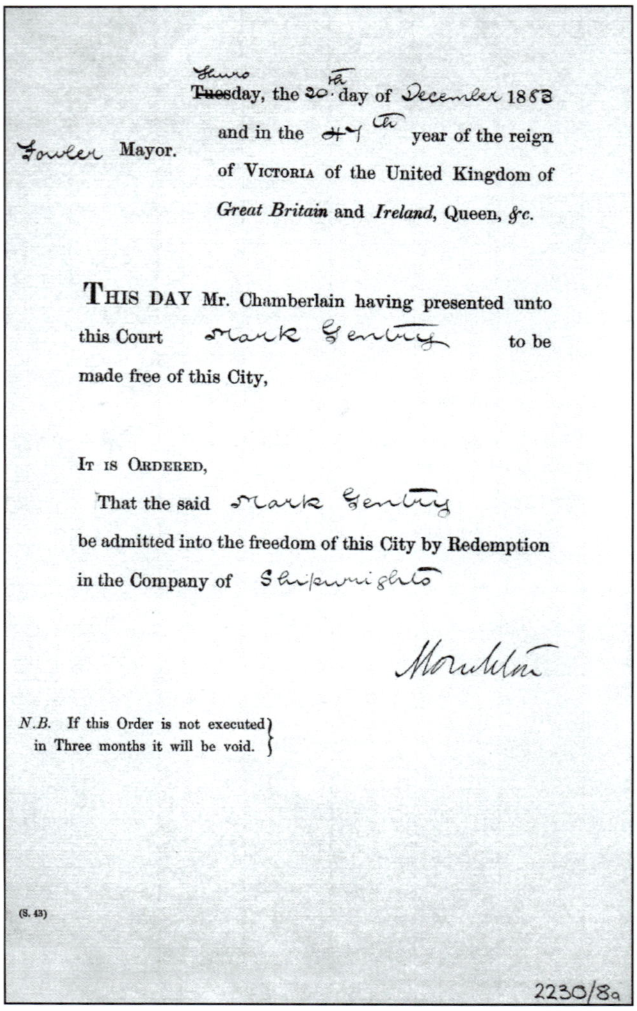

Fowler Mayor.

~~Tuesday~~ Saturday, the 20th day of December 1883 and in the 47th year of the reign of VICTORIA of the United Kingdom of *Great Britain* and *Ireland*, Queen, *&c.*

THIS DAY Mr. Chamberlain having presented unto this Court Mark Gentry to be made free of this City,

IT IS ORDERED,

That the said Mark Gentry be admitted into the freedom of this City by Redemption in the Company of Shipwrights

Monckton

N.B. If this Order is not executed in Three months it will be void.

(S. 43)

2230/8a

Certificate granting Mark Gentry the freedom of the City of London in 1883

Chapter 3

PROPERTIES OWNED AND OCCUPIED BY MARK GENTRY

Throughout his life, Mark Gentry, owned and occupied a number of properties in Stratford and later at Sible Hedingham. The first home of Mark and Jane Gentry was at 14 Saxon Road, North Bow, London, which was followed by 1 Buxton Villas, Leytonstone Road, Stratford. In c1881 they lived at Langthorne House, West Ham Lane, Stratford. (1) The Langthorne Works, his builder's yard at West Ham Lane, was leased by him. (2)

In February 1885 contracts were exchanged for his purchase of Rookwoods, Sible Hedingham from Captain Ulick John Burke, B.A., J.P., (1843-1913) a Barrister at Law. (3) Completion took place on 24th March 1885 when the freehold of 33a 3r 1p was conveyed for £5,000. On the same day Ulick Burke surrendered the copyhold part of Rookwoods to Mark Gentry comprising of 2a. 13r. 3¾p. for £150. Mark Gentry was admitted to the copyhold on 19th May 1885.

The caption under the original photograph states, "Rookwoods - As in Mr. Taylor's time", which dates it prior to 1870.

On 25th November 1869 John Taylor, a corn and seed merchant, maltster and landowner, and his wife Frances Jane Taylor sold Rookwoods for £3,500 of which the value of the freehold part of the property was £3,350 and the copyhold £150. The purchaser was John Barnard Stubbings of Castle Hedingham who died on 26th August 1878. On 23rd June 1879 his trustees sold Rookwoods to James St. George Burke of The Auberies, Bulmer for £4,175. The property was freehold with the exception of the cottages and the site of another cottage, which were copyhold of the Manor of Grays. Following the death of James St. George Burke on 25th February 1881 Rookwoods passed to his son Ulick John Burke.

When purchased by Mark Gentry, the Rookwoods Estate comprised of a large early nineteenth century mansion house built of gault brick, outbuildings, a cottage and just over 35 acres of grounds. This included Rookwoods Meadow, which was let to James Hearn. Among the staff employed at Rookwoods was George Norman, a gardener. Mark Gentry was a member of Halstead Chrysanthemum Society and they both had some success at the annual shows. Mark Gentry also owned three cottages in Yeldham Road, Sible Hedingham, which were occupied by George Dixey and others. Whilst living at Rookwoods, Mark Gentry carried out many improvements to it.

On 10th May 1886 he mortgaged both the freehold and copyhold of Rookwoods to John Turner, a brewer, of The Brewery, Heneage Street, Spitalfields, Middlesex (now London) and Thomas Glascott Venables, a gentleman, of The Park, Wanstead, Essex for £2,850. On 8th June 1892 John Turner and Thomas Venables transferred the mortgage to Mrs. Hannah Gouldsmith, a widow, of Trowbridge, Wiltshire. The principal sum remained at £2,850. (4)

Mark Gentry advertised Rookwoods for sale by auction on 23rd July 1892. It was described as *"a commodious well appointed family residence with 30 acres"*. The estate included *"ornamental groom's and gardener's cottages"* (See Chapter 10). Rookwoods was *"approached by carriage drive through massive entrance gates protected by ornamental lodge"*. (5) Rookwoods did not sell and it was afterwards offered for sale by private contract.

On 6th November 1894 Messrs. Balls disposed of 600 lots of antique furniture, oil paintings and other contents of Rookwoods, which until shortly before the sale had been in the occupation of Mark Gentry. (6)

On 21st November 1894 Mrs. Hannah Gouldsmith as mortgagee sold Rookwoods, inclusive of both freehold and copyhold for £3,500 made up as to £3,400 freehold and £100 copyhold. The purchaser was Miss. Elizabeth Scratton of Gosfield Cottage, Gosfield who was a daughter of the Rev. James Scratton (1825-1884) of Prittlewell Priory and Milton Hall, near Southend on Sea, the fifth son of Daniel Scratton, J.P., (1786-1868). Elizabeth Scratton only acquired 20a. 3r. 27p. including the mansion house, outbuildings, cottages and gardens. Mark Gentry retained ownership of Further Meadow of 9a. 1r. 37p. (field no 193) and Holy Bread Croft of 3a. 1r. 10p. (field no 198). This land of just over 12 acres presumably contributed to the difference in value of £1,650 between the £5,150 paid by Mark Gentry when he purchased Rookwoods in 1885 and the £3,500 when Hannah Gouldsmith sold in 1894. The consideration of £3,500 was sufficient to discharge the mortgage debt of £2,850 and interest thereon. The balance would have been paid to Mark Gentry but the amount is unknown. It is also possible that in 1894 a quick sale of Rookwoods took place at an under value to clear the mortgage debt. The twelve acres retained by Mark Gentry may not have amounted to £1,650 at 1894 values. It is likely that he also suffered a loss from the cost of improvements carried out by him during the late 1880s. (See chapter 10)

Rookwoods circa 1950s

Elizabeth Scratton died on 23rd October 1901 leaving Rookwoods to her nieces Florence Ellen Sparrow and Ethel Bertha Sparrow. They were admitted to the copyhold part of Rookwoods on 5th March 1902. The Misses Sparrow later owned field numbers 193 and 198 because they both formed part of the Rookwoods Estate when it was assented on 11th January 1949. In the meantime on 4th February 1919 the Misses Sparrow sold field number 193 to Arthur Frank Gibson, a Sible Hedingham builder for £145 but on 16th February 1925 he sold it back to the Misses Sparrow. (7)

In about 1885 Mark Gentry purchased a small freehold farm known as *"Washlings"* containing 40 acres. This farm was situated between Rookwoods and the road between the Church and High Street Green, opposite Washlands Farm. Washlings Farm, which included a timber and thatched barn, piggeries and cattle yard, was leased to John Perry for £66 per annum. (8) He was also a timber merchant and lived at the Three Sugar Loaves Public House of which he was landlord, (9) the owners being Adams and Sons of The Brewery, Trinity Street, Halstead. John Perry was also tenant of Washlands Farm owned by George Hicks Goodchild of Graves Hall and occupied Glebe land at Lower Farm of which the Rev. Henry Warburton was the proprietor. Mark Gentry offered *"Washlings"* for sale by auction on 23rd July 1892 when it was included in the same sale particulars as Rookwoods.

The Hanbury family had owned land in Sible Hedingham since 1834 when Hostage Farm was conveyed to them by Bakers Trustees. Robert Hanbury (10) purchased further land in Sible Hedingham and Great Maplestead in 1854, 1857 and 1865. He died on 20th January 1884, probate was granted on 10th March 1884 and on 24th August 1887 his extensive landed estates at Sible Hedingham and Great Maplestead amounting to 1093 acres were sold by auction. (11) The vendors were his executors namely George Hanbury of 21 Portman Square, Middlesex, Charles Addington Hanbury and Edmund Smith Hanbury both of The Brewery, Brick Lane, Middlesex. Mark Gentry purchased fourteen of the twenty one lots (12) and the amounts paid by him were as follows:

Lot 4 Hosdens Farm, Great Maplestead - 62 acres including dwelling house then in three cottages and various farm buildings £700

Lot 6 High Field, Great Maplestead and Sible Hedingham - 23 acres with a brick and slated barn - advertised as arable land believed to contain a considerable quantity of brick and tile earth £450
(See Chapter 7)

Lot 7 Further Harrow Field, Great Maplestead and Sible Hedingham - 8 acres of arable land believed to contain good brick and tile earth £400

Lot 8 Mussel Hill Field, Great Maplestead - 8 acres £125

Lot 10 Hostage Farm, Sible Hedingham - dwelling house, various farm buildings and 155 acres of arable and pasture land running through part of which there was supposed to be a vein of good Brick Earth £1,700

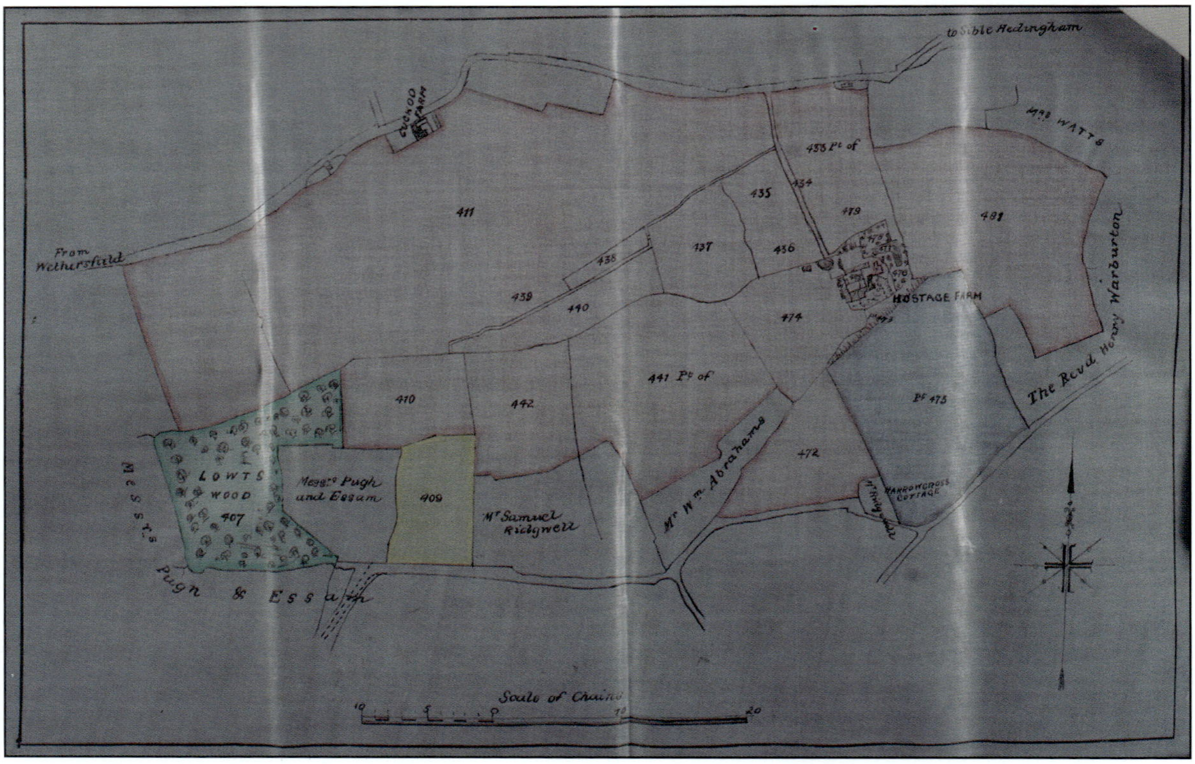

Map of Hostage Farm dated 1887 (from the deeds of 1887-1925 - ERO., D/DSf/T43). This map shows Hostage Farm coloured pink comprising of 155a. 1r. 6p., which Mark Gentry purchased from Robert Hanbury's executors on 1st November 1887. Stony Field being field no. 473 containing 18a. 0r. 18p. is coloured blue, Cracknells Field, field no. 409 of 5a. 3r. 35p. is yellow and Lowts Wood (407) of 13a. 2r. 19p. is green.

Lot 11 "Hazel Croft", Sible Hedingham - 6 acres of pasture supposed to contain a considerable quantity of brick and tile earth £420
Lot 12 "Stony Field", Sible Hedingham - 18 acres of arable land £380
Lot 14 "Cracknell's Field", Sible Hedingham - 5 acres grass land £170
Lot 15 "Lofts Wood", Sible Hedingham - 13 acres of woodland £200
(Lofts Wood is now known as Lowts Wood)
Lot 16 Seven parcels of arable land formerly parts of Perryfields and Pevers Farms, Sible Hedingham - 72 acres £700
Lot 17 Four fields of arable land formerly parts of Cuckoo and Hostage Farms, Sible Hedingham - 55 acres believed to contain good brick earth £500
Lot 19 The Cuckoo Farm Premises, Sible Hedingham - range of brick and tiled buildings £200
Lot 20 Freehold cottage near Cuckoo Farm, Sible Hedingham £60
Lot 21 Freehold cottage opposite Mark Gentry's (Langthorne) Brick Works, Sible Hedingham £55

Lot 7 being Further Harrow Field, also known as Harrow Field or The Harrow was conveyed to Jane Gentry by 1911. In c1916 she transferred ownership to her son, Mark John Glover Gentry who sold it in 1917 to Charles William Crawley who died later that year and it was then vested in his executors. Throughout this time Harrow Field was let to (Frederick) George Bishop. From 1919 it was owned and occupied by the executors of C. W. Crawley and from 1922 by Lewis Crawley. (13) (See chapter 7)

Lot 11 included 2a. 0r. 27p. of copyhold land known as Wethersfield Road Meadow. The sale price of £420 was apportioned as to £300 for freehold and £120 for copyhold land. The copyhold land, which was formerly in the occupation of Mark Elsden, was absolutely surrendered by Robert Hanbury's executors to Mark Gentry on 15th November 1887. Thereafter Mark Gentry was admitted as tenant on 27th February 1888 upon payment of 8/- to the Lord of the Manor of Prayors. Wethersfield Road Meadow was enfranchised on 31st October 1902 upon Mark Gentry paying £17 10s 8d. (14) The six acres of pasture known as *"Hazel Croft"* did prove to contain brick earth as advertised in the sale particulars. Mark Gentry retained 3.304 acres (being field no. 764 on the 1897 O.S. map) upon which he excavated clay for brickmaking. In about 1886 he sold the remaining 2.508 acres (being field no. 764) to Eli Cornish upon which he established The Tortoise Brick Works. Following the closure of the Langthorne Brick Works in 1911, Eli Cornish purchased field no. 764 to extend The Tortoise Brick Works, which continued to operate until 1938.

Mark Gentry purchased over 425 acres from Robert Hanbury's executors at the auction. He already owned Rookwoods of 35 acres, including an adjoining field called *"Holy Bread Croft"* of 3 acres and Washlings Farm of 40 acres together with several acres at the Langthorne Brick Works. He therefore owned well over 500 acres of land mainly in Sible Hedingham with some in Great Maplestead and for some years was described as one of the principal landowners in Sible Hedingham. (15) The total acreage of Hostage Farm amounted to about 260 acres and included lots 10 to 15 and 17. In c1891 he employed William Newman as his farm bailiff and Elijah Playle as stockman. They lived in Hostage Farm House and Hostage Farm Cottage respectively. (16)

On 27th February 1888 Mark Gentry was admitted tenant to four acres of land and meadow called Mussels Farm at Great Maplestead, which land was copyhold of the Manor of Prayors at Sible Hedingham and was enfranchised on 24th January 1890 upon payment of £22 9s 10d. (17) In 1887 Mark Gentry had purchased Mussel Hill Field at Great Maplestead extending to 8 acres, which was lot 8 in the Hanbury sale. Mussels Farm was either the copyhold part of this lot or other land very close by. Although four acres of Mussel Hill Field was copyhold the sale particulars state that it was copyhold of the Manor of Hedingham Upland, not the Manor of Prayors. However this may be academic because the Lords of both Manors were successive members of the Majendie family of Hedingham Castle.

At an auction held at the Rose and Crown Hotel, Sudbury on 25th April 1889 various properties were sold by John Dyer, a farmer of Aveley Hall, Assington, Suffolk of which three lots were purchased by Mark Gentry as follows:

> *Lot 11 A brick and tiled cottage at Sible Hedingham let at £3 10s 0d per annum sold to Mark Gentry for* *£40*
>
> *Lot 12 Two cottages at Sible Hedingham rents amounting to £7 per annum sold to Mark Gentry for* *£95*
>
> *Lot 13 A brick and tiled cottage with bake office let at £3 10s 0d per annum sold to Mark Gentry for* *£55* (18)

Lot 12 being 1 and 2 Brick Cottages, Wethersfield Road, photographed in 2012

These were four copyhold cottages situated on land twenty rods long by one rod wide between the Tortoise Brick Works of Eli Cornish and the highway at Wethersfield Road, Sible Hedingham. The cottages were formerly occupied by Edward Harrod, Joseph Giblin, Thomas Giblin and Robert Harvey and subsequently by the Widow Start, Daniel Cornish and Edward Ruffle. When purchased by Mark Gentry they were occupied by Eli Cornish, William Baldwin and Edward Ruffle. They were surrendered by John Dyer at the Manorial Court held on 8th May 1890 and at the following Manorial Court on 24th August 1890, Mark Gentry was admitted as tenant. (19) This land and cottages were enfranchised on 7th September 1910 upon Mark Gentry making payment of £23 16s 3d. (20) Ownership was then transferred to his son, Mark John Glover Gentry. In c1911 they were conveyed to Robert Balls and were later owned by William Henry Baines. (21) These four cottages are now known as Hillside, 1 and 2 Brick Cottages and Hare House.

On 28th September 1889 Mark Gentry attended an auction at Park Farm, Assington when the contents of Park and East Farms at Assington and Little Greys at Great Cornard were for sale by direction of the administratrix of the estate of John Dyer deceased. Mark Gentry purchased an 8 horse-power portable steam engine, a double blast threshing and finishing machine and an undercast elevator, all by Clayton and Shuttleworth for £85. He also purchased a 7 horse-power portable steam engine for £37 10s 0d and a 6 horse-power steam engine by Hornsby for £17. (22) The threshing machine and elevator were for use on his farms and the three portable steam engines were for the Langthorne Brick Works to drive the pug mills. In January 1890 he advertised for a young man (age 17 to 20) to drive portable engines and to work under an engineer. (23)

At an auction held in the Assembly Rooms, Sible Hedingham on 13th May 1890 Messrs. Balls and Newman sold the *"Long Field"* containing over 4½ acres, with a barn, the property of William Abraham. The lot was knocked down to Mark Gentry for £150. It was reported that some time previously William Abraham had purchased this field for £400. (24)

By 1889 until c1894 Mark Gentry also owned the following properties:

i. An orchard and pasture in Water Mill Lane (now Alderford Street), which was occupied by William Toswell, who was landlord of the Swan Public House and his son George Toswell a nurseryman. George Toswell who was an overseer of Sible Hedingham later purchased the orchard and pasture from Mark Gentry. At a meeting of the Halstead Board of Guardians held on 26th August 1898 it was reported that the Sible Hedingham overseers had requested the Board to engage the services of a professional valuer for the assessment of brickyards. George Toswell and Walter John Elsdon, a builder, overseers of Sible Hedingham, totally denied this statement and considered themselves capable of assessing all properties in the parish. Mark Gentry requested his name to be added to the denial. (25)

ii. A cottage, malting and buildings in Water Mill Lane occupied by (Frederick) George Bishop, a corn and coal merchant, maltster, miller, threshing machine proprietor and farmer.

iii. A house and garden occupied by George Ames in Water Mill Lane.

iv. Alderford House and garden occupied by William Robert Jones. By 1891 this was occupied by Edward Harry Haiden and thereafter by his executors. (26) Edward Haiden was a coal, corn and cake merchant. He was also a commission agent, assistant overseer, tax collector and Conservative registration agent for the Hedingham District of the Saffron Walden division. (27) George Bishop and Edward Haiden probably supplied Mark Gentry and his brickworks with coal. George Bishop and Mark Gentry were both members of Sible Hedingham Parish Council. Mark Gentry was a very active supporter of the Conservative party of which Edward Haiden was an agent.

On 6th June 1890 Mark Gentry charged some of his properties to London and County Banking Company Limited and further charges to the Bank were made on 25th September 1890 and 9th October 1891. This included depositing the deeds of Hostage Farm with the bank as security for moneys owing by him to the bank. On 29th May 1895 the Bank and Mark Gentry conveyed to Robert Leabon Curtis (28) of 119 London Wall, London, Surveyor, part of Hostage Farm namely 149a. 0r. 3p., together with Cracknells Field, Stony Field and Lofts Wood (now Lowts Wood) for which he paid £3,000 to the bank. On 5th December 1896 R. L. Curtis mortgaged these properties to Hannah Gouldsmith of Rodwell Hall, Trowbridge, Wiltshire for £3,000, which he covenanted to pay her on 5th June 1897 plus interest. On 5th August 1902 Robert L. Curtis and Hannah Gouldsmith sold 31a. 1r. 37p. including Wood Field, Cracknells Field, Lofts Wood, Willow Ground and part of Cuckoo's land to Robert Balls, Land Agent of Castle Hedingham. The consideration was £275 of which £250 was paid to Hannah Gouldsmith, which was still owing to her under the mortgage dated 5th December 1896 and the balance of £25 was paid to R. L. Curtis. (29)

When a receiving order in bankruptcy was made against Mark Gentry in 1892 it was stated that he had considerable stock at Hostage Farm, which was mortgaged. (30) In June 1892 he sold all his farm stock, cattle, sheep, pigs and machinery by auction, having let Hostage Farm to Foster William Badham. (31)

On 1st July 1892 umpire-age took place between James Mayhew Balls acting for Mark Gentry, the landlord and George Cardinal acting for Foster William Badham, the new tenant. It was recorded that Hostage Farm extended to 261a. 1r. 39p. and an annual rent of £280 was fixed, including cottage worth £20, tithe free. The usage of some of the fields was recorded namely barley, wheat, potatoes, white turnips and beans. Field names recorded were Chalkfields, Stoneyfield, Barn field, Meekly field, Earthy field, The Downs and Hop Ground. The rates for Hostage Farm were recorded as follows:

Poor Rate	£14 4s 3d
Poor Rate	£7 17s 0d
Highway Rate	£4 19s 5d
	£27 0s 8d

The cost of rates, as well as hay, chaff, labour and manure were all taken into account when fixing the rent. (32)

On 3rd October 1892 Foster William Badham committed suicide by shooting himself in the garden of Hostage Farm. Daniel Cornish, manager of Mark Gentry's brick works, picked up the gun and discharged the loaded cartridge. Badham who was 48 years of age had returned from New Zealand the previous year and had lived at Bures St. Mary until taking possession of Hostage Farm in June 1892. He had been considered by those who had to do business with him to be strange in his manners. At the inquest held on 5th October there was evidence of failing brain power and the jury returned a verdict of *"Temporary Insanity"*. (33)

On 16th January 1892 a receiving order in bankruptcy was made against the estate of Mark Gentry at the London Bankruptcy Court on his own petition. He stated that his unsecured debts amounted to about £11,000 and he had further fully secured debts of

£23,000. His assets were returned at £3,000 and it was anticipated that another £3,000 would result from contracts in hand. His brickworks at Sible Hedingham were freehold, but mortgaged, and upon those premises were plant, machinery and a large quantity of bricks. He owned the freehold of Hostage Farm amounting to 260 acres, which was mortgaged and where he had considerable stock. At his residence of Rookwoods he had household furniture to the value of £500. The Langthorne works at West Ham Lane, Stratford were held on two leases having nine years to run. (34)

Upon closer scrutiny it was revealed that Mark Gentry had liabilities of £38,572 8s 2d of which £14,659 16s 11d were unsecured and assets amounted to £6,324 2s 8d. The stock at the brickfields was worth from £750 to £1,000. He had spent between £6,000 and £7,000 on the brickfields and works. In December 1883 his building business made a surplus of £19,821, which by 1892 had converted into a deficiency of £3,335. He made a profit of £250 in 1889, a loss of £2,500 in 1890 and a loss of £17,000 in 1891. He drew £1,000 per annum from the business but his personal expenditure was only about £700 a year the balance being spent on repairs to properties the deeds of which were held by the Bank. Prior to 1891 he had a floating loan of £6,000 from the Bank and borrowed another £9,000 that year. The claim of the Bank was £15,000 less the value of deeds. He had borrowed money since 1888 from the Bank and others. In the whole course of his trading he only once had legal proceedings taken against him, which was in respect of a disputed account. (35) In connection with the London Impermeable Collar and Cuff Company he had losses amounting to about £2,500 and was under liabilities in respect of bank overdraft and the lease of premises. He had incurred losses of about £3,000 when he sold the West Ham Press Company in December 1890. He attributed his failure partly to these losses; partly to loss and outlay in respect of the brickworks and farm at Sible Hedingham, partly to depreciation in the value of his properties but chiefly to losses on contracts. The Official Receiver stated that the usual and proper books of accounts had been kept and that Mark Gentry had intimated his intention to submit a proposal at the first meeting of creditors. (36) When this was held on 12th February 1892 it was proposed to allow the case to go into bankruptcy and to appoint a trustee and committee of inspection. It was anticipated that Mark Gentry would probably make an offer with the assistance of friends to buy back the estate. (37)

On 12th February 1892 Mark Gentry was adjudicated bankrupt and Joseph Priestly of 92 Cheapside, London, Chartered Accountant was appointed as Trustee in Bankruptcy. On 25th April 1892 at an adjourned meeting of the creditors they accepted a proposal for a composition in satisfaction of his debts. The payment of the composition was secured by Robert Leabon Curtis and Henry Russell, a Solicitor of 14 Old Jewry Chambers, London of all Mark Gentry's property vested in them and all moneys in the hands of Joseph Priestly. On 19th May 1892 a hearing took place before Mr. Registrar Hope in the Bankruptcy Division of the High Court of Justice when he was asked to approve the scheme of arrangement, which had been agreed to by creditors. The scheme provided for the payment of 7s 6d in the £ by three equal instalments extending over two months. The scheme included the withdrawal of claims to the extent of £3,800. The Official Receiver reported that the debtor had contributed to his failure by rash and hazardous speculation. Nevertheless the Registrar approved the scheme and annulled the bankruptcy. (38) The second instalment under the composition was paid on 27th July 1892. (39)

During the course of the bankruptcy proceedings it was claimed that at its commencement *'Mark Gentry was or claimed to be siezed possessed or otherwise entitled to certain property comprising freehold or leasehold lands, messuages, tenements, stock in trade, machinery, trade fixtures, fittings, utensils, farming stock, growing crops, tenant right, household and office furniture and effects, shares, monies, debts due from debtors, rights under incomplete contracts and other things in possession and in action and other property rights subject as to certain of such property to mortgages, charges and incumbrances created thereon by the said Mark Gentry all of which as well as other property or rights thereinbefore described to which the said Mark Gentry was at the time aforesaid beneficially entitled were thereinafter called the property of the said Mark Gentry.'* (40)

A contributory factor to his bankruptcy was the non recovery of money owing to him. One example was the failure of Rippers Bros., builders of Castle Hedingham and Cambridge. Towards the end of 1893 a committee of inspection was appointed at the first meeting of creditors, which included Mark Gentry who was a creditor being owed £18 5s 8d. Other creditors included:

Mrs. Jane Gentry and Daniel Cornish	£49 1s 0d
George English, brickmaker, Bulmer	£30 3s 0d
Allen & Sons, brick merchants, Sudbury	£30 0s 0d
Eli Cornish, brickmaker, Sible Hedingham	£14 14s 0d
William Parr, beer retailer, Castle Hedingham	£11 14s 2d
Portway and Son, ironmongers, Halstead	£35 0s 0d (41)

In 1905 the bankruptcy orders against Edward and Tucker Ripper were discharged. In the meantime a joinery works was established in the name of their younger brother, Charlton Ripper, which became a large successful company. In 1919 Eli Cornish, Reuben Hunt, Charlton and Tucker Ripper became the first directors of the newly incorporated Sible Hedingham Red Brick Company Limited, which took over the former brickworks of Eli Cornish at Purls Hill and Mark Gentry at Highfields.

Mark Gentry's poor financial situation around 1892 was exacerbated when he became an unfortunate victim of two cases of fraud and false pretences against him. In the first case Henry Frederick Benson Goodwin, who claimed to be a builder and contractor of North Pole Road, Notting Hill fraudulently ordered bricks from Mark Gentry to the value of £50. The order was placed on the strength of references given upon Goodwin by William Henry Brownjohn of Oxford Road, Windsor who variously described himself as a commission agent and as a lime and cement merchant but was actually a fish hawker. They regularly gave false references for each other when ordering goods and disposed of goods as soon as they were delivered, without making payment. Goodwin elicited that Mark Gentry had failed for £40,000 and that he (Goodwin) had to pay the carriage which he said was two-thirds the value of the bricks. Other victims of the fraud were H. Bray & Co., brickmakers of Nottingham and Peterborough for the supply of 3,500 bricks and Hicks, Gardner & Company, brickmakers of Stratton, Huntingdonshire who supplied 12,000 bricks. The prisoners were charged at North London Police Court and remanded in custody. (42) The second fraud was committed jointly by William Mathew Webster, aged 70, a builder of Clock House, White Hart Lane, Tottenham and Andrew Edward Mann, aged 47, a builder of 81 Trinity Road, Tottenham. They failed to pay for 5,500 bricks supplied by Mark Gentry for which the original invoice was found in Webster's house when he was arrested. At a hearing at North London Police Court on 11th February 1893 bail was refused and the prisoners were remanded in custody. (43) In 1893 Mark Gentry was a creditor of John Mark Putney and James Henry Putney, builders, lime and coal merchants of Dorking. When a receiving order in bankruptcy was made against them, he was appointed onto the committee of inspection. (44)

When Rookwoods was sold by the mortgagee, the Gentry family moved to Grove House, (now 32 Potter Street), Sible Hedingham during or about November 1894. Grove House and garden was much smaller than Rookwoods but still a desirable house of reasonable size.

Grove House, Potter Street circa 1920

Grove House had been purchased by Timothy Maber on 30th December 1865 and when he died on 19th January 1892 it was inherited by his widow Harriet Caroline Maber. They also owned an eight roomed dwelling near Grove House, which was formerly occupied by the coachman and later let to Alfred Steward at £9 per annum. In addition they owned Tocat House on the opposite side of Potter Street. Mrs. Caroline Maber instructed Messrs. Balls to sell all three houses by auction, which took place on 7th August 1894 at the Assembly Rooms, Sible Hedingham in three lots. Grove House was lot 1 and was purchased by Mrs. Jane Gentry for £1,000. It included stables, chaise house, farmery, gardens and paddock covering an area of about 2a. 2r. 17p. Tocat House was sold by private contract on 8th September 1894 to Mrs. Emily Jane Young, wife of Alexander Gilmour Young of Haverhill for £460. (45) Interestingly, Basil Tilley, Managing Director of Tilley Lamp Co., of Hendon, London NW4 later owned and occupied Grove House from 1952 to 1960. (46) Tilley Lamp Co manufactured and supplied Portable Lamps and Floodlight Projectors. In particular the company advertised portable lighting for Brick, Tile and Clay Works. (47)

In early 1901 Brook Farm, described as adjoining Hedingham Railway Station, was advertised for sale. The auction was conducted by Robert Balls at the Assembly Rooms on 4th March 1901. The farm comprised of just over 74 acres of arable and pasture land, which was sold in 12 lots. (48) Three of the lots were purchased by Mark Gentry as follows:

Lot 3 Arable land, suitable for development of building plots, with a frontage of about 233 feet to the west side of Swan Street, extending to 3a. 3r. 32p. *£120*

Lot 5 Catch Croft being arable land of 12a. 0r. 19p. including a 30 feet wide entrance from Swan Street and a public chase way from Church Street *£170*

Lot 8 Building land with a frontage of 410 feet to the east side of Swan Street amounting to 4a. 2r. 10p. *£350*

By July 1901 all three lots were owned by Greville Montgomery (See chapter 13) and it is probable that Mark Gentry purchased them on his behalf. Mark Gentry also built and owned a number of properties in Sible and Castle Hedingham (See chapter 10)

THE GROVE,
SIBLE HEDINGHAM, ESSEX.
About 1¼ miles from Hedingham Station C.V.R.

Messrs. *BALLS and BALLS*

Have been favoured with instructions from Mrs. Gentry (the Residence having been let) to Sell by Auction, on TUESDAY, July 21st, 1914, at 11 o'clock precisely, the excellent HOUSEHOLD FURNITURE and EFFECTS, including:—

Turkey, Persian, Brussels and other carpets and mats, copper and brass coal scuttles, occasional lounge and other chairs, couches, gilt chair with wool and bead work seat and back,

Fine Tone GRAND PIANO by *Erard*, music cabinet, china cabinet, overmantels, engravings, oil-paintings, grandsire clock in mahogany, carved oak hall seat, barometer, mahogany dining table, dining chairs, massive mahogany sideboard with mirror panels, mahogany dinner waggon, card tables, knee-hole writing table, *Singer* treadle sewing machine.

The APPOINTMENTS of the BEDROOMS mahogany warbrobe, mahogany duchesse dressing table, chests of drawers, mahogany washstands, iron and brass and Arabian bed-steads, box spring and hair mattresses, suites in American walnut, and inlaid mahogany,

ANTIQUE INLAID LINEN CHEST with drawer. Kitchen and culinary utensils, glass and china, dessert services. Handsome Worcester dinner service of about 150 pieces.

OUTDOOR EFFECTS

including:—Garden frames and lights, garden seat, iron roll, *Green's* lawn mower, portable kennels and fencing, wire netting, chicken house and coops, various ferns and plants, light-running single brougham on rubber tyres, in excellent condition; and numerous effects.

Catalogues may be had of the Auctioneers, Castle Hedingham and Braintree, Essex; and Haverhill, Suffolk.

Horse brass inscribed 'MG' found on a field between Rookwoods and Brick Kiln Hill (photograph courtesy of Paul James, a keen metal detector enthusiast, who discovered this exciting find)

Advertisement dated 10th July 1914 for the sale of the contents of Grove House by Jane Gentry

Chapter 4

MARK GENTRY, MASTER BUILDER, CONTRACTOR AND TIMBER MERCHANT

In the 1871 census at the age of 20 years, Mark Gentry was described as a *'Builder's Foreman'*. (1) In 1878 he became a master builder, contractor and timber merchant on his own account beginning business with about £300 capital and £200 borrowed money. (2) By 1881 he was employing 30 men and 2 boys at his Langthorne Works, West Ham Lane, West Ham. (3) The first entry in the Post Office Directory for London is also 1881 when Mark Gentry is described as a builder and contractor at Langthorne Works, West Ham Lane, Stratford. The address of his business premises is stated variously in different records as West Ham and as Stratford. The name *'Langthorne'* is taken from Stratford Langthorne Abbey, which was founded in 1135 and became one of the richest and most important Cistercian establishments in England. It was sacked during the Peasants' Revolt of 1381 and dissolved in 1538. The whole monastic complex now lies beneath the Docklands Light Railway and Jubilee Line. (4) There was also a Langthorne Street, which no longer exists and was located off West Ham Lane.

By 1885 Mark Gentry had offices and showrooms at 2 Wormwood Street, London EC, which continued until 1892. He was tenant of 2 and 3 Wormwood Street, described as a house, which was owned by St. Bartholomew's Hospital. (5) He operated three businesses from this address namely the Hedingham Brick and Tile Works, the London Impermeable Collar and Cuff Company Limited and his building and contractors business. From 1890 until 1892 he also had offices and showrooms at 43 London Wall, EC. He later had offices in the basement of Dashwood House, New Broad Street, London. It was from this address that William G. Flint, who was Mark Gentry's London agent, operated. This building was also occupied by many other companies. From c1886 to c1890 Mark Gentry also had a depot at 28 Bishopsgate Goods Station, London.

In addition to being a builder and brickmaker, he also designed buildings. It is highly probable that these included the two lodges, cottage and stable blocks at Rookwoods. In 1886 he offered his services as architect for building a large hall between the two Hedinghams, which did not materialise. He was architect of the drawings for re-building Chilton Lodge, Sudbury in 1909 for which the work was carried out by Charles Deaves, builder, contractor and undertaker of Bures. (6) Until 1892 Mark Gentry carried on an extensive business as a builder and contractor and executed many large contracts in London, Middlesex and Essex. These contracts include the following:

1. A new first floor office and ironwork to galleries in the Registrar's office at the Mayor's and City of London County Court at the Guildhall, which was built in 1824. The contract was signed by Mark Gentry on 5th August 1881 (7)

2. In January 1882 Mark Gentry's tender of £1,480 was accepted for stabling and sheds at Church Street, Stoke Newington for the London General Omnibus Company for which Alfred Tosh was the architect. (8)

3. On 23rd January 1884 George Shaw, Chairman of the City Commissioners of Sewers, laid the foundation stone for a new block of artisans and labourers' dwellings between the Metropolitan Railway and Middlesex Street, London. The buildings were divided into five blocks of varying heights according to plans drawn by Col. William Haywood, M.I.C.E., F.R.I.B.A., the architect. (See 10 and 15 below). Mark Gentry was contractor for these buildings which cost £68,500 plus £106,818 for the site. The dwellings comprised of 521 rooms, 241 tenements of one, two and three rooms, 20 shops and accommodation for 937 persons. (9) They were formally opened on 26th January 1885. (10)

4. On 25th June 1884 two contracts were signed by Mark Gentry as contractor for work at London Central Market for the Corporation of London. One contract was for work on the elevation and side elevation and the other was for work on the basement and elevation both for the General Market. (11)

5. In 1884-85, Mark Gentry was the contractor for re-building 16 City of London Almshouses at Ferndale Road, Brixton. The original almshouses were pulled down and rebuilt. The foundation stone was laid on 17th December 1884 by the Chairman of the City of London Freeman's Orphan School Committee. The architects were Davis and Emanuel. These almshouses, together with two other sets of almshouses, are grouped around an open quadrangle facing Ferndale Road and are now known as the Freeman's Houses. (12)

6. The erection and fitting up of two swimming baths with necessary offices in Goulston Street, Whitechapel. The Commissioners of Public Baths and Washouses in the parish of St. Mary, Whitechapel (then in Middlesex) accepted Mark Gentry's tender for £4,289 on 9th February 1885. In accepting this tender it was stated that Mark Gentry was a substantial and respectable man who was likely to carry out his contract with the Commissioners in a satisfactory manner.

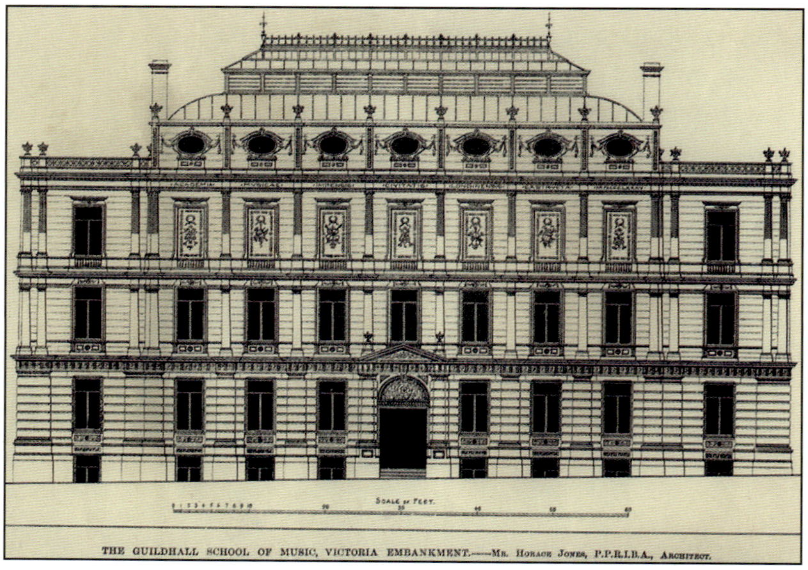

The Guildhall School of Music, Victoria Embankment, London built by Mark Gentry during 1885 and 1886. (Illustration from The Builder, 5th September, 1885)

7. During Autumn 1885, Mark Gentry was awarded the contract for the erection of the Guildhall School of Music on land belonging to the Corporation of the City of London adjoining the Thames Embankment. His tender amounted to £17,900 plus £2,500 if Portland instead of Bath Stone was used. (13) This new purpose built building in John Carpenter Street was designed by Sir Horace Jones (1819-1887) who was architect and surveyor to the Corporation from 1864 to 1887. The Guildhall School of Music was opened in December 1886 and took its name from the Corporation's historic headquarters at the Guildhall although it was never based there. The School of Music was the last important work of Sir Horace Jones although in collaboration with Sir John Wolfe-Barry he produced the designs for Tower Bridge but died within a month of the commencement of its construction.

8. In January 1886 the foundation stone for offices of Holborn Union Board of Guardians in Clerkenwell Road was laid and among the names inscribed on it were Saxon Snell & Sons, architects and Mark Gentry, builder. The ground and building cost £23,000 and provided the Board with office accommodation and board-room to administer the 8,000 inmates in its care. (14) The construction of the building commenced in 1885 with a base of blue engineering bricks. The remainder of the bricks were *'Hedingham reds'* supplied by Mark Gentry who completed the building in 1887. The beautifully formed bricks fit together perfectly with just a hint of lime mortar. The most ornate façade faces Clerkenwell Road with a plainer one facing Britton Street. The building now known as The Red House, was converted into 21 flats in 1994-5 by Croft Homes, using Michael Sierens Associates as architects.

St. James's Dwellings, Ingestre Place, Soho, London erected by Mark Gentry during 1886-1887. (Photograph courtesy of Survey of London Vol. 31: St. James, Westminster)

Detail of St. James's Dwellings, Ingestre Place, London, showing the decorative parapet. The name of the building is carved into the brickwork, and much of the architectural detail - scrolls, pediments, festoons, and finials - is in terracotta.

9. Mark Gentry was the builder and Hyman Henry Collins the architect for The St. James Dwellings, Ingestre Place, Soho, London being dwellings intended for the accommodation of the labouring poor. These dwellings were erected by the Vestry of St. James, Westminster with trust funds mainly derived from the sale of the parish burial ground in Hampstead Road. The foundation stone was laid by the Hon. Maude Stanley for these industrial dwellings, which were erected during 1886-87. (15) Modifications were subsequently made in the quantities and the tender of Mark Gentry to carry out the work on the revised quantities for the sum of £5,732, was accepted. The four-storey L – shaped building comprised 23 single-room tenements, 12 two-room tenements and a general wash-house and work-room. It has its main frontage to Ingestre Place, but the entrance and staircase, leading to open access galleries along the back, are at the extreme west end of the shorter frontage in Silver Place. Both elevations are in yellow stock brick with copious red brick and terra-cotta dressings, designed in an endeavour, according to *The Builder*, to make the architectural features *'pleasing, but not ornate'* and *'as homely in appearance as possible'*. These features include wide pilaster-strips, cornices above ground and top storeys, and a parapet with sections of brick and terra-cotta alternating with sections of iron railings. Decorative iron guard-rails in front of each window were intended *'to encourage a taste for window gardening'*. The sanitary arrangements were all centrally placed around a small area off the access galleries on the back. (16)

10. In 1886 the Corporation of London contracted Mark Gentry to construct public conveniences at Farringdon Street (Ludgate Circus), which involved work above and below the pavement. The City Engineer for this project was William Haywood (17) (see 15 below).

11. During Spring 1886 Mark Gentry's tenders were accepted for building two blocks of offices and chambers at 63 Lincolns Inn Fields as follows:

Front block	£9,975
Back block	£6,340

Concrete floors £1,700 (18)

The buildings, which were designed by William Simmons, were completed in 1888.

12. On 28th October 1886, Mark Gentry signed three contracts for work at the Annexe of the London Central Market for the Corporation of London. One contract included work over footway entrance, first floor windows of shop No. 19 and window on either side of main entrance. The next contract was for work in southern roadway and on western angle and chimney. The third contract was for work on 'street avenue' and elevation of one shop. The contract drawings were prepared by the Architects Office at the Guildhall. (19)

13. In early 1888, Mark Gentry's tender of £1,495 was accepted for the erection of new show-rooms at Grove House, Broadway, Stratford. (20)

14. During 1888, Mark Gentry constructed the New London Fish Market in Farringdon Street for the Corporation of the City of London. It was designed by Sir Horace Jones and cost about £26,000. The building was after the style of the Italian Renaissance with Portland stone pillasters supported on a granite base and surmounted by a cornice carrying balustrade and dormers, the panels between the pilasters being filled with moulded red brickwork. (21)

15. Mark Gentry was the contractor for building the mausoleum for Lt. Col. William Haywood (1821-1894) in the City of London Cemetery. (22) Lt. Col. Haywood was the architect for the cemetery, circa 1855, its Chapels, Catacombs and Gatehouse. He was born in 1821 and educated at Camberwell Grammar School. He joined the City of London Corporation as Assistant to the Surveyor to the Commissioner for Sewers and the next year was promoted to Surveyor. In 1849 he was asked to report on the burial provision within the City of London and following this report was tasked with finding and designing a suitable cemetery to accommodate the deceased of the City of London. His designs for the cemetery included those of his own mausoleum. This was built by Mark Gentry during 1889 with two different types of limestone namely Kentish Rag and Portland Stone. (23) William Haywood was Surveyor to the Commissioners of Sewers and City Engineer for the Corporation of London. (24) In these capacities he had worked with Mark Gentry in other contracts (see 3 and 10 above). The inscription over the entrance to the mausoleum states, *'The tomb of Lieutenant Colonel William Haywood 1889'*. The inscription on one side reads, *'Within this tomb lie the ashes of Lieutenant Colonel William Haywood once Commandant of the London Volunteer Rifle Brigade. He was by profession an Architect and Engineer and designed and laid out this Cemetery. Born 21st December 1821. Died 13th April 1894. Cremated at Woking 18th April 1894'*. The inscription on the other side of the tomb is, *'Here also lie the ashes of Jemima Emma Haywood. Born 6th June 1841. Died 10th May 1896. Cremated at Woking 15th May 1896'*. The mausoleum, which since 1984 has been a grade II listed building, is located along the main avenue to the north east of the main gates. The listing description, is as follows: *"Ragstone with ashlar dressings. Leaded pitched roof. Gabled Gothic single storeyed building, one bay wide. Pointed entrance arch. Solid tympanum bearing inscription. Original wrought iron gates. Side walls panelled with inscriptions. Corner pinnacles bearing monster gargoyles. Shelf to rear interior with male and female busts."* (25)

The mausoleum for Lt. Col. William Haywood (1821-1894), which was erected in 1889 by Mark Gentry in the City of London Cemetery.

16. During 1890-1891 Mark Gentry erected two blocks of artisans' dwellings in Quaker Street and Wilkes Street, Spitalfields, London for the Great Eastern Railway Company as part of the Liverpool Street Station enlargement works. (26) When the GER began an enlargement of Liverpool Street Station in 1887, the number of persons displaced by the demolition of 93 houses in St. Botolph's, Bishopsgate was estimated at 600 (27) for whom the company was required to provide alternative accommodation by the General Powers Act of the same year. Two of the three blocks of buildings built for this purpose was begun early in 1890 (28) at the northeast corner of Quaker Street and Wilkes Street. Each block of artisan's dwellings contained 24 one-room and 68 two-room tenements, giving accommodation for 320 persons. The buildings were completed by October 1890 (29) in compliance with the agreement made with the builder Mark Gentry, whose tender, was for £13,776. (30) The buildings consist of two long blocks, two rooms deep and four storeys high, placed at a right angle to Quaker Street with the fronts facing each other across an open-ended court. Each block is divided into three sections, with four tenements on each floor, and all the storeys were originally similar in arrangement. Every group of four tenements was allotted two water-closets and one scullery, leading off the main staircase landing. The elevations are of yellow stocks with bands of red brick just above the sills of the windows, which have segmental arches of red brick. Giant pilasters, also of red brick, are placed at each end of the front and back and flank the tall openings that light and ventilate the three staircases. The detailed bill of quantities (31) included the following red bricks and chimney pots, which may have been supplied by Mark Gentry's brickworks:

"5619 feet	*Extra to facing with best hard red bricks as contract*	*£58 10s 8d*
1390 feet	*Red brick axed arches*	*£69 10s 0d*
804 feet	*Red brick splayed plinth*	*£8 7s 6d*
59 feet	*Red brick moulded label course*	*£0 14s 9d*
592 feet	*Red brick moulded string 3½ inch x 6inch high round chimney cap*	*£14 16s 0d*
184	*Terra Cotta chimney pots and setting and flaunching with tile and setting*	*£36 16s 0d"*

The architect was John Wilson, engineer to the GER and the surveyors were Hovendon and Berridge of 30 Bishopsgate Street Without, London EC. The summary of the contract figures dated 31st March 1891 was as follows:

"Extracts from General Conditions and Sundry Items	*£189 15s 7d*
Excavator and Bricklayer	*£6,486 19s 1d*
Mason	*£815 18s 7d*
Carpenter	*£280 1s 9d*
Joiner and Ironmonger	*£1,765 0s 4d*
Founder and Smith	*£3,076 15s 3d*
Plumber	*£748 0s 8d*
Plasterer	*£1,079 15s 2d*
Glazier	*£58 5s 6d*
Painter	*£330 4s 2d*
	£14,831 6s 1d
Less 5%	*£741 11s 4d*
	£14,089 14s 9d
Plus Day Works	*£22 7s 11d*
	£14,112 2s 8d
Add Surveyor's charge @ 1% on above amount for measurements	*£141 2s 5d*
Add for copy of Bill	*£2 9s 4d*
	£14,255 14s 5d
By Cash on account	*£13,500 0s 0d*
Balance due to Mark Gentry	*£755 14s 5d"*

17. Blackwall Buildings, Thomas Street (later renamed Fulbourne Street), Whitechapel were built in 1890-91 and demolished in 1969. The builder was highly likely to have been Mark Gentry because he built similar style philanthropic flats. In 1885 the London and Blackwall Railway applied to Parliament to widen its line between Fenchurch Street and Stepney. This was granted and the houses demolished had to be replaced and Blackwall Buildings were the result. The London and Blackwall Railway was leased to the GER by whom all the major construction work was carried out. There is no proof that Mark Gentry was the builder of Blackwall Buildings but it is known that he carried out other building work for the GER such as the artisans dwellings in Quaker Street, Spitalfields (see 16 above).

18. Mark Gentry's tender of £5,900 was accepted for the erection of five houses and shops at Maryland Point, Stratford for Edward Jex of 37 Chobham Road, Stratford. John Hudson of 80 Lemon Street and 36 Romford Road, Stratford was the architect and the quantities were prepared by Franklin and Andrews.

19. One of the last contracts in 1891-92 was building a post office at Mount Pleasant. His estimate was £50,000 and he always based his contracts on the anticipation of 10% profit. He made a loss of £10,000 on this contract, which contributed to his bankruptcy. However it was completed after his bankruptcy making a profit of £1,500 for the estate. (32)

Not all the tenders submitted by Mark Gentry were successful. Amongst unsuccessful tenders were the following:

a. The erection of a block of school buildings, known as Colegrave Road Schools,

Stratford New Town, West Ham for West Ham School Board for which John Thomas Newman of 224 Romford Road, Stratford was the architect and quantities were supplied by R. L. Curtis & Sons. There were twenty one tenders ranging from £6,445 to £8,548 of which Mark Gentry's tender was £6,650. (33)

b. The erection of stabling and a dwelling house at Gorham Place, Notting Dale for London General Omnibus Company, for which Alfred Tosh was the architect. The nine tenders ranged from £2,983 to £4,019 9s 0d of which Mark Gentry's was £3,250. (34)

c. The erection of a new ice factory in Lower Shadwell, London E in 1886. The tenders were Chafen £12,987 and Gentry £18,900. (35)

He continued his business of builder, contractor and timber merchant at Langthorne Works until his unfortunate bankruptcy in 1892. He held the Langthorne Works on two leases which in 1892 had nine years left to run. (36) On 17th March 1892 George Elliott Curtis and Sharp, auctioneers of 51 Broadway, Stratford sold by auction, his builders stock, machinery and plant at the Langthorne Works. (37)

The name *'Langthorne Works'* was then used from sometime during or between 1892 and 1896 by Arthur Webb, a builder and contractor at 30 Romford Road, Stratford. He was born at Wethersfield in 1863, a son of Henry Webb and Eliza Webb formerly Cockerton who lived at Codham Croft, Wethersfield. (38) By 1881 Arthur was a carpenter living and working in West Ham. (39) He commenced business in 1885 (40) in partnership with Charles Bishop trading as Bishop and Webb. They were initially described as carpenters and joiners (41) but later as builders operating from 30 Romford Road. (42) Their partnership was dissolved by mutual consent on 22nd August 1896 when their address was recorded as Langthorne Works, Stratford. (43) Thereafter Arthur Webb continued trading as a sole proprietor until his business was incorporated as Arthur Webb Limited. By 1971 the company was described as Building and Plant Contractors, Joinery and Shopfitters and Maintenance Contractors, which was still operating from Langthorne Works, 30 Romford Road, Stratford. The white weather boarded house, which was the home of the Webb family (44) was built between 1690 and 1720. In the 1860s it was a dispensary and in recent years became the offices of the Newham Museum Service. (45)

Langthorne Works at 30 Romford Road, Stratford in 1971
(Photograph courtesy of Newham Library Service)

Chapter 5

MARK GENTRY, MASTER BRICKMAKER

Mark Gentry owned two brickworks in Sible Hedingham where he traded under the names of *'The Hedingham Brick and Tile Works'* and *'The Hedingham Brick, Tile and Terra Cotta Works'*. His first brickworks, was the Langthorne Brick Works at Wethersfield Road, Sible Hedingham, which he purchased in 1884 (See chapter 6) and the second was the Highfield Brick Works on the border of Sible Hedingham and Great Maplestead, which he established in 1894. (See chapter 7)

If events had taken a different course, Mark Gentry could have owned other brickworks in the area. In the nearby village of Gestingthorpe there were two old established brickworks and a pottery. In 1898 he gave evidence at a public inquiry that if the Sible Hedingham to Long Melford Light Railway is built he was prepared to take on the Gestingthorpe works if the line runs through to them. The line was never built and consequently he did not take over the Gestingthorpe works (See chapter 15)

In circa 1892 Mark Gentry entered into possession of land for brickmaking purposes, which was owned by William Rayner of Maiden Ley, Castle Hedingham. In March 1893, the Essex Assize Court, before Baron Pollock, heard a land dispute when William Rayner sued Mark Gentry for trespass and applied for an injunction against him. The dispute concerned the possession of three or four acres of land of which the plaintiff was owner. William Rayner alleged the defendant had taken the land for brickmaking purposes having staked out and dug on the land. Mark Gentry maintained that it had been agreed that he should have the land and insisted on his right to possession. However Daniel Cornish, Mark Gentry's manager, said the plaintiff refused to let the land until he had consulted his son, William John Rayner, and in the meantime the defendant had entered into possession. There was no evidence of any agreement that the defendant should have the land and Judgment was therefore given to the plaintiff with costs. (1) A similar account of this action adds, *"that the defendant set up a counterclaim alleging that there was an agreement for a lease, and calling upon the plaintiff for specific performance. The evidence showed that there were negotiations to let the land for use as a Brick Yard for a term of years, terms were drafted before an absolute agreement was entered into and the plaintiff alleged that he had declined to take the matter any further. Although the Court gave Judgment for the plaintiff with costs the question of damages was waived."* (2) The exact location of this land is uncertain but it is highly likely to be where William Rayner established his own brickworks at Maiden Ley later in 1893. If the proposed lease with William Rayner had been implemented it would have resulted in Mark Gentry opening up another brickworks.

On 22nd December 1895, William Rayner was seen trespassing in Mark Gentry's brickworks. William Rayner was charged with damaging a hedge and pleaded not guilty at a hearing at Hedingham Petty Sessions on 14th January 1896. Mark Gentry's employees namely Charles Murrell, Ernest Harper, Walter Spring and Thomas Bareham, gave evidence that they saw the defendant look at pits and wash troughs and then go towards the wash mill and behind the engine shed. Upon leaving the property it was alleged that he damaged a hedge by leaving a gap in it. The Bench found the defendant guilty and he was fined 1d with 19s 6d costs. (3)

With these two court cases it is assumed that, relations between these two master brickmakers, was not good. In later years (from 1904) when Mark Gentry's trade in Hedingham was declining he partially blamed the competition from other brickworks which had opened since he had established his brickworks. One of the competing brickworks was Rayners at Maiden Ley, which achieved a significant output of red facing and ornamental bricks and also had the advantage of a siding onto the CV&HR. When the Langthorne Brick Works closed in 1911 William John Rayner attended the sale, with his young son, George Henry Rayner, who eventually became the last owner of the Maiden Ley Brick Works, which closed in 1952.

In August 1906 Mark Gentry advertised for *"a foreman brickmaker to make two million red sand facing and moulded bricks along the Tilbury and Southend Railway"*. (4) The exact location and whether or not manufacture took place is not known.

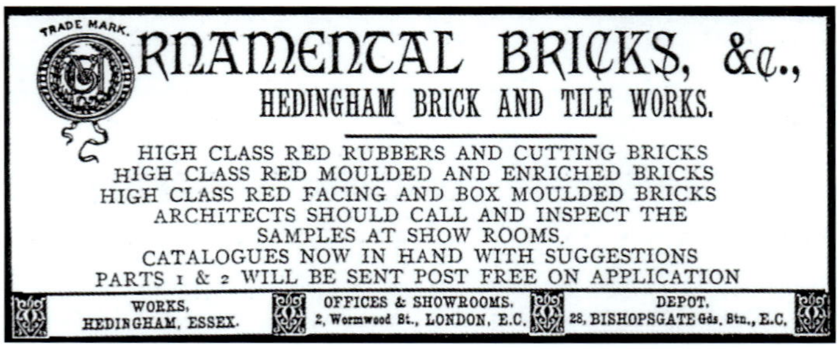

An advertisement for Hedingham Brick and Tile Works c1886 to c1890

An advertisement for Hedingham Brick and Tile Works c1886 to c1890

The majority of bricks made at both of Mark Gentry's brickworks contained the brickmarks *'M.G.'* (Mark Gentry) and *'M.G.H.'* (Mark Gentry Hedingham). The trade mark was also *'M.G.'*. Mark Gentry published a number of catalogues over the years but none appear to have survived. It is known that one catalogue available in 1898 contained 60 pages with some 6,000 examples of brickwork. (5) All bricks made at both brickworks were red bricks. They included hand-made facings, hand-pressed facings, red moulded and ornamental, red rubbers and arch bricks. In addition chimney pots and tiles were also supplied. *'The Architect'* of 16th July 1886 gives an account of the ornamental bricks made by Mark Gentry and concludes, *'We are glad to call attention to the rich colour and fineness of the bricks and their excellence of design'*. During the early 1890s Mark Gentry advertised supplying, *'arch brick for gauged work made to any shape in three weeks'*. (6)

By the late 1890s he was advertising, *'Arch bricks made to any shape, length, or radius, in 14 days from receipt of order'*. (7) This indicates that during the 1890s he improved brickmaking processes to shorten the time from receipt of order to supply.

He always maintained a London office and showroom where examples of his bricks were displayed. These were shared with his building business until its closure in 1892. (See Chapters 2 and 4) Thereafter a London office and showroom continued to promote his brickworks. During the 1900s they were located at 11 & 12 Finsbury Square, London EC. (8)

By the early 1900s, Mark Gentry advertised making red facings, hand-made and hand-pressed rubbers, arch bricks and moulded bricks, plain roofing tiles and ridge, valley and hip tiles. (9) During 1903 he was actively involved in meetings to discuss the standardising of the size of bricks. A joint committee was formed representing the Royal Institute of British Architects, the Institution of Civil Engineers and the Institute of Clayworkers. Mark Gentry stated, *"I agree that 8 ⅞in. by 4 ⅜in. by 2¾in. should be the size of facing bricks, and inside bricks 2 ⅝in. in thickness. My business compels me to make a number of different sizes and thicknesses to please architects and I do not see how this is to be altered."* (10)

He expended many thousands of pounds in the development of the industry and made a specialty of moulded and ornamental bricks. When he died one obituary stated, *"Born at Stratford, Essex, Mr. Gentry was for many years successfully engaged in the building trade, subsequently abandoning this occupation for that of brickmaking at Sible Hedingham. Here he was actively engaged for over a quarter of a century, the M.G. red rubbers gaining a well deserved reputation in the London market. In later years, however, keen competition and a general decline of building activity considerably narrowed his field of operations. A man of genial and optimistic temperament he could always make the best of things, and no one was more welcome at the councils of the Institute of Clayworkers of which he was a committeeman from the year 1900, serving as its chairman in 1903. There was nothing indeed affecting the interests of the Institute that he did not actively and whole-heartedly support, and he combined with a keen business instinct a generosity and good nature that made him many friends."* (11)

TRADE MARK.

Ornamental Bricks, &c

MARK GENTRY,

Sible Hedingham,
Essex

NOTED M.G. RUBBERS,

HAND-MADE HAND-PRESSED FACINGS

AND MOULDED BRICKS.

Arch Bricks made to any shape, length, or radius, in 14 days from receipt of order.

Any Moulded Bricks not in stock can be made in 14 days from receipt of order.

Special Plant for making Pressed Facings any size or thickness, 4, 5, or 6 courses to the foot, in 14 to 21 days from receipt of order.

Chimney Pots. Architects' own Designs made.

COMPLETE CATALOGUE, PARTS I., II., & III., NOW READY, SENT FREE ON APPLICATION.

Architects' own Designs Carefully Executed.

MARK GENTRY, Sible Hedingham, **ESSEX.**

An advertisement from THE BRICKBUILDER of April 1898

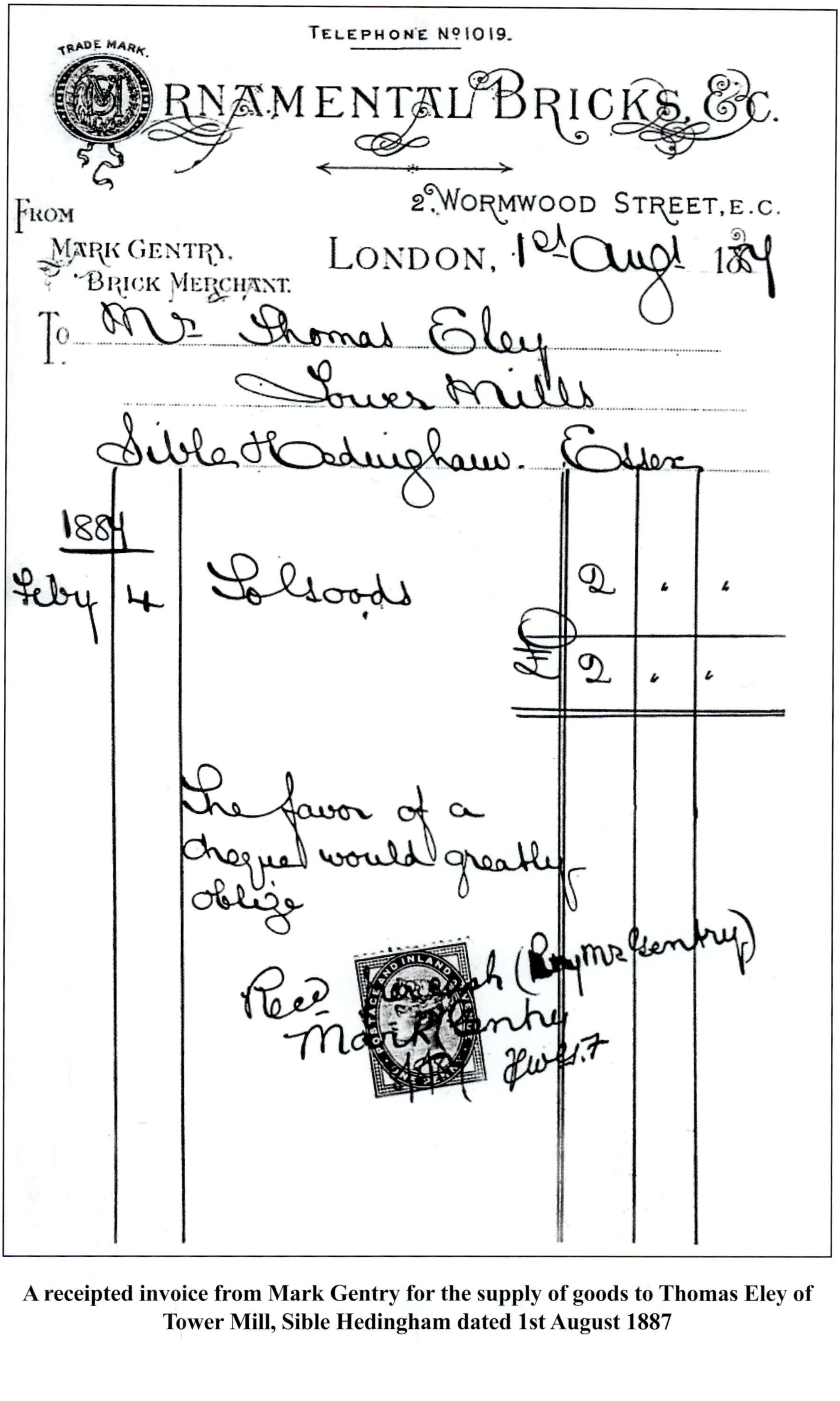

TELEPHONE No. 1019.

TRADE MARK.

ORNAMENTAL BRICKS, &c.

2, WORMWOOD STREET, E.C.

FROM MARK GENTRY, BRICK MERCHANT.

LONDON, 1st Aug 1887

To Mr Thomas Eley
Tower Mills
Sible Hedingham. Essex

1887					
Feby	4	To Goods	2	"	"
			£ 2	"	"

The favor of a cheque would greatly oblige

Recd cash (by Mr Gentry)
Mark Gentry

A receipted invoice from Mark Gentry for the supply of goods to Thomas Eley of Tower Mill, Sible Hedingham dated 1st August 1887

Terracotta

Mark Gentry mainly advertised the manufacture of terracotta during the period between 1885 and 1892. Terracotta was a higher class of ware than ordinary bricks and not only used in the construction of buildings but also in the form of statues and garden ornaments. The following are examples of Mark Gentry's terracotta work.

A terracotta central oval date plaque with '1888' intertwined surrounded by ornamental brickwork, including sunflower keystone brick at Rookwoods Cottage, Sible Hedingham

A former ornamental terracotta fountain now used as a flower pot in a pond at Rookwoods photographed 1986

A terracotta lion on the corner of a brick wall at Rookwoods photographed 1986

Chapter 6

THE LANGTHORNE BRICK WORKS, SIBLE HEDINGHAM

In about 1883 Orbell Cornish (1832-1923) established a brickworks in Wethersfield Road, Sible Hedingham in which he employed his sons and daughters. The following year Mark Gentry arrived in the village with the intention of starting a brickworks. He met Orbell Cornish who had only recently started the brickworks on his own account and was very reluctant to sell. Eventually Mark Gentry not only persuaded him to sell but also employed him as manager. Orbell Cornish then lived at Hostage Farm, which was owned by Mark Gentry who had purchased a considerable tract of land. By February 1885 Mark Gentry had arranged for the brickworks, under the management of Orbell Cornish to be extended. (1)

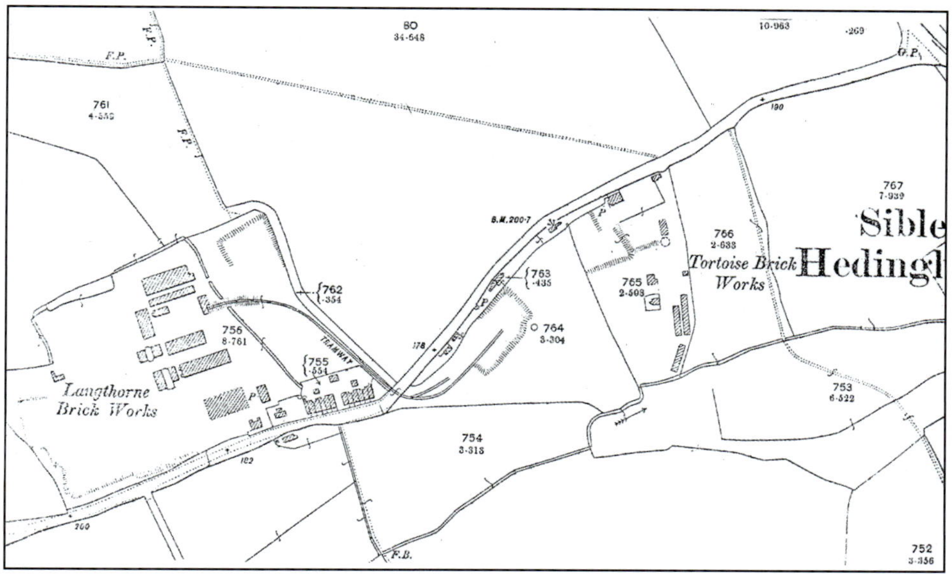

The Langthorne Brick Works of Mark Gentry and The Tortoise Brick Works of Eli Cornish from the 25 inch to one mile Ordnance Survey Map of 1897

It was Mark Gentry who named the brickworks The Langthorne Brick Works, the name coming from Stratford. (2) The following paragraph is quoted from the East Essex and Halstead Times of 19th December 1885: "..... *rapid progress has been made towards the establishment of an extensive business. Large drying sheds have been erected so that brick making can proceed regardless of frost or other unfavourable weather. Machinery driven by a powerful engine has been erected for the carrying on of the various processes necessary for the production of a perfect brick. New kilns have sprung up and many other preparations made, all pointing to a determined effort on the part of the proprietor to set going a concern which shall not merely be a paying one, but which shall turn out work of the best kind on the most approved plans. Proof of this may be seen in the many samples of ornamental bricks of varied and artistic design already turned out on the premises, not to speak of the large quantities of ordinary brick. Under the experienced management of Orbell Cornish there seems to be every prospect of the speculation growing into a prosperous industry that will give employment to many hands and be of some benefit to the neighbourhood."*

A view of Langthorne Brick Works from Wethersfield Road showing a large kiln on the right and rows of hacks for drying bricks on the left

In his first year (1885) Mark Gentry employed over 40 men and in December that year he provided a dinner for them at the White Horse Inn. He presided at the dinner with Orbell Cornish and Henry Ranger (3) occupying the vice-chairs. Other guests at the dinner included Rev. Henry Lake (Castle Hedingham), Rev. James Burgess (Congregational, Castle Hedingham), Dr. John Bourne Bromley (Castle Hedingham), Dr. Sidney Thorp (Sible Hedingham), Joseph Pittock (Station Master, Sible Hedingham), William Corder (proprietor of Southey Green Brick, Tile and Pottery Works, Sible Hedingham), Tom, Eli and Daniel Cornish (sons of the manager). During the after dinner speeches and loyal toasts which followed, those present expressed their support to the new Halstead Cottage Hospital which had opened the previous year. (4) Dr. Bromley stated that if any of the brickmakers should meet with an accident and are taken to the hospital they would receive proper attention and nursing which many of them could not have in their own homes. (5)

On 21st July 1887, Ernest Radley, a boy of 10 years of age was amusing himself in the brickyard by walking along the edge of one of the pits from which brick earth had been excavated and which contained some four or five feet of water. He fell in, unobserved, and his body was later found in the water, the boy having drowned. On 22nd July an inquest was held but it did not appear that anyone was to blame for the sad occurrence and the jury returned a verdict of accidental death. (6)

The Langthorne Brick Works with the hacks centre left and kilns behind. In the right background is the tower of Sible Hedingham Church and in front some of the cottages built by Mark Gentry for his employees. The timber runway in the foreground was to facilitate pushing barrow loads of clay from the clay pits to the brickmaking area.

The kilns with stacks of newly fired bricks in the foreground. On the left are hacks for drying 'green' bricks.

The hacks (described as the outdoor drying ground) with the kilns in the background. The shed on the extreme right was the stock shed.

The stock shed for storing specially moulded bricks is on the left. The house in the centre was occupied by the manager and the cottages on the right by other employees.

On Thursday, 17th July 1890 there was a large storm over Sible Hedingham, the heavy rain caused serious floods and great damage to property. Church Street was like a river and cottages were flooded up to a depth of three feet. A number of hens and turkeys were drowned and at Southey Green potatoes were washed out of the ground. A crop of hay was entirely swept away and many fields flooded. The following night the storm raged again and cottages in Church Street were again flooded. The greatest damage however occurred at the Langthorne Brick Works. The fires in the kilns containing some 30,000 bricks were extinguished, some ornamental bricks which were drying were rendered shapeless and damage was sustained to numerous buildings. It was estimated that over one thousand pounds worth of damage was done at the brickworks and the men were unable to get onto the premises to work on the Friday and Saturday. (7)

Orbell Cornish continued as manager until 1890 when he was succeeded by his son Daniel Cornish (8) who was manager from 1890 until 1894. In January 1891 it was recorded that the brickworks had for some time been pressed to idleness through frost. Daniel Cornish, determined to show his sympathy with the men, invited all their children to his house *"to partake of a substantial meal. The guests numbered between 30 and 40 and it was needless to say their appetites were very keen. Mr. Cornish did his best to satisfy them with a plentiful supply of meat puddings and other things with the result that the children had what may be literally termed a fill."* (9)

The Langthorne Brick Works gradually expanded and eventually employed between 70 and 100 men. After a few years it was necessary to dig clay from pits on the opposite side of Wethersfield Road. To transport clay from the pits into the brickworks a narrow gauge tramway was constructed. (See chapter 16) Initially the lines went across the road in the form of a level crossing, but later as the clay pits became deeper, a tunnel was constructed under the road for the tramway.

The following is a description of the Langthorne Brick Works in 1898: *"The kilns are of the old-fashioned up-draught type. Four are open-top of 20,000 each, and there are three covered-in kilns* (with brick domes) *of 45,000 capacity. We understand that Mr. Gentry is prepared to receive particulars of continuous kilns with the idea of adopting the same. .... What enterprise and energy have accomplished is best evidenced by the fact that an output of about 750,000 per year has grown into something nearly approaching five millions. The works are one of the largest of their kind in the Eastern Counties, standing upon an estate of 300 acres, of which, however, only about 12 acres are at present utilized for brickmaking. .... The clay is taken from a 30 foot clear face, and is as plastic as putty. Only the clay for arch bricks and better class of work generally is washed. .... The power is provided by a 30 h.p. engine in the centre of the yard, driving a shaft 200 feet each way. .... The only class of bricks made at these works are, hand made reds, hand pressed, and machine-made bricks, together with moulded varieties, rubbers and arch bricks. The manufacture of chimney pots also finds a place. The bricks are sand-faced, and the distinguishing feature of the business is the manufacture of moulded and arch bricks made to architects specifications. Of these large quantities are made, some of the arch bricks being 24 inches long .... The manufacture of so many moulds necessitates a department to itself. The pattern makers' shop is supplied with a saw bench and other labour-saving machines, and contains over 6,000 moulds."* (10)

On 8th April 1899 during a gale, a large chimney shaft was blown down at the Langthorne Brick Works. The strong wind was stated to have almost twisted the tall chimney on its foundation before it was hurled onto the carpenter's shop with a great crash. Fortunately no one was in the carpenter's shop at the time.

Johnson's Steam Sand-Faced Brick Press.

A Johnson's Steam Sand-Faced Brick Press

One of the machines purchased by Mark Gentry for use at his Langthorne Brick Works was a *'Johnson's Steam Sand-Faced Brick Press'*, manufactured by Johnson of Leeds. (11) In 1894 he advertised this machine for sale stating it *"can be seen at work by application. Low price will be taken if sold at once before removal. Apply to Hedingham Brick Works, Sible Hedingham."* (12) In 1898 Mark Gentry still had two other brick machines by Johnson of Leeds making 12,000 bricks a day and six hand presses. (13) In October 1899 he advertised for sale the two Johnson's hand-screw brick presses, with open sides, in good condition and one Johnson's steam press, circular table, with open and closing moulds. (14)

On 19th February 1905 there was a fire at the at the brick works. The fire engine and brigade of the Joint Castle and Sible Hedingham Fire Brigade attended with the captain, Robert Balls, (15) in charge. The firemen and pumpers were initially paid £5 2s 6d plus a further £1 17s 0d for the balance of expenses. In addition William Radley (16) was paid £2 2s 0d for the hire of his horse to pull the engine to the fire. The Royal Exchange Assurance Co. paid the 'Hedingham Fire Engine Joint Committee' £10 15s 6d for extinguishing the fire.

By 1908 Mark Gentry was giving his attention to gas-fired kilns, and hoped to be able to set up a successful kiln of this type. (17) It is unlikely that this was achieved because the works closed three years later during the autumn of 1911. The site was sold to (Arthur) Frank Gibson, a builder of Oakdene, Sible Hedingham, the son of George Gibson, a carpenter and builder who died in 1915. The site later became a chicken farm, followed by garages for Aubrey Letch's omnibuses now Hedingham and District Omnibus Company. (See chapter 21)

Chapter 7

THE HIGHFIELD BRICK WORKS, SIBLE HEDINGHAM

Highfield, adjacent to Purls Hill, has been so named since at least 1574 when it was recorded as *'Greate Highfeild'* and *'Litle Highfeild'*. (1) It was partly in Great Maplestead and partly in Sible Hedingham. On 24th August 1887, Mark Gentry purchased *'High Field'* from the estate of Robert Hanbury, when it comprised of 23 acres with a brick and slated barn and was advertised as arable land believed to contain a considerable quantity of brick and tile earth. (See chapter 3) Robert Hanbury had purchased Highfield in Great Maplestead on 2nd April 1878. The copyhold part of this land amounting to four acres was surrendered by his executors on 15th November 1887 when Mark Gentry was admitted as tenant. (2)

Mark Gentry farmed the land until 1894 when he established his second brickworks on the site, some ten years after he had acquired the Langthorne Brick Works. Although Highfield Brick Works was not quite as large as the Langthorne Brick Works, it was still quite extensive and eventually had six updraught kilns.

Highfield Brick Works with workmen using crowding barrows to removing newly fired bricks from the kilns and loading them into trucks on the siding from the Colne Valley and Halstead Railway. The man on top of the kiln is John Corder (1863-1957) and on the left is his eldest son Edward John Corder (1886-1938).

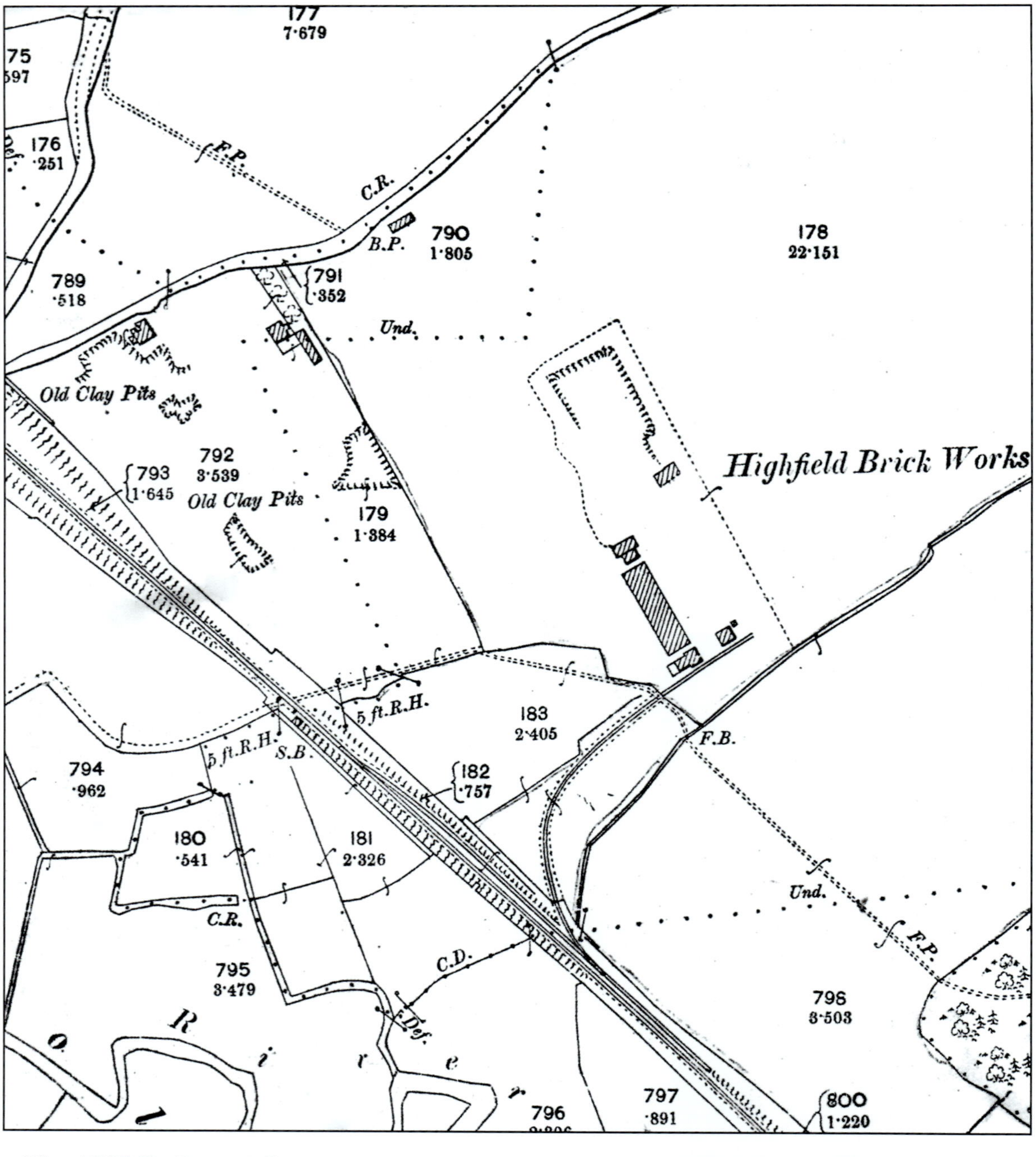

The 1897 Ordnance Survey map of 25 inches to one mile showing the Highfield Brick Works with its siding from the Colne Valley and Halstead Railway. The "Old Clay Pits" were on the site of the former brickworks at Alderford Farm. (See chapter 19)

The Highfield Brick Works had the considerable advantage of having a standard gauge siding from the CV&HR and its route is clearly shown on the map on the north east side of the main line. The signal and points for the siding were controlled from a small signal box or ground frame marked *"S.B."* on the map. This was a red brick building on the south west side of the main line. It was south east of the footpath from New England, immediately before it crossed over the main line to Highfield Brick Works. The footpath crossed over the siding south west of the brickworks and then across a footbridge over a stream before continuing to Purls Hill Plantation. The signal box was built circa mid 1890s with bricks made by Mark Gentry and the arches over the door and window contained his distinctive and well recognized sunflower keystone bricks. LNER later described this building as *"Ground Frame (2 levers)"*. (3) It was used to operate the points and signal for this busy siding. In c1953 when the siding was no longer required, it was removed together with the mechanism for the signal and points, which left the red brick signal box as an empty building for many years. It survived for a few years after the railway was dismantled in 1965, before it was demolished c1970s.

In 1894 the freehold of Highfield Brick Works was conveyed to Jane Gentry (1852-1934), presumably as a result of her husband's bankruptcy in 1892. On 25th April 1894 a conveyance was made between The London and County Banking Company Limited of the first part, Robert Leabon Curtis and Henry Russell of the second part, Mark Gentry of the third part and Jane Gentry of the fourth part. On 26th April 1894 a mortgage was made between Jane Gentry of the first part, Mark Gentry of the second part and Mary Jane Benson of the third part. On 11th April 1895 the mortgage was transferred by Mary Jane Tompson formerly Benson to William Orbell and Joseph Orbell. They transferred the mortgage on 29th June 1905 to Jane Coldham and Mary Coldham. On 6th June 1907 a reconveyance was made between Jane and Mary Coldham and Jane Gentry. On the following day a mortgage was made between Jane Gentry and Flavius Josephus Kingsford.

In 1896 an adjacent brickworks was opened at Purls Hill by Ernest West, a builder and contractor of Fairfield Works Chelmsford and Witham. West was a director of the Purls Hill Brick, Tile and Terra Cotta Company Limited which was incorporated on 12th April 1898 and dissolved on 17th November 1899. (4) He then became a director of the Hedingham Brick Company Limited when it was incorporated in 1899. (5) This company was purchased by Eli Cornish (1860-1939) in 1904 and continued by him until 1909. From 1909 he traded under his own name as proprietor of the Purls Hill and Sidings Works. In 1920 he sold the property to Rippers Limited and The Sible Hedingham Red Brick Company Limited, the latter having been incorporated in 1919 to take over the former brickworks of Mark Gentry and Eli Cornish at Highfield and Purls Hill respectively. (6)

The majority of workmen employed by Mark Gentry and Eli Cornish at Highfield Brick Works and Purls Hill Brick Works, walked to work via New England. At a meeting of Sible Hedingham Parish Council held on 16th March 1906 under the chairmanship of Mark Gentry, Councillor Eli Cornish referred to the bad condition of the footpath at New England. He stated that seven or eight carts go in the entrance every day and something like one hundred and fifty men walk backwards and forwards and he considered it a disgraceful thing for workmen having to walk through the mud and for children to play in it. The Council agreed to write to the owners asking if they would repair the path. (7)

In February 1911 the Parish Council considered the acquisition of land for use as allotments. A petition had been received signed by twelve inhabitants expressing a wish that *'Harrow Field'* be obtained. This field, which abutted the railway bridge at New England, belonged to Jane Gentry. The Parish Council was informed that part of this field would be required for brickmaking purposes at about the end of the following year (1912) and could not therefore be let for allotments. An alternative three acres was offered at the end of Highfield for £2 15s 0d per acre including rates and tithe. (8) *'Harrow Field'* was never used for brickmaking purposes possibly because of the death of Mark Gentry on 1st June 1912.

Following his death the Highfield Brick Works was continued by his only son Mark John Glover Gentry (1881-1918). (See chapter 17). At the Building Trades Exhibition 1913, W. T. Lamb & Sons showed bricks and tiles by different manufacturers, including Mark Gentry junior. (9) In February 1914 Mark Gentry junior advertised for a new brick making machine as follows:

> *"Wanted. Norris or similar brick making machine must be in good order cheap for cash. Highfields Brickworks, Sible Hedingham, Essex."* (10)

Jane Gentry continued to own the freehold of Highfield Brick Works until she conveyed it to her son on 17th June 1916. In August 1917 Mark Gentry junior agreed to sell the Highfield Brick Works to Charles William Crawley (1864-1917) and the purchase was completed on 25th October 1917. The conveyance was made between Flavius Josephus Kingsford of the first part, Mark John Glover Gentry of the second part and Charles William Crawley of the third part.

Charles Crawley lived at Chelmshoe Farm, Great Maplestead, which he farmed together with Rushley Green Farm at Castle Hedingham. He was well known in the Hedingham area in agricultural circles, besides farming extensively he was always on the alert to find ways of improving agricultural implements. He was a member of Castle Hedingham and Great Maplestead Parish Councils, President of Halstead and District Free Church Council and a Commissioner of Taxes. (11) He was also a merchant and haulage contractor, owning a small 5 ton compound Aveling and Porter Steam Tractor. (12)

Unfortunately, Charles Crawley only owned the brickworks for a short time as he died on 28th December 1917 at the age of 53 years. On 16th May 1918 Arthur Henry Crawley and Albert Edward Crawley, the brothers and two of the Executors of Charles William Crawley, sold the Highfield Brick Works and land in Great Maplestead and Sible Hedingham extending to 23 acres 3 roods and 32 perches to Rippers Limited for £1,000. On 10th July 1918 Rippers Limited purchased Alderford Farm comprising of 20 acres 1 rood and 32 perches of land from (Arthur) Frank Gibson for £500. Frank Gibson had purchased Alderford Farm from Henrietta Frances Capes on 24th December 1914. The farm was the site of the former brickworks owned by Charles Augustus Hilton, Orbell Cornish and John Taylor successively. (See chapter 19). On 23rd March 1920 Rippers Limited sold Alderford Farm and the Highfield Brick Works to The Sible Hedingham Red Brick Company Limited. (SHRBC) On the same day Eli Cornish and his mortgagee conveyed the Purls Hill and Sidings Brick Works to Rippers Limited and SHRBC. (13) Therefore in 1920 the Highfield Brick Works merged with the adjacent Purls Hill and Sidings Brick Works to form one brickworks operated by SHRBC. (14) (See chapter 20)

SHRBC, as successor to Mark Gentry senior and junior, used many of their brick moulds throughout the period 1920 to 1954. Thereafter many of these moulds were sold to the Bulmer Brick and Tile Company Limited where some of them are still in use.

Chapter 8

INVENTIONS AND PATENTS

It was mainly through Mark Gentry's judgment, foresight and energy that brickmaking at Sible Hedingham developed into a very large and important industry. Few people tried harder to make a cheaper and better brick for the market. He experimented with every type of machinery imaginable, taking out several patents, in fact every kind of machine which it was thought might be suitable for the clay, but still the Hedingham bricks were too good and costly for the market. (1)

One experiment was a long concrete tunnel with a fan at one end to try and dry bricks more quickly but this failed because the tunnel system was not suitable to the particular clay at Hedingham. Mark Gentry found his best return to drying bricks was from a steam floor. (2) He also purchased machinery to make 'wire cut' bricks but this was not a great success because the clay was not completely suitable for this process. From 1898 all his bricks were handmade and hand-pressed. (3) Most of the money which Mark Gentry put into the manufacture of bricks was lost by reason of these costly experiments and the general depression in the building trade which occurred from time to time. The patents applied for by Mark Gentry include the following:

"31st May 1893 - No. 10,668 - Mark Gentry - Down-draught smokeless kiln for brick burning" (4)

"April 1894 - No. 8,379 - Mark Gentry - Improvement in Down-draught kilns for Burning Bricks" (5)

"Patent Specifications Published June and July 1894 - 14,256 - Mark Gentry, Sible Hedingham, Essex - Improved cover or screen for use in drying bricks" (6)

16,674. Gentry, M., and Grunwell, H.
July 14

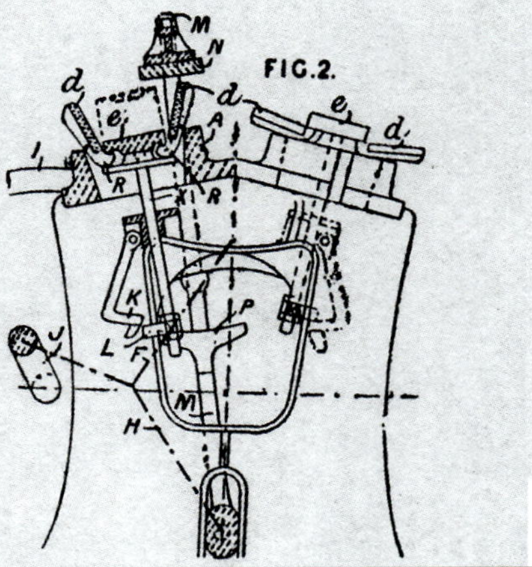

Moulding bricks, tiles, &c.—The mould linings *d* are provided with knuckles R, or rollers working in recesses in the bottom plate or die *e*, and the linings fall outwards when the bottom is raised clear of the casing A. The moulds are in duplicate and so arranged that one mould is open for the removal of a pressed brick while a brick is being pressed in the corresponding mould on the other side. The top pressing-die N is attached to rods M, operated by a hand-wheel, a crank J, and a toggle joint F, H. The mould is raised by a curved plate P of the rods M, acting on a projection L of the guide-rod X, and is supported in a raised open position by a catch K engaging with the projection L. This catch is pushed back by the curved plate P when the rods M are swung over from one side to the other. The sides of the mould and casing are tapered and fitted with guide-pins and friction rollers.

"14th July 1897 - No. 16,674 - Mark Gentry and Hartley Grunwell, 85 Gladstone Avenue, Noel Park, Wood Green - Improvements in brick presses for moulding bricks, tiles, &c" (7)

These were improved hand and power presses. Mark Gentry entrusted the manufacture of these sand-faced brick presses to Thomas C. Fawcett Limited of Leeds. By April 1900 the Gentry and Fawcett's patent presses had been put on the market and were working very satisfactorily in a number of brickworks. They were primarily for brickmakers who manufactured sand-faced bricks. The machines were a great improvement on those designed for a similar purpose which preceded them, being built with an idea to the reduction of wear and tear and securing perfect regularity of pressure and a clean arris. It was claimed that the machine would press from either machine or from hand mould 4,000 to 5,000 perfect sand-faced bricks per day of ten hours, the labour required being one man and two boys. The patent power and sand-faced brick press, with double action lever would press 5,000 to 6,000 perfect sand-faced bricks a day with the aid of two boys. The machine possessed collapsible moulds, the pressing surfaces being lined with hard steel plates. They were built on wheels, so they could be easily moved from one place to another. (8)

The Fawcett advertisement in *"The British Clayworker"* of November 1900 (page xxi) stated:
"…….Gentry and Fawcett's Patent Power Sand-Faced Brick Press with collapsible moulds. Two boys can press six thousand to eight thousand bricks per day without the risk of accident. Also adapted for pressing wire cut bricks straight from the machine."

At the Building Trades Exhibition of April 1901 this press was exhibited in motion. In fact Thomas C. Fawcett Limited had one of the largest working exhibits of brick machinery generally at the exhibition. (9) A report of the exhibition stated about this brick press that:
"The novel feature of this press is that the moulds are collapsible and fitted with a special form of knuckle, instead of pins (which in practise were generally found objectionable). There was an ingenious device which ensured perfect regularity of pressure on each brick, and thus no damage of arrises or corners is possible in the machine. The press only weighs a ton and will turn out about 10,000 bricks per day when worked by a man and a couple of boys." (10)

During three seasons (1900, 1901 and 1902) over 50 of these machines, which were designed from 1897 to 1899, had been made and put into operation, many of the orders being repeats. It was through Mark Gentry's practical experience in his brickworks that he was able to suggest many valuable improvements embodied in the press, which was designed by himself and Thomas C. Fawcett Limited. (11)

Two of Gentry and Fawcett's power presses were used in the manufacture of wire-cut and pressed facing bricks at the brickworks of William Cottis and Sons of Epping. (12) In November 1907 William Delhi Cornish of Bury Farm, Lower Edmonton, London advertised for sale three Gentry and Fawcett presses driven by belt. He had no further use for them as the clay had been used up. (13)

Mark Gentry was constantly experimenting in an endeavour to make improvements to all aspects of brick making techniques, drying and brick burning but unfortunately some of his innovations were not successful.

THOMAS C. FAWCETT, LTD.,

ENGINEERS,

HUNSLET ROAD, LEEDS.

NEW SPECIALITIES—

Fawcett's Patent Automatic Cutting Table.

NO WASTE ENDS, SAVES LABOUR, SAVES OIL, AND INCREASES PRODUCTION OF WIRE-CUT MACHINES.

NO SMALL WORKING PARTS TO GET OUT OF ORDER. CAN BE FITTED TO ANY MAKE OF WIRE-CUT MACHINE.

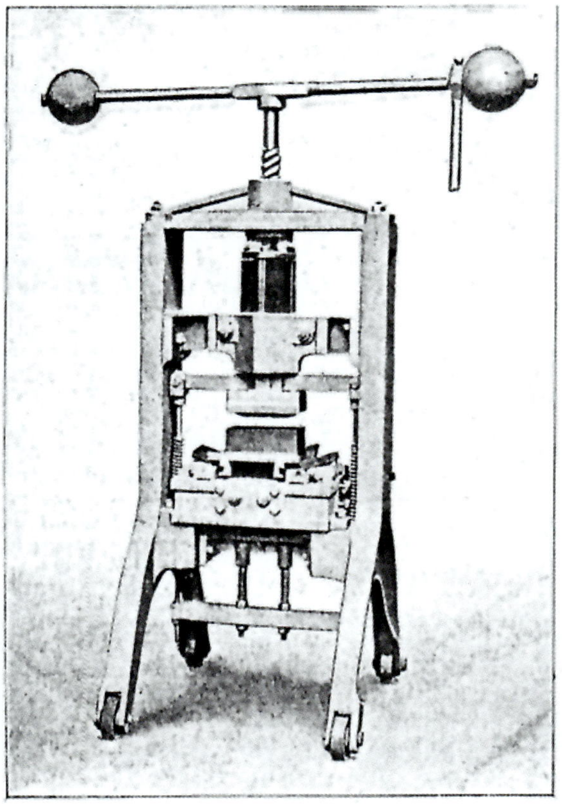

Makers of Gentry and Fawcett's

PATENT SAND-FACE BRICK PRESS

with collapsible moulds as illustrated. Will press from either machine or from hand mould 4,000 to 5,000 perfect sand-faced bricks per day, with the aid of one man and two boys.

Also makers of—

Semi-dry, Stiff Plastic & Wire-cut Machinery,

PRESSES,

PLANTS SUITABLE FOR ALL MATERIALS,

Large or Small Outputs.

SITES REPORTED UPON. CLAYS TESTED. PLANS, ESTIMATES AND FULL CATALOGUE ON APPLICATION.

An advertisement of Thomas C. Fawcett Limited from The British Clayworker of May 1900 including an illustration of Gentry and Fawcett's hand brick press

THOMAS C. FAWCETT, LTD.,

ENGINEERS,

HUNSLET ROAD, LEEDS.

NEW SPECIALITIES—

Fawcett's Patent Automatic Cutting Table.

NO WASTE ENDS, SAVES LABOUR, SAVES OIL, AND INCREASES PRODUCTION OF WIRE-CUT MACHINES.

NO SMALL WORKING PARTS TO GET OUT OF ORDER. CAN BE FITTED TO ANY MAKE OF WIRE-CUT MACHINE.

Gentry and Fawcett's

PATENT POWER SAND-FACED BRICK PRESS

with collapsible moulds. Will press 5,000 to 6,000 perfect sand-faced bricks per day, with the aid of two boys.

Also makers of—

Semi-dry, Stiff Plastic & Wire-cut Machinery,

PRESSES,

PLANTS SUITABLE FOR ALL MATERIALS,

Large or Small Outputs.

SITES REPORTED UPON. CLAYS TESTED. PLANS, ESTIMATES AND FULL CATALOGUE ON APPLICATION.

An advertisement of Thomas C. Fawcett Limited from The British Clayworker of September 1900 with an illustration of Gentry and Fawcett's power brick press

Chapter 9

MARK GENTRY'S EMPLOYEES

Mark Gentry employed a large number of men at his two brickworks in Sible Hedingham at various times. As brickmaking was largely seasonal work the majority of men were employed during the Spring, Summer and Autumn. A smaller number were employed during the Winter digging out clay and carrying out maintenance work. In his first year (1885) he employed forty men, which later increased to between seventy and one hundred men as the Langthorne Brick Works expanded. Upon the opening of the Highfield Brick Works in 1894 he employed a similar number. When the industry was at its peak between 1894 and 1904 Mark Gentry probably employed a total of up to about two hundred men

The following are the known employees some of whom lived in cottages owned by Mark Gentry at Wethersfield Road (then often recorded as Oldens Road), Sible Hedingham:

Langthorne Brick Works

Ambrose Alfred Thomas (later a machinist at Rippers Limited)
Bantock Robert, traction engine driver
Bareham Bertie Albert or Alfred, brickyard labourer, later employed by SHRBC
Barker Percy, brickfield labourer
Beadle Bunny, engine driver of 'Tin Pot' (See chapter 16)
Boreham Harry, brickyard labourer
Boreham Herbert, brickyard labourer (later a thatcher)
Broyd Charles, brickmaker's labourer
Broyd Ernest
Broyd Harry 'Higgler'. During 1968 the author interviewed Harry Broyd, one of the last surviving employees, who was then in his 80s and still lived in a Brickyard Cottage, which has been built by Mark Gentry. He told the author that there were latterly four kilns working, one called "Jumbo" holding 60,000 bricks, another with 28,000 bricks and the other two of about 20 to 24,000 bricks each. He mentioned two brothers who walked to and from Sudbury to work. They were nicknamed *"Thunder and Lightening"* because they walked in all weathers. Unfortunately he could not remember their real names. The working hours were then 6am to 6pm weekdays and 6am to 1pm on Saturdays.
Carter Albert, brickmaker's labourer
Carter Charles, foreman brickmaker
Carter Ernest, brickmaker's labourer
Carter Herbert J., brickmaker's labourer
Carter Meshack, brickmaker
Carter Nathaniel, brickmaker
Carter Percy, brickmaker
Carter William, brickmaker
Chatters Alfred, brickmaker's labourer
Coote Fred, brickmaker's labourer
Corder George, brick burner – firing the kilns 1895 to 1911 (1)
Cornish Daniel, manager 1890 to 1894
Cornish Orbell, manager 1884 to 1890

George Corder (1863-1938) **John Corder (1863-1957)**

George and John Corder were first cousins and brick burners for Mark Gentry at the Langthorne Brick Works and the Highfield Brick Works respectively. Firing the kilns was the most important and responsible position in every brickworks.

Cox Walter, brickmaker from late 1880s until c1892, thereafter for about twenty years he was employed by Colliers Limited at Home Yard Brick Works, Hutton where he was killed by machinery on 10th April 1913. He was working at a wire-cut brick machine close to a revolving shaft, which was unfenced. He became entangled in the shaft and was thrown round and killed. His employers were summoned under the Factory Acts for neglecting to provide fencing to the machinery and were fined £50 with 10s costs. He was one of a family of twenty; his parents and brothers remaining in Sible Hedingham. He left a widow and nine children one of whom also had an accident necessitating the amputation of a leg. (2)
Cutler Charles
Eves James, brick moulder
Finch Charles, brickmaker's labourer
Finch George, brickmaker
Firman Albert, on 28th June 1890 he got his hand caught in a brick press and was seriously injured. Dr. Jones was promptly in attendance to stitch up the wounds and it was hoped that amputation would not be necessary. (3)
French Charles, brickmaker's labourer
Golding Robert, brickmaker
Harper Ernest, stationery engine driver, engineer and fitter who worked for Mark Gentry for about 25 years and thereafter in a similar capacity for Rippers Limited for 22 years.
Harper Herbert, engine driver
Harrington Louis or Lewis, steersman and later traction engine driver (See chapter 16)
Mead Edward, brickyard labourer and later brickmaker
Murrells Harry, brick labourer
Partridge Dan, brickmaker
Pettitt (Herbert) Thomas, a brickmaker, was born at Woolpit, Suffolk in January 1868. He started work as a brickmaker at 12 years of age and in 1893 moved to Sible Hedingham

where he was employed by Mark Gentry for three years. In 1896 he commenced work for Eli Cornish in whose service he remained as a brickmaker for 30 years.
Pilgrim James, brickmaker
Pilgrim Nathaniel, brickmaker
Ruffle 'Batty'
Ruffle Frederick, in 1900 he had an accident at work and Robert Webb (manager) sent Ruffle to Doctor Henry Twamley. Ruffle failed to pay Dr. Twamley's account for 15s 0d for medical attendances and Court proceedings were issued. At a hearing at Halstead County Court in September 1904 Ruffle said he thought the Doctor would be paid out of an accident fund. Ruffle was asked if he disputed the bill and replied with all simplicity, *"Well, he did'nt do me any good"*. Evidentally Ruffle thought Doctors ought to work upon the payment by results system.
Ruffle George, brickmaker
Rust Charles H., brickfield labourer
Sargeant Harry, brickmaker's labourer
Scillitoe Maurice, brickmaker
Scrivener Alfred, brick labourer
Sewell Arthur, brick labourer
Smith Harry, brickmaker's labourer
Spring Albert
Spring Alfred White, worker at brickworks at kiln
Spring Walter, brickmaker and brick burner
Springett Henry known as Harry, traction engine driver. (See chapter 16) He later became an engine driver for Essex County Council for over 30 years. He lived latterly at Fenn Cottage, Cobbs Fenn and died on 12th April 1947 aged 77 years. (4)
Springett Maurice, third hand on traction engine circa 1905. He was the eldest of the five sons of Harry Springett (above). Maurice later transferred to the Highfield Brick Works where he was a stationery engine man.
Stuck Alfred, brickmaker's labourer
Stuck William, brickmaker's labourer
Talbot George, a carpenter who made brick moulds, built sheds, hacks, brickmaker's tables and carried out all necessary carpentry work.
Turner Thomas, brickfield labourer
Webb Robert Lewis (1873-1945), a native of Haverhill who moved to Hedingham in the early 1890s when he was employed by the CV&HR. After a short time he left the railway and found employment with Mark Gentry as a clerk and eventually became manager of both brickworks. During the First World War he took up employment in the offices of Rippers Limited where he stayed until 1935. He was Secretary to the Assembly Rooms until the late 1930s, which had originally been established by Mark Gentry. Robert Webb initially lived in one of Mark Gentry's houses in Wethersfield Road, until he became landlord of the Sugar Loaves Public House where he lived until moving to Sydney Villa, Swan Street. He helped form the Loyal Webster Lodge of Oddfellows of which he was Secretary for many years until 1937. The Lodge had many brickmakers among its members.
Wilding Ernest, traction engine driver (See chapter 16)
Wilding Walter, employed as a general labourer loading and unloading the kilns, c1899 to 1911. He also worked on a new machine acquired by Mark Gentry to make 'pressed'

bricks, which had to be 'dipped'. He was later employed by Eli Cornish at the Tortoise Brick Works. One of his sons, Stanley Wilding, was employed by Bert Corder, a Sible Hedingham builder, until 1946. In that year Stanley Wilding commenced his own business as a builder operating from a yard established on the site of one of Mark Gentry's clay pits in Wethersfield Road.
Willsher Ted, brickyard labourer
Wiseman William James 'Swagger' (5)
Wright Arthur H., brickmaker

Highfield Brick Works
Bareham Arthur E. brickmaker, son of William Bareham (below)
Bareham Percy William, brickmaker, son of William Bareham (below). Percy followed his father into the brickmaking industry and later became manager of a brickworks at Sudbury for two and a half years. He then became a general hawker and died in 1953 aged 72.
Bareham Sidney Frank (known as Peter) son of William Bareham (below); Peter worked in the Highfield Brick Works until he took over a newsagents business from Mark Gentry junior and continued this business until retiring through ill health. He died on 1950 aged 64. (6)
Bareham William, moved from Cornard in 1896 and became manager of Highfield Brick Works. He later leased the Adam and Eve Nursery in Sible Hedingham. (7)

Charles Humphrey Boreham (1888-1917), known as Humphrey, was a brickmaker for Mark Gentry at his Highfield Brick Works. He is about to remove a 'green' brick from a mould and place it on a pallet board on a cradle barrow.

Boreham Charles Humphrey, brickmaker, killed 1917 whilst serving in the army during the First World War. Three of his brothers were also brickmakers. (8)
Corder Edward, a foreman (9)
Corder John, brick burner – firing the kilns between 1894 and 1938 latterly for The Sible Hedingham Red Brick Company Limited; his three sons, Edward, Bert and Percy also scintled bricks (10)

Walter Edward Letch (1878-1961)

William Wright Raynham, D.C.M. (1877-1953)

Letch Walter, known as 'Captain' Letch, lived at Cobbs Fenn, Sible Hedingham, later worked for SHRBC and then for Rippers Limited.
Raynham William Wright, foreman. He had previously served in the South African and Egyptian campaigns. He rejoined the Northumberland Fusiliers in the First World War when he was awarded the D.C.M., and was afterwards employed by Rippers Limited. (11)
Springett Maurice, stationery engine driver. On 6th May 1908 he met with an alarming accident, which could have been more serious. He was engaged in oiling the shafting of a pug mill when his clothes caught in the machinery and he was whirled round and round the shafting. The machine was quickly stopped by a fellow workman who was nearby but not before Springett's clothing had been practically torn from his body. In the circumstances he was extremely fortunate in escaping with a few bruises.
Springett Roger, employed until towards the end of 1912, when he joined the 2nd Suffolk Regiment and lost his life on France in 1914 aged 24 years. (12)

Brickworks unknown
The following worked for Mark Gentry but it is not known in which of his two brickworks.
Bearman Thomas, a foreman
Boreham Harry, ganger, general labourer and brickmaker
Byford Henry, a clay digger
Earey Samuel, who lived at Nunnery Street, Castle Hedingham
Finch Charles, a clay digger
Hume John, a brickmaker from Ballingdon
Murrells Charles, a brickmaker
Springett Walter, a brickmaker and a son of Harry Springett (above)
Steward Harold Ernest, a bricklayer commencing with Mark Gentry. He later went into business on his own account, lived at Rose Cottage, Swan Chase and died in 1953. (13)
At a hearing at Hedingham Petty Sessions on 14th January 1896, John Hume a brickmaker from Ballingdon, claimed 12s 0d wages for work done at the rate of 6d a yard (clay

digging at 6d per cubic yard). Mark Gentry's solicitor argued that he was not liable, because he left the job to the ganger, who might employ whom he liked. The bench found for Mark Gentry stating that they had no doubt that the man (John Hume) had broken his contract. If he and others did not finish the contract Mr. Gentry might possibly have a very strong case against them. Charles Finch and Harry Byford had entered similar claims but withdrew them. Mark Gentry generously did not ask for costs. (14) Another report stated that *"Hedingham Bench room was crowded by brickmakers and others to hear some cases from Mark Gentry's brickyard. It appeared that a number of workmen contracted to excavate a quantity of brick earth at 6d per yard. The job was commenced but some of the men grew tired of having to 'dig deep' and practically struck work. They each sued Mark Gentry for 12s 0d wages due and lost their cases. At the same Court Mark Gentry charged William Rayner, his rival, with breaking down his hedge and trespassing in his brickfield"* (See Chapter 5)

George Kendall and Dennis Partridge were both employed as brickmakers by Mark Gentry. One day in 1905 they both walked into the White Horse Inn on their way home from work and a dispute arose about work and wages. Abusive language was used and Kendall assaulted Partridge. At a hearing at Castle Hedingham Magistrates Court on 11th April 1905 Kendall was fined 5s 0d and 7s 0d costs. (15)

Employees of Mark Gentry, with four brickmakers holding moulds, during the 1890s. The cradle barrow, with springs to minimise vibration, was for carrying 'green' bricks.

On 9th March 1891 a serious trap accident occurred near the Langthorne Brick Works. Upon the arrival of the half past six down train at Hedingham Railway Station, Mark Gentry was met by his coachman in a pony chaise. They proceeded to the brickworks and whilst there darkness set in, resulting in the overturning of the trap soon after reaching the road. Mark Gentry sustained little injury with the exception of a severe shaking, the pony was little hurt, but the coachman fractured his leg in two places and suffered other injuries. The trap was badly damaged. (16) Once a year Mark Gentry and Eli Cornish jointly hired a special train from the CV&HR to take all their workmen to Clacton on Sea for a day where they gave them a good meal and arranged entertainment.

Chapter 10

HOUSES AND BUILDINGS CONSTRUCTED BY MARK GENTRY AT ROOKWOODS, HOSTAGE FARM AND WETHERSFIELD ROAD, SIBLE HEDINGHAM AND AT NUNNERY STREET, CASTLE HEDINGHAM

The lack of cottages was severely felt in the Hedinghams and soon after his arrival Mark Gentry commenced building homes for his employees. In 1886 he built a block of six houses (Nos. 1 to 6 Wethersfield Road) in front of the Langthorne Brick Works and in 1887 he built a second block of six houses (Nos. 7 to 12 Wethersfield Road) adjacent. These dwellings were known as Brickyard Cottages. Each terrace is of red brick under slate roofs. The houses at the end of each terrace (Nos. 1, 6, 7 & 12) do not have their doors facing the road, but in the side elevations. They were built with bricks made at the Langthorne Brick Works and contain some fine ornamental red brickwork. They are an excellent example of industrial workers' housing development of the late Victorian era. (1) These houses were connected to the water supply. At a meeting of Halstead Board of Guardians held on 25th March 1887, the Surveyor, Charles Wash (2) reported that a *"proper water supply"* had been provided for six new cottages built by Mark Gentry at Wethersfield Road. A certificate under the Public Health (Water) Act was granted to him. (3) By 1910 ownership of the twelve Brickyard Cottages was transferred to Mark Gentry junior. They were then occupied by Bert Bareham, George Ruffle, Alf Ambrose, Harry Springett, Maurice Scillitoe, Nathaniel Pilgrim, Charles Cutler, Herbert Boreham, George Corder, Walter Wilding, Harry Broyd and Ernest Harper who were all employed by Mark Gentry senior at the Langthorne Brick Works. (4) In the late 1880s, Mark Gentry also built and owned one house named *'Langthorne House'*, (No. 14 Wethersfield Road), which was occupied by his manager, Daniel Cornish.

Brickyard Cottages, Wethersfield Road, built by Mark Gentry for his employees in 1886 and 1887. In the background is Langthorne House, which was occupied by his manager.

Alice Ann Corder (1861-1927) in front of her home, Brickyard Cottages, prior to 1911. Note the moulded brickwork to form ornamental detail either side of the first floor windows and the sunflower in the key-brick or voussoir of the gauged brickwork of the Georgian or flat arch over each door and window.

Good specimens of his work are to be seen at Rookwoods where he displayed his skill and knowledge in the erection in 1887 and 1888 of two lodges, two stable blocks and encased an existing pair of lathe and plaster cottages in brick. He used a large quantity of ornamental red brick and terracotta in the construction of these ancillary buildings.

The gates to Rookwoods Mansion, Rookwoods Lodge and Rookwoods Cottage from a postcard postmarked 15th November 1906.

One lodge, formerly called *'Oxford Lane Bungalow'* and now known as *'The Nook'*, was built on the south side of Oxford Lane and is not listed. It was built by Mark Gentry and owned by successive owners of Rookwoods until John Cooper Bland, M.C., sold it c1960 to Arthur Lawrence Cleghorn of Rockbank, Broad Road, Bocking.

During the late 1880s, Mark Gentry erected long lengths of red brick walls along both sides of Oxford Lane. These were surmounted with iron railings, which were removed during the Second World War to help the war effort but the brick walls survive.

Oxford Lane with the brick walls and iron railings erected by Mark Gentry on both sides of the lane, which is adjacent to Rookwoods. It was named Oxford Lane after the Earls of Oxford from nearby Hedingham Castle and was once part of the main route between the Castle and London.

The other lodge, always known as *'Rookwoods Lodge'*, was built on the north side of the main entrance gate to Rookwoods. This lodge, together with Rookwoods Cottage and the two stable blocks were listed as they form part of a complex of good examples of moulded brickwork in the Queen Anne style. The listing entry for *'Rookwoods Lodge'* is as follows: *"Lodge cottage. Circa 1887. Red brick. Hipped red plain tiled roof with pierced ridge tiles and acroteria. Moulded brick coping to central forward gable surmounted by a ball finial. Large central rectangular red brick chimney stack with 5 pilaster strips and fleur de lis panels over. Moulded eaves cornice with roundel and hexaglyph band under. Moulded string course at cill level. All mouldings follow through returns. Single storey. The gable with a two light vertically sliding sash window, glazing bars to upper sashes, in heavily moulded brick surround. Frieze with moulded panels, moulded segmental head with swag panel over. Angle porch to left of gable, with balusters to wall supporting two moulded shafts with moulded flat canopy over. Half glazed panelled door. To right of gable is an ornate moulded panel with intertwined date 1887 and a smaller panel over. Notable for its ornate moulded brickwork "* (5)

Oxford Lane Bungalow built by Mark Gentry in 1887.

Rookwoods Lodge built by Mark Gentry in 1887

In 1888 he placed a very decorative brick facing over two old lathe and plaster cottages, which was then converted into one cottage named *'Rookwoods Cottage'* (which was sometimes known as *'Coachman's Cottage'*). This cottage is situated about forty yards north of the main entrance gate to Rookwoods. The listing entry is as follows: *"Lodge Cottage. Circa 1888. Red brick with red plain tiled roof and pierced ridge tiles. Moulded brick coping to parapet verges. Rear red brick chimney stack. 2 storeys. 3 window range to first floor with central plain casement. 2 range to ground floor of vertically sliding sashes, the top sash with glazing bars. This Queen Anne style building is notable for the moulded brickwork...... Dentilled and moulded eaves cornice with hexaglyph and roundel band under. Three string courses. All follow through return walls. First floor windows right and left with gauged brick arches and floral motif to keystone. Ornate forward ground floor window surrounds continue to first floor cills with fleuron panels below ground floor cills and swags below first floor cills. Chamfered mouldings to windows. Central oval date plaque with intertwined 1888 between fluted pilasters, frieze with floral keystone and enrichments to pediment. Return walls with eaves height pilaster strips to right and left of central ground floor windows. Similar ornate framing to windows but with small fleuron panels over, horizontal swag and roundel panels and vertical flower vase panels.Gables with moulded surrounds and canopies to fleuron panels......"* (6)

Rookwoods Cottage, previously Coachman's Cottage, encased with ornamental brick and terracotta in 1888. This view also shows the recent rear extension, which was built in keeping with the original cottage.

The outbuildings at Rookwoods sit in their own complex to one side and behind the main house. These buildings are mainly located around a courtyard and are concealed from the house by their orientation. They include barns, a coach house, a stable block, a flower room, a shed now used as a tractor shed, the gardener's cottage formerly the small stable block and adjacent kennels. All these buildings are listed and are mainly constructed of red brick with good examples of moulded brickwork decoration.

In 1887 Mark Gentry built two stable blocks at Rookwoods with equally fine examples of ornamental brickwork as for the dwellings. These stable blocks were also worthy of listing and the entry for the largest stable block, closest to Rookwoods Mansion House (which is also a listed building) is as follows: *"Stable block. C1887. Red brick with fine moulded brickwork. Grey slate roof hipped to west. Red brick chimney. The ornate two storey east face symmetrical with central pediment to Dutch gable. Four pilasters with moulded and enriched capitals surmounted by stone ball finials. Plinth with moulded brickwork. Flower vase panels between the pilasters at ground floor level. Band with swag decoration at eaves level above which to left and right are fleuron panels. Central circular window with glazing bars, swag panel over. Moulded and dentilled pediment enriched with egg and dart motif and fleuron panels. Weathervane finial. South face two semi-circular headed windows with glazing bars in rectangular recessed moulded panels. Two vertically boarded doors in moulded surrounds. There is a small single storey extension to west with red tiled roof hipped to left, a stable door and a two light small paned vertically sliding sash window. ……."* (5)

The stable block built by Mark Gentry at Rookwoods in 1886.

A flower vase panel of moulded between the pilasters at ground floor level.

(Both photographs were taken by the author in 1986)

The second stable block is smaller but has an attached kennel. The listing entry is as follows: *"Stable block and attached kennel. C1887. Red brick with some flint. Hipped red tiled roof with gablets, pierced ridge tiles and finials. Gabled roof to vertically boarded loft door. Moulded eaves cornice. Three vertically boarded doors. Two windows, one with moulded brick keystone over. Attached kennel to right with moulded brick cornice and moulded brick capping to enclosure plinth. Two half kennel doors and vertically boarded enclosure door. An attached wall to left of four panels with moulded brick capping to support and gate pillars, the moulding to dentilled with egg and dart ornamentation....."* (8)

The Gardener's Cottage from the walled kitchen garden. It was formerly the small stable block standing to the west of the main house and is grade II listed. It is constructed of red brick and flint walls with a clay plain tile hipped roof decorated with ridge tiles and finials with gablets at each end. It has a loft door at the north end of the east slope. There is some decorative moulded brickwork, but compared with other buildings in the complex it is relatively plain and despite alterations is a handsome and elegant building.

In 1890 Mark Gentry built a terrace of four red brick houses, also including ornamental brickwork, adjacent to the former CV&HR on the south side of Nunnery Street, Castle Hedingham. They are now numbered 87, 89, 91 & 93 Nunnery Street and were built of red brick under slate roofs. They are similar in style to those in Wethersfield Road, having main doors in the side rather than the front elevation in each end-of-terrace house. (9) The same year he also built one cottage at Hostage Farm, which was occupied by his stockman. At a meeting of Halstead Board of Guardians held on 17th April 1891 it was reported that four cottages belonging to Mark Gentry at Nunnery Street and one cottage at Hostage Farm, newly built, were provided with a sufficient supply of water and certificates under the Public Health (Water) Act were granted. (10) The four houses in Nunnery Street were later owned by James Mayhew Balls who sold them on 10th April 1922 for £350 to George Reynolds Westrop, a nurseryman of Castle Hedingham. (11)

The four cottages built by Mark Gentry at Nunnery Street, Castle Hedingham with the former railway bridge, which carried the CV&HR over the road. These four cottages remain as another good example of moulded and ornamental brickwork.

In 1887 Mark Gentry purchased *'the Cuckoo Farm premises'*, a cottage near the farm and arable land formerly part of it. (See chapter 3) He later built *'Cuckoo Cottages'* at Cuckoo Hill, which are a pair of red brick cottages, with identical key bricks to the other cottages built by him in Wethersfield Road. Unfortunately *'Cuckoo Cottages'* have recently been ruined by the application of plaster over the original red brickwork.

Members of the Carter family, who were employed by Mark Gentry, resided in *'Cuckoo Cottages'*. During the early 1900s Charles and Kate Martin and their five children moved from Tagley Cottage, Stambourne to Cuckoo Farm where Charles was employed as a horseman. His eldest daughter, Maud Lizzie Martin (1890-1981) married Herbert Charles Corder (1889-1970) in 1921.

By 1903 Mark Gentry owned a total of 19 cottages along Wethersfield Road, the majority of which he built and a few were existing cottages, which he had purchased. He was prepared to make reasonable arrangements such as laying pipes for drainage if Halstead RDC would provide an outfall. (12)

The houses, cottages, lodges, stables and kennel described in this chapter contain some of the finest and most attractive red brickwork that can be found anywhere. They were clearly good advertisements for Mark Gentry and his craft as a brickmaker.

Chapter 11

BUILDINGS CONSTRUCTED WITH MARK GENTRY'S BRICKS

Mark Gentry supplied bricks in large quantities to builders and contractors throughout England and in particular London and the Eastern Counties. He even exported bricks by ship to Africa, Egypt and Ireland where he provided the facing bricks for Dublin Barracks. (1) Large purchasers in London were the Corporation, the County Council, the School Board, the Tower Bridge Committee, GER and other public bodies. (2) In addition a further 3,000,000 bricks were used by the Great Central Railway in the building of their stations and lesser quantities supplied to the East Ham School Board. (3) Mark Gentry executed a large amount of work for board schools in London and a fine example was at East Ham where all the arches and moulded bricks, when made to shape, required setting with one eighth joints. (4) He provided bricks for school buildings in West Ham (5) and also for the following:

Chelmsford, Essex – Barclays Bank, 2 High Street

Barclays Bank at Chelmsford, built 1905, has a very fine elevation of Gothic architecture using Mark Gentry's bricks. It was designed by Arthur C. Blomfield, M.A., who was also architect to the Bank of England. (6)

Cheveley, Cambridgeshire – Cheveley Hall

Cheveley Hall, south east of Newmarket, was one of the best known mansions built with *"MG"* bricks. It was the residence of the millionaire, Col. Harry Leslie Blundell McCalmont, C.B., M.P., J.P., D.L., (1861-1902) who was Member of Parliament for the Newmarket Division from 1895 to 1902 and Colonel of the 6th Battalion, Royal Warwickshire Regiment. (7) Some 3,000,000 bricks were used to build Cheveley Hall upon the specification of the architect, Colonel Robert W. Edis. (8) This was one of the finest mansions designed by him during the latter years of his active professional career. (9) The bricks were made six courses to the foot and were described as *"very pleasing size, much in favour with some architects"* They were hand-made and hand-pressed (10) and laid with 3/16 inch joints. (11) The tiles for the roofs were also made by Mark Gentry and were sand-faced, hand-made tiles. (12) The Cheveley Estate was owned by successive Dukes of Rutland and was leased by the 7th Duke to Col. McCalmont in 1890, which was followed by the sale to him in 1893. The estate comprised of 7,800 acres, including the well wooded park of about 700 acres. McCalmont demolished the earlier house and built the replacement of considerable dimensions on its site between 1896 and 1898. It was a large and lavishly appointed neo-classical mansion, which had a 70ft long banqueting hall with a minstrel's gallery. It included 43 bedrooms and 365 windows. In order to facilitate the transportation of building materials, railway lines were laid along Central Drive to the mansion. A locomotive was used to haul wagon loads of materials from Newmarket Railway Station. Upon completion, among many distinguished visitors was King Edward VII. McCalmont died suddenly in his London home during December 1902 and Cheveley Hall became the residence of his widow who disclaimed her life interest in 1919. His trustees and heir, Major D.M.B. McCalmont, sold the estate in 1920 to the Jockey Club, which later resold most of it in smaller lots. The Hall was stripped of its contents in 1920 and demolished in 1925 as it was not economically viable. The site is now occupied by woodland. (13) By the late 1920's Cheveley Park was the property of various owners and a large portion was developed as a building estate. (14) Many of the red brick estate cottages, gatehouses, grandstand, stud buildings, outbuildings and park walls survive. (15)

The south front of Cheveley Hall under construction in 1897. Note the locomotive for transporting building materials just left of centre.

The north front in 1897 with high scaffolding on the right around the construction of the main entrance.

Entrance gates to the Central Drive through Cheveley Park showing the railway lines for transporting building materials circa 1897.

The south front upon completion in 1898.

Coggeshall, Essex - The Pumping Station at the Water Works
Mark Gentry supplied the bricks for the Pumping Station at Coggeshall Water Works. It was built in 1910 under the direction of the former Braintree Rural District Council at a cost of £8,000. Great and Little Coggeshall, Feering and Kelvedon were supplied with water from an artesian well, in Dead Lane, from which the water was pumped into a reservoir near Colne Road. On one occasion whilst delivering bricks, Mark Gentry's traction engine was involved in an accident. (See chapter 16)

Dublin, Eire – The Barracks
Mark Gentry supplied the facing bricks for Dublin Barracks. In 1997 Bulmer Brick and Tile Company Limited supplied 4,500 bricks for repairing the barracks.

Earls Colne, Essex - New house for headmaster of Grammar School
During 1897-98 a new house was built for the headmaster of Earls Colne Grammar School by Reuben Hunt. The building was faced with Mark Gentry's red bricks and covered with *"Perfector"* roofing tiles from Thomas Peake of Tunstall, Staffordshire. The inscription on the tablet stated *"This building was erected by Reuben Hunt, 1897, to commemorate the 60th year of Queen Victoria's reign. Henry A. Cheers, Architect, Twickenham."* The builder was Zachariah Rogers of Earls Colne and the total cost was upwards of £5,000. (16) The building included a boarding-house and Reuben Hunt provided an additional £1,000 for a repairing fund. (17)

Elveden, Suffolk - The Brick Kilns
Bricks with the brickmarks *'M.G.'* (Mark Gentry) and *'R'* (William Rayner & Son of Maiden Ley Brick Works, Castle Hedingham) were found in the four kilns at the former Elveden Brick Works when they were demolished in 1982. Prior to demolition the kilns were surveyed by Martin Hammond and Bill Blowers, two members of the British Brick Society. They believed that the kilns were constructed about 1896/97 prior to a large extension being added to Elveden Hall and it was for that purpose that the kilns were erected. (18) In 1894 the Executors of Maharajah Duleep Singh sold the Elveden Estate to Edward Cecil Guiness, later the First Earl of Iveagh. He established the estate brickworks making red bricks with the brickmark *'ELVEDEN'*. A light railway was constructed to facilitate the transportation of bricks and other materials to various building sites on the estate. He more than doubled the size of the Hall, built impressive servants' quarters and new cottages for employees. A branch railway line from Barnham Station to Elveden was constructed to transport building materials to the estate. However the elaborate red brick water tower was not built with Elveden bricks because it was erected in 1895 before the brickworks was established.

Halstead, Essex - Courtaulds Factory
Some of the buildings at the Halstead Mill of Samuel Courtauld & Co. Limited including the Lodge and First Aid Rooms were built with Mark Gentry's bricks. These two buildings were amongst those which survived when the remaining mill buildings were demolished in c1985. The former boiler house, which was built with his bricks in 1904 was mainly demolished c1985, although one wall between Factory Lane East and Solar Car Park remains.

London - Blackwall Tunnel

The Blackwall Tunnel, which was opened by HRH the Prince of Wales (later King Edward VII) on behalf of Queen Victoria in 1897, contains some *'M.G.'* red facing bricks. These bricks were used in the vaulting of the roof of the two archway entrances at the north and south side of the River Thames. These archways combine a pleasing ornamental entrance with a gauge arch to measure the height of loads before they descend the slopes leading to the tunnel itself. (19)

London – Claridge's Hotel, Brook Street, Westminster, W1

Claridge's Hotel was built between 1894 and 1898, the architects being C. W. Stephens and Sir Ernest George & Yeates. It was constructed of red brick facings, supplied by Mark Gentry, together with red Mansfield stone, rubbed brick dressings, cast iron balconies, slate roofs with entrances in Portland stone and black granite dressings. It is a large building principally of six storeys, with two storeys of attics set into a mansard roof and basements. It was enlarged in 1931 to the design of architect, Oswald Milne. (20) The exterior of the building remains substantially as it was finished, a massive four-square block faced in red bricks (21) made by Mark Gentry. In 2011, alterations and renovations commenced with red bricks supplied by Bulmer Brick and Tile Company Limited using some the old *"M.G."* moulds. During the course of this work many of the original Hedingham bricks with the brick marks, *"M.G."* were found. (22)

Claridge's Hotel, Brook Street, London

London - The former Holborn Board of Guardians offices and boardroom at Clerkenwell Road now known as The Red House, 49-53 Clerkenwell Road
Built by Mark Gentry with red bricks supplied by him from 1885-87. (See chapter 4)

London – Fire Station in Bishopsgate Street, EC
In 1907 red facing bricks were supplied for the London County Council's Fire Station. (23)

London - Paddington Recreation Grounds
In c1902 bricks were supplied for new buildings at Paddington Recreation Grounds. These included some pretty ornamental designs which were specially made. (24)

London - St. Patrick's Roman Catholic Church, Soho Square, W1
St. Patrick's R.C. Church was rebuilt between 1891 and 1893 to the designs of John Kelly of Messrs. Kelly and Birchall, architects of Leeds. (25) The contractor was W. H. Gaze, builder of High Street, Kingston on Thames (26) and the bricks were supplied by Mark Gentry. The red brick exterior is a sort of simplified Renaissance, with the Sutton Row side basically arched. All cornices and mouldings are of brick, Portland stone being used only for the pedimented Corinthian portico at the foot of the tower. On 19th November 1940 a powerful bomb pierced the roof of the church and buried itself in the nave but failed to detonate. A major refurbishment took place between 28th February 2011 and 31st May 2012. As part of the refurbishment the red brick campanile (bell tower) was restored with bricks made by Bulmer Brick and Tile Company Limited. (27) This church is a grade two star listed building.

London – United Methodist Free Church, off South Lambeth Road

This Church, built circa 1902, was one of the finest examples of a suburban church building in the Metropolis at the time. It marked a very distinct advance upon the typical chapel structure, for South London was not rich in artistic buildings. It was built at the junction of two streets, the builder being A. O. Robinson of Peckham. The facing bricks to the whole of the elevations visible from the main roads were Mark Gentry's best dark red facings, size 8¾ inch by 4½ inch by 2¾ inch and about 55,000 of these were used. Fletton bricks were adopted for the internal walls and facings of back walls. The contract for the whole block including boundary walls was £6,586. The architects were Messrs. George Baines, F.R.I.B.A., and R. Palmer Baines of 5 Clements' Inn, Strand. The perpendicular period of Gothic architecture, freely treated, was adopted. The church of quaint outline, was flanked on one side by a bold square tower, which was terminated by a small spirelet and weathervane. A staircase in the tower led up to a small end gallery. A projecting Narthex containing the two main entrances formed a prominent feature of the design. The dressings were of Bath stone. The seating was arranged circular on plan so that the whole of the congregation immediately faced the preacher. The preacher's platform or rostrum was placed centrally in an octagonal apse, where the choir was also accommodated. The organ chamber was arranged on one side of the apse, having organ fronts into both church and apse. The vestries were placed immediately behind the apse. A large schoolroom, with gallery, together with additional classrooms, conveniences and a suitable church parlour were also provided. (28)

United Methodist Free Church, off South Lambeth Road, London.

London – Whitfield Tabernacle, Tottenham Court Road

This was built inside and out with *"MG"* bricks. (29)

Sible Hedingham - The Pest House, Watery Lane
This was originally a lath and plaster house, which during the 1820s and 1830s provided accommodation for smallpox cases, as it was and still is situated in an isolated position. It later became two cottages, which by the 1890s were occupied by (Herbert) Thomas Pettitt and William Joshua Mead. Thomas Pettitt was a brickmaker, employed by Mark Gentry and in the course of his work made many of the bricks for his house. In c1895, Thomas Pettitt and William Mead purchased bricks from Mark Gentry for the cottages to be encased in brick. When alterations have since been carried out, the bricks were found to contain the brick mark, *"M.G."* in the frogs. The Pest House was sometimes known as The Paste House.

Stisted, Essex – Rayne Hatch House
This house was built in 1906 and contains some very fine ornamental brickwork. Whilst delivering some of the bricks it was claimed that Mark Gentry's traction engine smashed two culverts in Petersfield Road, Gosfield. (See chapter 16)

Stratford, Essex - Grove Picture Palace
The former Grove Picture Palace was built in 1910 of red brick and terracotta. It was designed by Gilbert and Constanduros, one of the most important firms of cinema architects. It is located between the junctions of The Grove with Manbey Park Road and Manbey Grove, south of Maryland Railway Station and is now used as a Doctor's Surgery.

Tilbury, Essex – Roman Catholic Church, Dock Road
The Roman Catholic Church at Tilbury is of yellow brick but has all its tracery windows in Mark Gentry's red brick and is extremely effective. (30) The Presbytery and Convent of Mercy is also of yellow brick with red brick dressings. They were designed by Robert L. Curtis and built 1906-7. (31)

Chapter 12

THE INSTITUTE OF CLAYWORKERS AND THE BUILDING TRADES EXHIBITIONS

The Institute of Clayworkers was inaugurated early in 1895 with Greville Montgomery (See Chapter 13) as Hon. Secretary. The following year he became Hon. Treasurer and George M. Callender (1862-1923) succeeded him as Hon. Secretary. George Callender who was born in Scotland became a Civil Engineer and lived in Putney. The offices of the Institute were the same as those of "The British Clayworker" namely 222 Strand, London (opposite the Royal Courts of Justice) and later at 43 Essex Street, London WC2. It was largely through the efforts of Greville Montgomery that the majority of the principal brickmakers in the country joined the Institute, including Mark Gentry, Robert A. Allen and Sons of Ballingdon and Bures and William Homan Collier of Marks Tey.

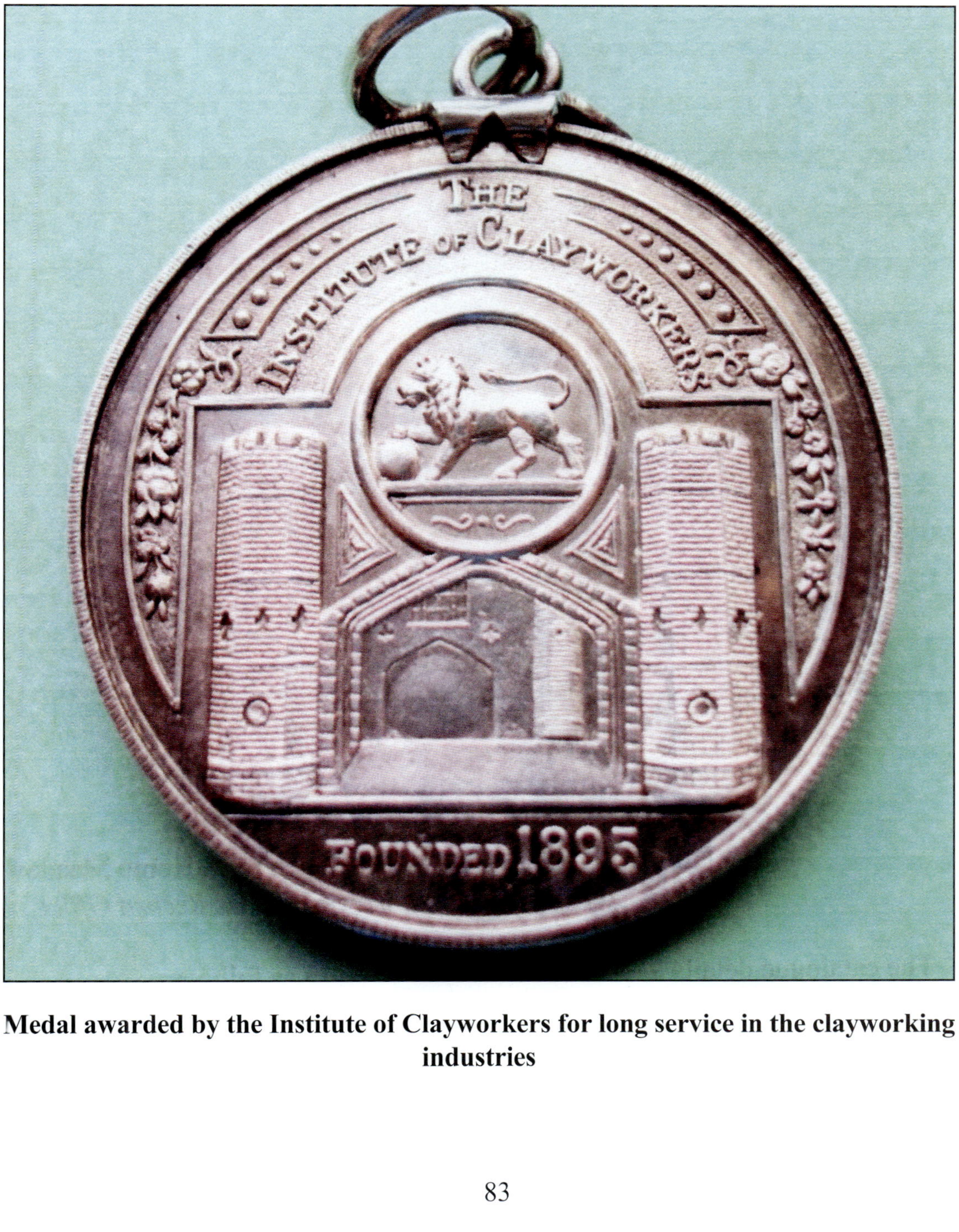

Medal awarded by the Institute of Clayworkers for long service in the clayworking industries

In the interests of brickmaking, Mark Gentry sometimes travelled abroad. In 1897, with William Barnsley Hughes of Tunbridge Wells, he inspected the 'Belgian' kiln at Hennvyeres, Belgium. (1) During Easter 1898 Mark Gentry, Greville Montgomery, William Homan Collier and over 40 other brickmakers from England and Wales visited various brickworks in Denmark during a trip organized by Greville Montgomery. (2) On 1st November 1901 Mark Gentry, Greville Montgomery, Eli, Edward and Daniel Cornish were among clayworkers who visited Felbrigg Brick Works near Cromer to inspect the yard of George Riches, J.P., and the practical working of one of William Barnsley Hughes patent down draught continuous kilns. (3) Mark Gentry took many other trips both home and abroad organized by the Institute of Clayworkers. His never failing good humour and keen participation in all that was going forward made him a much sought-after companion. (4)

Members of the Institute of Clayworkers photographed at Brook Hill Brick Works, Buckley, near Chester on 2nd June 1906. Upon leaving Chester members went to Ireland and visited Belfast and Dublin. Seated in the front row, from third on the left, is Mark Gentry, John Cathles Hill (President), Major John Merriman Gibson (Vice President) and Henry Greville Montgomery, M.P., (Hon. Secretary). Major Gibson was a Director of Buckley Brick and Tile Company Limited, which was incorporated in 1865. In the 1890s he commanded the 1st Flintshire (Buckley) Engineer Volunteers, many of whom later served in the Boer War. John Hill (1858-1915) was a director of the London Brick Company Limited, which during the early 1900s owned a brickworks at Great Bentley, Essex making red sand-faced bricks. (Photograph from The British Clayworker, June 1906 - reproduced courtesy of The British Library Board).

By 1897 Mark Gentry had become a member of The Institute of Clayworkers. At the fourth Annual General Meeting of the Institute held on 3rd May 1899 he was elected as a new member to serve on the Committee. (5) He was subsequently re-elected each successive year until his death in 1912. He regularly attended the meetings of the Institute and contributed much to the discussions. He often represented the Institute (with the Hon. Secretary, Greville Montgomery) at meetings of other bodies such as railway companies to get improved conditions, facilities and rates for brickmakers generally.

On 3rd February 1898 a deputation of Essex brickmakers organised by the Institute of Clayworkers met Sir William Birt of the GER at Liverpool Street Station to discuss grievances including a reduction of charges, computed weights and rebate on sidings. Among those attending were Mark Gentry, William Rayner of Castle Hedingham, Robert Allen of Ballingdon, William Collier of Marks Tey, Crispus Cottis of William Cottis & Sons of Epping and George King, proprietor of Harold Wood Brick Co. (6) Following two further meetings a computed weight for bricks carried on the GER was agreed. The question was, were bricks to be weighed from kiln or from stock? Sir William thought from either or both but Mark Gentry pointed out that when customers were quoted 12 months ahead, the actual deliveries could include bricks from kiln and stock and if only the latter (with bricks having been in stock all winter) the consignee would suffer. Eventually an agreement was reached of weighing the bricks from the kiln and adding 1cwt to the weight per thousand as a make-weight for bricks absorbing moisture in bad weather. (7)

Two years later Mark Gentry was a member of another deputation regarding damage to goods in transit and met Mr. W. Gardiner, the goods manager of GER. Mark Gentry stated that he had sent six chimney pots of special design, each packed in a crate by itself. Upon arrival at the destination, a distance of about 20 miles, all six chimney pots were broken. Six more were dispatched and met the same fate. On consigning a further six half of them arrived in good condition. Other brickmakers gave similar examples of their grievances, which Mr. Gardiner promised to endeavour to remedy.

Mark Gentry also had trouble with other railways. On 16th July 1900 he consigned a truck of best red facing bricks to a station on the London and North Western Railway. On arrival at a junction the truck turned over and the bricks thrown down an embankment. A month later he was informed that the truck had been delivered but a claim was made against him for demurrage. The Railway Company informed him that the goods were consigned at owner's risk and they were not responsible. (8)

At a meeting of the Institute of Clayworkers held 1st November 1900, Mark Gentry drew attention to the inconvenience and loss arising from the breakage of goods in transit, sent at owners risk. He pointed out this arose very largely from the use of steam brakes by railway companies. This resulted in an approach to GER for an interview. (9)

On 10th March 1903 Mark Gentry and Greville Montgomery were among the representatives of the Institute who attended a meeting with Midland Railway to discuss grievances on behalf of brickmakers. (10) At these meetings the railway companies initially relied upon their form of official defence namely that guards and shunters had been cautioned to exercise reasonable care and to report cases of rough shunting. They also claimed that most of the damage arose through bad packing and the delay in goods being removed by consignees. However the railway companies assured brickmakers that they would do their best to minimise breakages. Many years later it was reported that the

vigorous representations made by Mark Gentry and others on behalf of the Institute of Clayworkers produced beneficial results. (11)
In March 1900, Mark Gentry was elected to a sub-committee of the Institute to consider *"extraordinary traffic and excessive weights on roads"* and the Boiler Registration and Inspection Bill, which was then before the House of Commons. It was noted that as well as traction engines, the use of horses and carts between a brickworks and railway stations may cause *"extraordinary traffic"*. The Bill was opposed by the Institute when it came before the Select Committee. (12)

In 1902 Mark Gentry was a subscriber to the cost of a portrait of Edgar Webster, Ex-President of the Institute. The same year he gave a donation to the Institute Benevolent Fund of £10 10s 0d and Greville Montgomery donated £105 0s 0d. In 1903 Mark Gentry gave another £5 5s 0d. It came as no surprise, when, at a meeting of the Institute held on 26th March 1903, Mark Gentry was unanimously elected as chairman for the ensuing year. In the June of his year as Chairman he was present at a large dinner held at the Café Royal, London for some 30 members of the French Institute, the Union Ceramique de France.

Horace Rendall Mansfield, M.P., (13) was President of the Institute of Clayworkers when Mark Gentry was Chairman. In June 1904 he took the chair at the AGM of the Institute when Parliamentary business in London prevented Horace Mansfield from being present. This meeting took place at Leicester when members took the opportunity to visit Leicester brickworks and were entertained at the home of Mr. & Mrs. Horace Mansfield. In later years Mark Gentry occasionally took the chair if the chairman was absent and last took the chair at a meeting of the committee of the Institute in April 1911.

Mark Gentry's stand at the Building Trades Exhibition April 1897. (Photograph from The British Clayworker, April 1897 - reproduced courtesy of The British Library Board).

In 1895 Greville Montgomery revived the Building Trades Exhibition and through his organization it became a great success during the ensuing years. Mark Gentry frequently displayed his bricks at the Building Trades Exhibitions, which were held in London every two years. A report of the April 1897 exhibition stated, *"Mark Gentry of Hedingham, Essex made an effective show of his well-known rubbers, facing and moulded bricks. These famous reds created a great deal of attention from architects."* (14) At the conclusion of the highly successful 1897 exhibition many exhibitors decided to express their appreciation to Greville Montgomery and George Callender by arranging a complimentary dinner for them. This took place in the Venetian Room at the Grand Midland Hotel, St. Pancras, London and among the fifty attending was Mark Gentry. (15)

Mark Gentry's stand at the exhibition held at the Royal Agricultural Hall, London on 26th April 1899. (Photograph fromThe Brickbuilder, May 1899 - reproduced courtesy of The British Library Board).

The Brickbuilder reported that, *"Mark Gentry of Sible Hedingham had a most creditable exhibition. Here we were struck by the ornamental bricks especially. For some years we have advocated the employment of what is generally known to the public as 'carved bricks', such as were used so successfully by mediaeval Italian architects, and Mr. Gentry has certainly gone a long way to produce our ideal, albeit his ornamental bricks are not 'carved'. The great difficulty in many cases, with this sort of clay goods is the production of a uniform tint. A large relief pattern – for instance, a cornucopia with attendant flowers and fruits – must be made in several pieces to have a good effect. If the colour of adjacent pieces is not exactly alike much of the value of the work is lost. But, with the specimens exhibited there was no such fault as this, and indeed the goods of various descriptions on this stall were practically uniform in colour throughout. Moreover, the patterns were in high relief and sharp, the 'undercuts' being as clear as the rest. This stand amongst other things contained bricks of deep red colour, lettered relief bricks, orange rubbers, red hand-made facings and hand pressed facings, red rubbers which are made in various shapes, red moulded bricks, chimney pots, & c. These are all first-class red goods, sand faced. The arch bricks alone were of a special character, some of them being 2 feet in length and in section tapered towards one end."* (16)

Mark Gentry's stand at the 1901 exhibition. (Photograph from The British Clayworker, June 1901 - reproduced courtesy of The British Library Board).

The British Clayworker reported that, *"In addition to his well known "M.G." red bricks, there were many ornate bricks, small panels of floral design, both simple and composite, tiles with letters, etc., in high relief, all of red tint of great uniformity. We were particularly struck by the regularity exhibited in joining different pieces in complicated patterns; not only did the work in high relief on adjacent pieces fit well together, but there was an absolute continuity of colour, and at a distance it was difficult to appreciate that the several parts were not one piece. It is work of this sort that reminds us of those old Italian examples of art brickwork about which Street has written so much. We should like to see artistic bricks employed in greater quantity by the British architect than at present, and there is certainly a tendency in that direction. Without saying a word in disparagement of terra-cotta, which has its own peculiar and unique uses, we cannot help remarking that such beautiful and uniform ornate bricks and floral panels as Mr. Mark Gentry exhibited seem to us to carry out the best traditions of Italian mediaeval art brickwork, and can be thoroughly recommended to present-day art architects."* (17)

A local newspaper report recorded the presence of Hedingham Bricks at the Building Trades Exhibition as follows, *"At the International Building Trades Exhibition, which is being held this week at the Agricultural Hall, Mr. Mark Gentry of Sible Hedingham has a stand, upon which is shown a very fine collection of high-class red facings, and ornamental bricks and of a quality the 'Building News' says that will satisfy the most exacting architect. 'Mr. Gentry' remarks that authority 'has reached perfection in the attainment of uniform colour, by which means he can insure in a large relief design, as that of a cornucopia, made in several blocks of perfect uniformity of colour throughout which is seldom possible'. The exhibition comprises a vast assortment of the productions of the brickyard, all of which have been turned out at the Langthorne Brickfield, Sible Hedingham."* (18)

Mark Gentry's stand at the exhibition held at the Royal Agricultural Hall, London on 26th April 1899. (Photograph from The Brickbuilder, May 1899 - reproduced courtesy of The British Library Board).

The exhibition report stated, *"Mr. Gentry's exhibit was a good one, as it always is. The goods shown were remarkable for their excellent colour and finish. Indeed, although it is difficult amongst so many good exhibits to say which is entitled to the greatest merit, we must say that the ornamental brickwork and other things which Mr. Gentry had on his stand would take a lot of beating. One feature on the stand amused us. Mr. Gentry is making blue-black bricks – and why not, if he can do so. He knows something of ancient bricks too, for he treated us to some account of what our forefathers did and these black-*

faced bricks came to the forefront. When we first saw them we asked whether they were intended for paving purposes and were told "certainly not". So far so good. These black bricks are merely intended for decoration in walls. Then we ventured to ask by what process the black was introduced to the brick, and what the black was. But this great secret still rests within Mr. Gentry's bosom." (19)

He did not exhibit at the 1905 Building Trades Exhibition but did so again in 1907, with red facings, rubbers and moulded bricks. The report of the exhibition, which was held at Olympia between 6th and 20th April 1907, stated of his display, *"……… Many of these facing bricks are of unusual sizes and shapes and run from four to six courses to the foot, the making of such bricks being a speciality with this firm. With such a clay as that at Sible Hedingham it is only natural that this stand should also show an unusually good set of moulded bricks and blocks, including a sharp, clear-cut re-production of the East Ham coat-of-arms, and some excellent "egg and tongue" work for copings and borders. All these are executed in a light red clay of pleasing colour, which renders it specially adaptable for blocks for monograms, date plates, and similar carved and moulded work."* (20) *Another report of the exhibition stated, "Moulded bricks of striking quality were shown by Mark Gentry, whose yards have long been known for the crispness and sharpness of the work they turn out. It is indeed seldom that a firm can be found who will produce such excellent moulded work in red clay as the letterings and shields exhibited by Mr. Gentry, and he is to be congratulated, not alone on his wonderful clay, but on the skill of the mould-makers and the actual workers in the clay."* (21)

King George V, when Prince of Wales, visited the Building Trades Exhibition at Olympia in 1907 and 1909. He took a keen and sympathetic interest in the building industry. (22)

Mark Gentry also had a good display of samples of his products on view at 11 and 12 Finsbury Square, which were his London offices and showrooms, where he was represented by Charles Haslop until c1906 and thereafter by Phillip Chilton Gross (1857-1943) and William Potter Corby (1872-1910). (23) Phillip Gross, who was born at Greenwich, was a builder's clerk living at Lambeth in 1891. (24) By 1901 he was a brick agent living in Leyton. (25) He died in the Camberwell District of London in 1943 aged 85 years. Towards the end of 1910 William Corby committed suicide in the Blean District of Kent aged 37 years. He was born at Stepney and by 1891 was employed as an architect's pupil living with his parents at Hampton Road, East Ham. (26) In 1901 he was employed as a sanitary engineer living with his wife and young son at Claremont Road, East Ham. (27) As well as being brick agent for Mark Gentry he was also agent for The Leeds Pottery, Middleton Fire-Clay Works, Messrs. F. Winkle and Company, earthenware manufacturers of Colonial Pottery, Stoke on Trent and others. (28) Mark Gentry was the London representative of The Pioneer Glazed Brick Co., manufacturers of leadless glazed white enamelled bricks, coloured enamelled bricks and salt-glazed bricks. This company shared his London office at 11 and 12 Finsbury Square and his London agents Phillip Gross and William Corby. (29) It was also the office for Robert L. Curtis & Sons, surveyors and for Robert Leabon Curtis, junior, a quantity surveyor.

The Royal Agricultural Hall, Islington, where the early Building Trades Exhibitions were held between 1895 and 1905.

On 23rd December 1910, W. P. Corby & Co. Limited was incorporated and its directors included Arthur Ernest Winkle and Lawrence Hubert Winkle, earthenware manufacturers of Stoke on Trent. The objects were, *"To carry on business as manufacturers' agents, sanitary specialists and agents for the supply of builders' materials, glazed bricks, paving bricks, red hand-made facings, red hand-pressed facings, red moulded and ornamental bricks, red rubbers, arch bricks and all other kinds of bricks, chimney pots, terra cotta, faience, sanitary ware, baths, basins, urinals and lavatories, fireclay goods, crockery ware, telegraph and telephone insulators and conduits, drain pipes and all other materials and things used in building and other works; also to carry on business as builders and contractors………"* (30)

The company's office was at 27 Chancery Lane, London WC and by 1913 it became the sole agent for J. & N. Nadin & Co. Limited, fireclay tile manufacturers of Stanton Colliery, Burton on Trent. (31) W. P. Corby Limited was dissolved in July 1919. (32)

Rippers Limited, joinery manufacturers, became regular exhibitors at Building Trades Exhibitions held at Olympia until the early 1970s. (See Appendix Two).

On 1st and 2nd December 1903 an exhibition was held at the Shire Hall, Chelmsford to encourage the application of art to manufacturers. Mark Gentry displayed ornamental bricks, panels and shields and the Essex Art Pottery Co. of Castle Hedingham, operated by the Bingham family, exhibited their pottery. (33) The displays of bricks at various exhibitions clearly promoted Mark Gentry's *'Hedingham Reds'* to architects and builders.

MARK GENTRY,

Red Brick Maker,

Sible Hedingham, ESSEX.

RED HAND-MADE FACINGS. RED HAND-PRESSED FACINGS. RED MOULDED & ORNAMENTAL BRICKS. RED RUBBERS & ARCH BRICKS, & CHIMNEY POTS.

Complete Catalogue will be forwarded to Architects on application.

See Stand No. 58, Row B, at Olympia, April 6th to 20th.

THE PIONEER GLAZED BRICK Co.

MANUFACTURERS OF

Leadless Glazed White Enamelled Bricks,

Coloured Enamelled Bricks,

Improved Salt-Glazed Bricks.

London Office: 11 & 12, FINSBURY SQUARE, E.C. London Representative, MARK GENTRY. London Agents: P. C. GROSS and W. P. CORBY.

See Stand No. 58, Row B, at Olympia, April 6th to 20th

Advertisements from The Brickbuilder & Cement Maker, April 1907 p. viii

Chapter 13

H. GREVILLE MONTGOMERY, M.P., J.P., HON. A.R.I.B.A., (1863-1951)

Henry Greville Montgomery, known as Greville Montgomery, was born in 1863, a son of Hugh and Susannah Montgomery. Hugh was a printer and proof reader. The family lived in Westminster where Greville was educated, following which his first occupation was as private secretary to William Sproston Caine, M.P. His subsequent appointments were with the Earl of Yarborough and the Dowager Duchess of Montrose.

Greville lived at Bakers Farm, Lamb Lane, Sible Hedingham during the late 1890s and early 1900s. (1) He was a tenant of Mrs. Hannah Johnson, widow of Edward Killingworth Johnson (1825-1896), the well known artist, whose family had owned Bakers for some three hundred years. (2) Greville only occupied the house and garden. The farm buildings and land was let to John Kendall and later to John and his son Richard Kendall, who farmed Bakers Farm. (3)

Bakers Farm, Sible Hedingham c1900 when occupied by Greville Montgomery

Whilst living in Sible Hedingham, Greville Montgomery established a special fund for temporary relief by the distribution of coal for sick people. This was in addition to the Sible Hedingham Widow's Coal Fund, which was administered by Miss. Eleanor Webster of The Bays. A joint distribution took place during the last week of November 1904 when about 64 aged, infirm and sick people each received 2 cwt of coal. (4) By the 1920s the two funds had amalgamated and were known as the 'Sible Hedingham Coal Charity'.

Greville was a newspaper proprietor and in 1892 founded *"The British Clayworker"*, the organ of the Brick and Tile Trades, of which he was proprietor and editor. As a result the

Institute of Clayworkers was inaugurated in 1895 with Greville Montgomery as Hon. Secretary. (See chapter 12) He founded *"The Brickbuilder"*, which from 1895 was a supplement of *"The British Clayworker"*. This supplement was later renamed *"The Brickbuilder and Cement Maker"*. (For details of other publications by Greville Montgomery see appendix one)

In 1895 he revived the biennial Building Trades Exhibition in London and through his organization it became a great success. Apparently he was a dissatisfied exhibitor at earlier trade fairs so he decided to arrange the 1895 exhibition himself and continued to do so for the next 50 years. It became the UKs largest business to business exhibition and one of the worlds most important trade shows for the building and construction industry. (See chapter 12) He also inaugurated the first Colliery Exhibition held in this country. Greville and his brother Hugh were also the managing organisers for the International Exhibitions of Rubber and other Tropical Products and Allied Industries. The fifth exhibition was held at the Royal Agricultural Hall, Islington in June 1921 under the patronage of King George V. The exhibition offices were at 43 Essex Street, Strand, London, which were shared with The British Clayworker and the Institute of Clayworkers. Greville Montgomery occupied 43 Essex Street as tenant of Duncan Irvine. (5) (For further information about exhibitions arranged by the Montgomery family see appendix two)

Henry Greville Montgomery, M.P., J.P., Hon. A.R.I.B.A., (1863-1951). (Photograph from The British Clayworker, April 1895 - reproduced courtesy of The British Library Board)

When the British Clayworkers' Mutual Insurance Corporation Limited was formed in 1898 to indemnify persons in the brick, tile and pottery making industry from loss and injury, Greville Montgomery became a Director and Shareholder. In fact it was inaugurated by him in conjunction with the Institute of Clayworkers shortly before the Workmen's Compensation Act 1897 came into force in July 1898. At the first General Meeting held on 20th October 1898 he was Manager and Secretary and by 1900 was Managing Director. (6) He remained a Director and Shareholder until his death in 1951 and the following year the company was voluntarily wound up. (7) (For further information see appendix three)

He was Liberal Member of Parliament for Bridgwater, Somerset from 1906 to 1910 during Sir Henry Campbell-Bannerman and Herbert Asquith's administrations, and favoured nationalization of Railways and Canals and Electoral Reform. He was also a Member of the Council of the Royal Drawing Society of which he was Chairman circa 1909. He was a Honorary Associate of the Institute of Structural Engineers and of the Royal Institute of British Architects. He was also a Justice of the Peace for Norfolk where he lived latterly at Bacton Hall near Norwich. In 1909 he was elected President of the Somerset Agricultural Society and was Patron of the Living of Norton Malreward, Somerset for nearly sixty years. He was a Liveryman of the Worshipful Company of Tylers and Bricklayers of which he was Master in 1927/28. It was one of the oldest and perhaps the nearest associated with brickmaking of all the City companies. He was a member of the Reform Club and also a member of the Savage Club of which he was a trustee. (8) He was a kind and generous man whose benefactions often went unseen and for many years he was a staunch supporter of the Architects Benevolent Society of which he was Vice President. (9) In 1934 he was elected the first honorary member of the Guild of Bricklayers. (10)

Of all his positions and achievements perhaps the two principal ones, apart from being a Member of Parliament, were his founding of *"The British Clayworker"* and his skilful organization over half a century of the Building Exhibition. This exhibition was originally arranged in partnership with his brother, Hugh C. Montgomery, also a publisher of trade journals and books and later with his son, Hugh Roger Greville Montgomery. In 1911 he was an agricultural student but later joined his father arranging exhibitions. The early exhibitions were held at the Royal Agricultural Hall, Islington and from 1907 at Olympia, West Kensington.

Greville Montgomery was a member of the Light Railways Association during the 1890s which met in one of the committee rooms at the House of Commons under the chairmanship of Sir Albert Rollit, M.P. This association gave the first real impetus to the construction of light railways. (11) Amongst those considered were the various proposed light railways for north Essex, which, if built, some would have served brickworks in Hedingham and Gestingthorpe. (See chapter 15)

In 1904 the Royal Commission on Trade Disputes and Trade Combinations called upon Greville Montgomery to give evidence on behalf of the clayworking industries. Bills, which the House of Commons considered, included the legislation of peaceful picketing, the immunity of members of Trade Unions from responsibility in damages and an amendment of the law of conspiracy. (12)

During early 1918 Greville Montgomery was appointed a member of the Building Materials (Bricks) Supply Committee of the Ministry of Reconstruction. At that time he was also giving his services to the War Office (Contracts Branch) at Imperial House, Westminster. (13)

He regularly attended meetings of the Essex Brickmakers Association, which by July 1919 became the Essex and Suffolk Brickmakers' Association. Amongst the members were, William Homan Collier (Chairman) and Ernest W. Collier of Marks Tey, Eli Cornish of Sible Hedingham and William John Rayner of Castle Hedingham. The Association, under the guidance of Greville Montgomery considered such questions as wages, prices, transportation by rail and the acquisition and price of coal.

During the 1920s, Greville Montgomery was Secretary of the South Eastern Federation of the Building and Engineering Trade of England and Wales, which also shared offices at 43 Essex Street, Strand, London.

It is interesting to note that Greville Montgomery was living in Sible Hedingham when the brickmaking industry there was at its peak. He did a vast amount of work to promote the trade and no account of brickmaking in Hedingham would be complete without reference to his association with the village and the industry.

Greville Montgomery married twice. His first wife was Florence Thomasine Shepherd, daughter of Charles Messingham Shepherd (1823-1887). They married in 1888 and sadly she died in 1890 aged 28 years. Their son Hugh Roger Greville Montgomery, known as Roger, was born in 1890 and married Molly Audrey Neele in 1927. They had a son Hugh Bryan Greville Montgomery, known as Bryan, who was born in 1929. Roger, Molly and Bryan became actively involved with Trade Exhibitions. Following the death of Roger on 13th February 1952 at Funchal, Madeira, his widow Molly Montgomery, O.B.E., Hon. A.R.I.B.A., and son Bryan Montgomery, M.A., (Oxon) continued arranging exhibitions as directors of The Building Trades Exhibitions Limited. Molly Montgomery was well-

Descendants of Hugh Montgomery

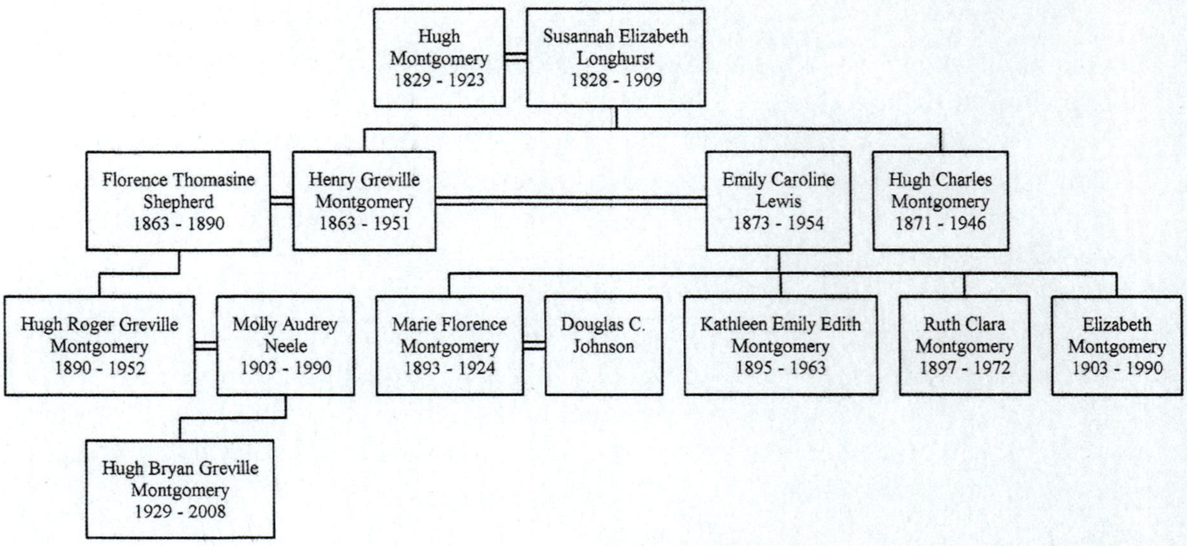

travelled, internationally minded and expanded exhibitions abroad. In 1963 the Building Trades Exhibition became The International Building Exhibition and in 1973 Interbuild. (See appendix two). Bryan became a Freeman of the City of London in 1952 and a member of the Tylers' and Bricklayers' Company. He died on 14th December 2008 and was succeeded by the fourth and fifth generations of the Montgomery family to arrange exhibitions under the holding company of Angus Montgomery Limited.

Greville married his second wife, Emily Caroline Lewis, daughter of David Lewis, in 1892 and they had four daughters, Marie, Kathleen, Ruth and Elizabeth. Greville Montgomery retired as editor proprietor of The British Clayworker in October 1948 (14) and as Secretary of the Institute of Clayworkers in November 1948. To mark the Institutes appreciation of his 50 years in office he was unanimously elected an honorary member. (15) He died 2nd December 1951. (16)

Greville Montgomery in Parliament

Greville Montgomery was approached on behalf of a number of constituencies before he decided to accept the invitation of the Liberals in the Bridgwater Division of Somerset to become their candidate. His choice of a brick and tile district like Bridgwater was most appropriate. After leaving Sible Hedingham he moved to Thornfalcon Cottage, Henlade almost in the centre of the Bridgwater Division. (17) It has been a Conservative seat since 1868 from when the Tory candidate had been returned unopposed on several occasions. The Liberal opponent in 1892 was defeated by a crushing majority, so by 1906 Greville Montgomery *"had his work cut out"*.

FOR THE . . . .
BRIDGWATER DIVISION.

HE STANDS **AGAINST**

Taxes on Food,
Sectarian Education,
Chinese Labour,
Reckless Expenditure,
Government Jobbery,
Snubbing of Volunteers,
Conscription,
Tied Houses,
and . . .
HOME RULE.

Greville Montgomery's election card when he stood for Bridgwater in 1906.

The fight proved a desperate one, for with 90% of the available electorate going to the poll Greville Montgomery's majority was just 17 over the Tory candidate. There were 10,180 electors and the result was as follows:

H. G. Montgomery	Liberal	4422
R. A. Sanders	Conservative	4405
	Liberal majority	17

During the contest Greville Montgomery wrote and published two leaflets himself on railway rates and cement. His views on railway rates and the allied question of canal development proved a feature of his Parliamentary career. (18)

However, his maiden speech in the House of Commons was upon Workmen's Compensation, a subject in which he had been actively involved for some years. (19)

On 19th June 1907 he gave evidence before the Royal Commission on Canals and Waterways which was chaired by Lord Shuttleworth. His evidence was collected from members of the brick and tile trade throughout the country. He pressed for improved canals for brickmakers not only to reduce railway rates but to increase brickmakers area of distribution. (20)

On 24th February 1909 in the House of Commons he put a question to the Rt. Hon. Winston Churchill, M.P., (as he then was), the President of the Board of Trade. The question related to railways and owners risk rates. Clayworkers wished to see a Bill compelling railway companies to pay, like other people, for the results of their own carelessness. (21)

During 1909 Greville Montgomery led the opposition to the proposed tax on clay royalties, which on 22nd September that year induced the Government to drop the tax. (22)

With a busy Parliamentary career he still found time to continue his work as Hon. Secretary of the Institute of Clayworkers and Editor of The British Clayworker. Towards the end of 1907 he visited brickworks and mines in South Africa.

In 1909 the following limerick appeared:

"We all know Montgomery, H. G.,
And a thorough good fellow is he,
Irrespective of party,
our wishes are hearty,
To see him Montgomery, M.P." (23)

At the General Election in 1910 this hardworking *'Clayworking'* Member of Parliament did not seek re-election.

Chapter 14

THE ALEXANDRA BUILDING ESTATE AT SIBLE HEDINGHAM

At an auction held on 4th March 1901 at the Assembly Rooms, Sible Hedingham, the personal representatives of John Green Emson namely Susan Emson, Frank Everitt Emson and Charles Ilderton Croft sold Brook Farm extending to some 74 acres in 12 lots. Three lots were purchased by Mark Gentry (See chapter 3). Lot 4 comprising of 4a 0r 14p with a frontage of about 240 feet to the west side of Swan Street was sold to Oliver Wallace for £115. By 10th July 1901 these four lots were owned by Greville Montgomery. This land was situated along both sides of Swan Street and also along both sides of what became known as Alexandra Road. The entire area purchased by him was named *"The Alexandra Building Estate"*, which he divided into building plots and sold during 1901 and 1902.

Zeerust House, Swan Street, which was built on Lot 1 by Henry Walter William Gooch for his own occupation. (Reproduced courtesy of Essex Record Office ref: D/DU 1935/1)

On 30th July 1901 an auction conducted by Messrs. Balls took place at the Assembly Rooms when 56 lots of freehold land were for sale of which 14 plots were in Swan Street and 41 in Alexandra Road. Lot 1 was sold to Harry Gooch, upon which he built his red brick house named Zeerust and established his joiners and builders business at the rear. A pair of red brick houses were built on Lot 2, which are now 146 and 148 Swan Street. Lot 3 was sold to William Mower, the local Police Sergeant upon which he built Colne Cottage in 1904. Lot 51, having a frontage to the south side of Alexandra Road of about 50 feet and a depth of about 197 feet was sold to Charles William Everitt of Castle Hedingham for £14 0s 0d. He paid a deposit of £1 4s 0d and the balance of £10 16s 0d upon completion. The final lot namely lot 56 of just over 5 acres of arable land being part of *"Catch Croft"* is now the Recreation Ground, which since 1927 has been owned by Sible Hedingham Parish Council. For the auction on 30th July a special train was arranged from Chappel Junction to Hedingham (which connected with trains from Liverpool Street and Colchester), which gives an indication of the importance of this sale.

The following extract is from a report of July 1902 (1) *"The Development of Sible Hedingham - Those who have visited Sible Hedingham recently must have been struck by the number of new houses that are making their appearance there, consequent upon the opening up for building purposes of a large area of land adjoining Swan Street. This estate was brought under the hammer, in convenient plots, sometime ago, and already there is considerable evidence of the builder's presence. ……….. The application of bricks and mortar to the erection of house property in a village is noteworthy. But Sible Hedingham is more fortunate than most of its neighbours in this respect. Here there has for some years been a steadily growing demand for workmen's cottages, as well as dwellings of a better class, owing to the expansion of the brickmaking trade, which may now be regarded as the staple industry of the place; and the development, consequent upon this extension, and for other reasons, is to be seen on the Alexandra Estate……. The first sale took place about a year ago, when the promoters had staked out a large number of plots and driven a well-made road through the middle of it.* (Alexandra Road). *Nearly sixty plots have been sold and there are now very few remaining………… About a dozen houses are complete or nearing that state, the builders of these being J. Deeks and Son of Halstead and Hedingham* (2) *and Harry Gooch of Sible Hedingham.* (3) …………. *The Colne Valley Railway system is conveniently handy, the telephone - that herald of advancing commercialism - is said to be on the way. …………."*

"Victoria Villas" were the first houses built on the south side of Alexandra Road in 1901

A further ten building plots were sold by Greville Montgomery on 28th July 1902 of which some faced Swan Street and others Alexandra Road. On the same day the executors of John Emson sold the last two lots of Brook Farm amounting to 12a 1r 19p. Lot 1 was Cross Path Field of 8a 2r 9p and Lot 2 was land on the east side of Swan Street at the top of Brook Hill of 3a 3r 10p. The majority of Cross Path Field was later occupied by Rippers Joinery Works and Lot 2 became the site of 1-24 Brook Terrace and 154-188 Swan Street (evens) being industrial housing built by Rippers Limited for employees. Both sales were conducted by Messrs. Balls at the Assembly Room.

Following the sale of the earlier building plots in 1901 the first red brick houses in Alexandra Road were built. It was given the name Alexandra from Queen Alexandra although for many years the road was commonly called the *"New Road"*. The first houses to be built on the south side of Alexandra Road were a pair of houses with bay windows named *"Victoria Villas"*, which were built of red brick in 1901. They are now 41 and 43 Alexandra Road.

They were followed by a block of four red brick houses named *"Rose Cottages"*, which were built in 1902 and are now 33, 35, 37 and 39 Alexandra Road. When Rose Cottages were advertise for sale in 1930 the tenants were as follows:

No. 1	Herbert Charles Corder, a brick burner and a son of George Corder (below)
No. 2	William Bailey Theobald
No. 3	Alfred George Carter
No. 4	Robert Drury

In 1904 another block of four houses of red brick and slate construction were built known as *"Ethel Cottages"*, which are now 25, 27, 29 and 31 Alexandra Road. When Ethel Cottages were advertised for sale in 1930 they were described as *"Four Freehold Villas"* having a frontage of 54 feet, a depth of about 180 feet, with gardens front and rear. The tenants were as follows:

No. 1	John Redgewell
No. 2	Bert William Corder (builder and contractor)
No. 3	Rev. James Grinnell (minister of Sible Hedingham Baptist Church)
No. 4	George Corder (brickmaker and brick burner)

In 1911, when Mark Gentry sold the Langthorne Brick Works, George Corder moved out of Brickyard Cottages, Wethersfield Road and into 4 Ethel Cottages. His family continued to reside there until his daughter Edith Ethel May Corder moved to Stisted Hall in 1984.

The eight *"Villas"* known as Rose and Ethel Cottages were owned by Alfred Miller until his death in 1929. He was a baker and confectioner in St. James's Street, Castle Hedingham, whose business was continued by his son Bert Miller. His family sold Rose and Ethel Cottages the following year on 4th September 1930. George Springett (1876-1943) and Alice Maud Springett (1882-1965), a daughter of Alfred Miller, lived in the detached house known as *"The Laurels"*, which was built during the early 1900s in red brick with a slate roof. Unlike other houses in Alexandra Road, *"The Laurels"* had its gable end facing the road. A Gospel Hall erected in the garden was removed in 1930 when the property was sold upon George and Alice Springett moving to Bramfield, near

Halesworth, Suffolk. *"The Laurels"* was demolished during the 1960s to make way for the access road to Spurgeon Close. Ethel Cottages were owned by George Elsdon, a builder and undertaker, until his death in 1970.

On 12th January 1937 Bert Corder purchased land in Alexandra Road from Mrs. Alice Maud Springett, upon which he built a large detached house named *"Baytos"*, now 32 Alexandra Road, which remained in the ownership of the Corder family until it was sold following the death of his widow, Florence Emma Corder in 1968.

Alexandra Road looking towards Swan Street prior to the road being made up in 1921, with the north side on the left and the south on the right. The bungalow is Downfield, which faces Swan Street and the garage opposite belonged to Mark Gentry junior. To the right of the garage is a house built for Lewis Wiseman, now sadly demolished.

One the north side of Alexandra Road, are two terraces of red brick houses. The western terrace comprised of seven houses, which are now 18, 20, 22, 24, 26, 28 and 30 Alexandra Road. This terrace included three pairs of houses and one single house at the western end. One house was named *"Rohilla"*, which is now 20 Alexandra Road. It was owned by W. Parsonson and another who sold it on 29th September 1905 to John Corder (1863-1957) a brickmaker and brick burner. On 22nd March 1957 his executors conveyed it to his grandson Kenneth Frederick Corder and his wife Ivy Muriel Corder. It remained in the ownership of Kenneth Corder until his death in January 2011 and therefore this house was in the ownership of the Corder family for well over one hundred years. An early name for 18 Alexandra Road was *"Le Cateau"*, which was probably named following the First World War battle.

At the eastern end of the north side of Alexandra Road is a terrace of three red brick houses, which were built in 1904 and named *"Cathay Cottages"*. Numbers 1, 2 and 3 Cathay Cottages are now 14, 12 and 10 Alexandra Road respectively. On 5th November 1901 Greville Montgomery conveyed the building plot upon which 3 Cathay Cottages (now number 10 Alexandra Road stands) to Percy Hicks. On 30th June 1904 Percy Hicks conveyed it to Frederick George Hicks. On 17th May 1905 Frederick George Hicks a baker of Little Waltham conveyed it back to Percy Hicks a carpenter of Little Waltham for £250. On 20th August 1913 Percy Hicks then of Asthall School House, Burford, Oxfordshire conveyed the property back to Frederick George Hicks for £230. (4) This house was owned and occupied by Percy James Corder, a bricklayer and builder from 1922 to 1952. Since the early 1960s it has been owned by his great niece, Shirley Ann Radley (formerly Corder).

A total of twenty one red brick houses were built on the Alexandra Building Estate between 1901 and 1904 namely ten on the north side and eleven on the south side of Alexandra Road. With the exception of *"The Laurels"*, the remaining twenty houses survive. Apart from these twenty one houses no more houses were built in Alexandra Road until the early 1920s. By 1921, the former Halstead RDC purchased exactly four acres of the field, known as Catch Croft, which had originally extended to over 11 acres. In 1921 twenty Council Houses were built on this land on both sides of Alexandra Road. (5) The remaining 7a 2r 10p was owned by Frank Gibson (6) who built Gibson Road on part of this land and in 1927 conveyed the remaining 5 acres to Sible Hedingham Parish Council to form the Recreation Ground. Alexandra Road was made up and taken over by Halstead Rural District Council in 1921 when owners of property abutting the road were required to pay a contribution.

In 1922 Frank Gibson built a house for James Sandford, which is now 55 Alexandra Road. (7) The following year he built a pair of houses named Belle Vue, which are now 47 and 49 Alexandra Road. (8) By this time Dorothy Villas, now 51 and 53 Alexandra Road had already been built as had the chalet bungalow, now 45 Alexandra Road. On the opposite side of the road Frank Gibson also built a detached house for Miss. Hester Adelaide Purnell in 1922, which she named *'Staverton'*, and is now 8 Alexandra Road. (9)

On 5th November 1901, Lot 19 was sold by Greville Montgomery to Charles Henry Dodd, a builder of Great Maplestead. On 25th January 1905 C. H. Dodd sold this land to Frederick George Hicks who on 31st March 1924 sold it to Percy James Corder in whose ownership it remained until his death in 1989. In September 1949 a bungalow was designed for Percy Corder for which he was granted a *'private building licence'* in February 1951. He built the bungalow during 1951-52 and it is situated between the two original terraces of red brick houses on the north side of Alexandra Road. The bungalow was named *"Runcorn"*, now 16 Alexandra Road, which he occupied from 1952 until 1989. The facing bricks were some of the last to be made at Rayner's Brick Works at Maiden Ley, Castle Hedingham before it closed in 1952.

Some of the land owned by Greville Montgomery was purchased by him from Oliver Wallace (10) of Brook Farm, Sible Hedingham on 10th July 1901. This included land on the east side of Swan Street. On 6th November 1908 Greville Montgomery then of Bacton, Norfolk sold part of this land, having a frontage onto Swan Street of 150 foot to Jane Gentry (wife of Mark Gentry) for £95. (This is the land upon which Sible Hedingham Post Office, the Chemist's Shop with adjoining house, 136 and 138 Swan Street now stands). On 1st December 1908 Jane Gentry sold this land to Alice Springett £85. (11) The reason for a £10 loss within a month is not known. The site immediately to the north, with a 100 foot frontage, was owned by Gentry and Perkins, upon which their garage was built. (See chapter 17)

The owners of land in this part of Swan Street in May 1908 (12) were as follows:

Plan No	*Description of property*	*Owner*
51	*Field and footpath*	*Robert Balls, H Greville Montgomery & A Frank Gibson*
52	*Field*	*Robert Balls, H Greville Montgomery & A Frank Gibson*
54	*Field*	*Robert Balls, G. Boreham, W. Mower, Bareham, Henry Gooch, M. J. Gentry, Perkins & H. Greville Montgomery*
55	*Field*	*Robert Balls, G. Boreham, W. Mower, Bareham, Henry Gooch, M. J. Gentry, Perkins & H. Greville Montgomery*

A pair of red brick houses was also built on the west side of Swan Street during the Edwardian era, which are now 129 and 131 Swan Street and were owned until the mid 1960s by George Elsdon, a builder of the Adam and Eve Works, Sible Hedingham. A bungalow was built on the corner of Alexandra Road and Swan Street by 1915. It was named *'Downfield'* and faced Swan Street. It was occupied by John Fuller and later by Louise Jackson.

Greville Montgomery still owned some freehold land in Swan Street until 1915 or later. After his decision not to seek re-election to Parliament in 1910 he left Henlade, Somerset and returned to Bacton Hall, Bacton, Norfolk, which remained his home until his death in 1951. In 1926 a pair of cottages were built for him at Bacton to the design of H. Austen Hall, F.R.I.B.A., as an experiment in the use of hollow blocks. These were supplied by W. H. Collier of Marks Tey and the Heather Brick and Terra Cotta Co., of Leicester. The roof was of reed thatch in preference to the use of foreign tiles. (13)

A pair of houses being built on Lot 13 of the Alexandra Building Estate, now 119 and 121 Swan Street. (Reproduced courtesy of Essex Record Office ref: D/DU 1935/1)

Chapter 15

THE PROPOSED CENTRAL ESSEX, THE HEDINGHAM TO LONG MELFORD AND OTHER LIGHT RAILWAYS

The great disadvantage to the Langthorne Brick Works of Mark Gentry, the Tortoise Brick Works of Eli Cornish and the Southey Green Brick, Tile and Pottery Works of William Corder, were the large distances away from Sible and Castle Hedingham Station on the Colne Valley and Halstead Railway. (CV&HR) All goods manufactured were transported by horses and carts but the use of horse power proved a matter of some difficulty and cartage was expensive.

Sible and Castle Hedingham Railway Station, with bi-directional 'station signal' and goods shed. On the side of this shed is an advertisement for 'Hedingham Brick, Tile and Terra Cotta Works'. This photograph was taken between 1885 and 1892 when Mark Gentry had his London Offices at 2 Wormwood Street and depot at Bishopsgate Goods Station.

The brick manufacturing industry in Hedingham gave the CV&HR a large traffic of coal inwards from the Haverhill direction and a large traffic of bricks outwards through Halstead, Chappel and Wakes Colne. In 1887 the brick traffic by rail from Hedingham was 5,000 tons a year, which increased to over 20,000 tons a year by 1898. At the half yearly meeting of the CV&HR held on 31st August 1898 it was reported that the *"brickfields traffic at Hedingham was going up by leaps and bounds"*. As it increased more rolling stock was required to carry it. The Great Eastern Railway (GER) had helped as far as it reasonably could, but it was also short of rolling stock and could not help any more. During the half year the CV&HR had ordered 20 more wagons but these were not sufficient. If more wagons could be found the prospects of the CV&HR looked good and it reported that no other brickfields were known, which had the advantage of Hedingham. The railway had an application before it for an entirely new brickfield at Hedingham estimated to make ten million bricks a year. (1)

In 1901 between 30 and 40 truck loads of bricks were dispatched from Hedingham daily when the industry was employing about 500 men. (2) Unfortunately through lack of sufficient rolling stock the railway lost much revenue throughout the time that the brick industry was at its peak. Although special 'brick' trains ran from Hedingham, the CV&HR could not cope with the extent of the brick production. It was necessary for the railway to purchase a larger and more powerful engine but this was not delivered until 1908. (3)

The 1908 0-6-2T locomotive built by Hudswell Clark being No. 5 of the CV&HR entering Halstead Station with the 12.20pm Haverhill to Chappel goods train on 6th August 1909. This "up" goods train included several trucks of bricks from Purls Hill Siding, Sible Hedingham.

The Master Brickmakers therefore supported the proposed light railways for north Essex. (see appendix five) Light Railways were not necessarily narrow gauge but had a limit weight of about 5 tons per axle. One advantage of light railways was that they were usually more economical to construct and the wagons were frequently lighter but had a better carrying capacity than standard railways. During the 1890s numerous public meetings and inquiries were held in the Hedingham area to consider various schemes. These meetings and inquiries were generally well attended particularly by the landowners and farmers across whose land the railways would have run and also by local industrialists and merchants, including brickmakers, who would have used the railways to transport their goods. (4)

On 9th September 1896 Sir Walter Gilbey, Bt., D.L., J.P., of Elsenham Hall presided at a meeting in Thaxted to consider the construction of a light railway between Elsenham and Thaxted, Bardfield and Finchingfield. He guaranteed £50 towards preliminary expenses and it was resolved to submit the scheme to the Government. (5) The estimate for 2ft 6in gauge was £25,000 or £2,500 per mile to include seven sidings, small goods sheds, platforms, shelters and the fencing of the line. For 4ft 8½ in gauge £500 per mile was added making £3,000 per mile and the total cost £30,000. (6)

A very crowded meeting to consider Light Railways was held in the Town Hall, Halstead in August 1896 under the chairmanship of Charles Portway, J.P., C.C., the well known Halstead iron founder. He was supported by Walter Hopkins (engineer) and Douglas Franklin (hon. secretary to the committee of promoters). Others present included Daniel Unwin, Thomas Goodchild, Frederick Payne, Walter Whitlock, Joseph Blomfield (all farmers), Owen Clover (miller), Stanley Moger (estate agent), Harry Harvey Portway (iron founder), Robert Lake Hughes (Clerk to Halstead RDC), Charles Runnacles (builder) and George Copus (representing the CV&HR). The meeting was arranged to ascertain the support from the districts of Wethersfield, Hedingham and Halstead to a proposed Light Railway from Elsenham by Thaxted, Bardfield, Finchingfield, Wethersfield, Hedingham to Halstead. Mark Gentry stated that his tonnage placed on the CV&HR amounted to between eleven and twelve thousand tons. If the Light Railway was built it would pass right through his Langthorne Brick Works and he would not employ horses and carts to transport bricks to Hedingham Station. Mark Gentry also supported the proposed Light Railway because it would give him *"two ends open for his traffic to London"* (The Light Railway and the CV&HR). Mark Gentry and many other landowners, including Guy's Hospital, consented to give land owned by them on the route of the Light Railway to the company, free of charge, in return for shares in the line. It was reported that in the Thaxted, Bardfield, Finchingfield and Wethersfield districts that the cost of coal was £1 10s 0d a ton but if the Light Railway was built it should only cost £1 a ton. It was understood that the cost of construction would be about £3,000 a mile and the proposal to support the railway was carried. (7)

When an earlier meeting was held in Great Bardfield during July 1896, it was Mark Gentry who had suggested that the railway should be carried through Wethersfield to Hedingham and connect with the CV&HR. This scheme became known as the Bardfield and Sible Hedingham Light Railway which was a projected continuation of the line it was proposed to build from Elsenham to Great Bardfield. He pointed out the desirability of continuing the line to Hedingham instead of making a "dead end" at Bardfield. He suggested that if running powers could be obtained over the CV&HR it would form an excellent route for the barley growers of Thaxted, Bardfield, Finchingfield and Wethersfield areas with Mistley from where large quantities of malt were shipped. Among the supporters were Charles Wing Gray, M.P., and Col. Samuel Brise Ruggles-Brise, C.B., D.L., J.P., of Spains Hall, Finchingfield. (8) Mark Gentry stated that he could guarantee placing on the line something like 12,000 tons a year. (9)

A Light Railway from Hedingham to Long Melford was also promoted. This was supported by Gestingthorpe Parish Council, which passed a resolution in favour of the line because in its opinion the Gestingthorpe district was in need of increased railway facilities and the railway would be beneficial to the community and improve trade. The correspondence between Gestingthorpe Parish Council and the Solicitor to the Promoters took place between May and July 1898. The Clerk of Gestingthorpe Parish Council was Alfred Digby Finch, who was also manager of Rayners Brick and Tile Works in the village. (10)

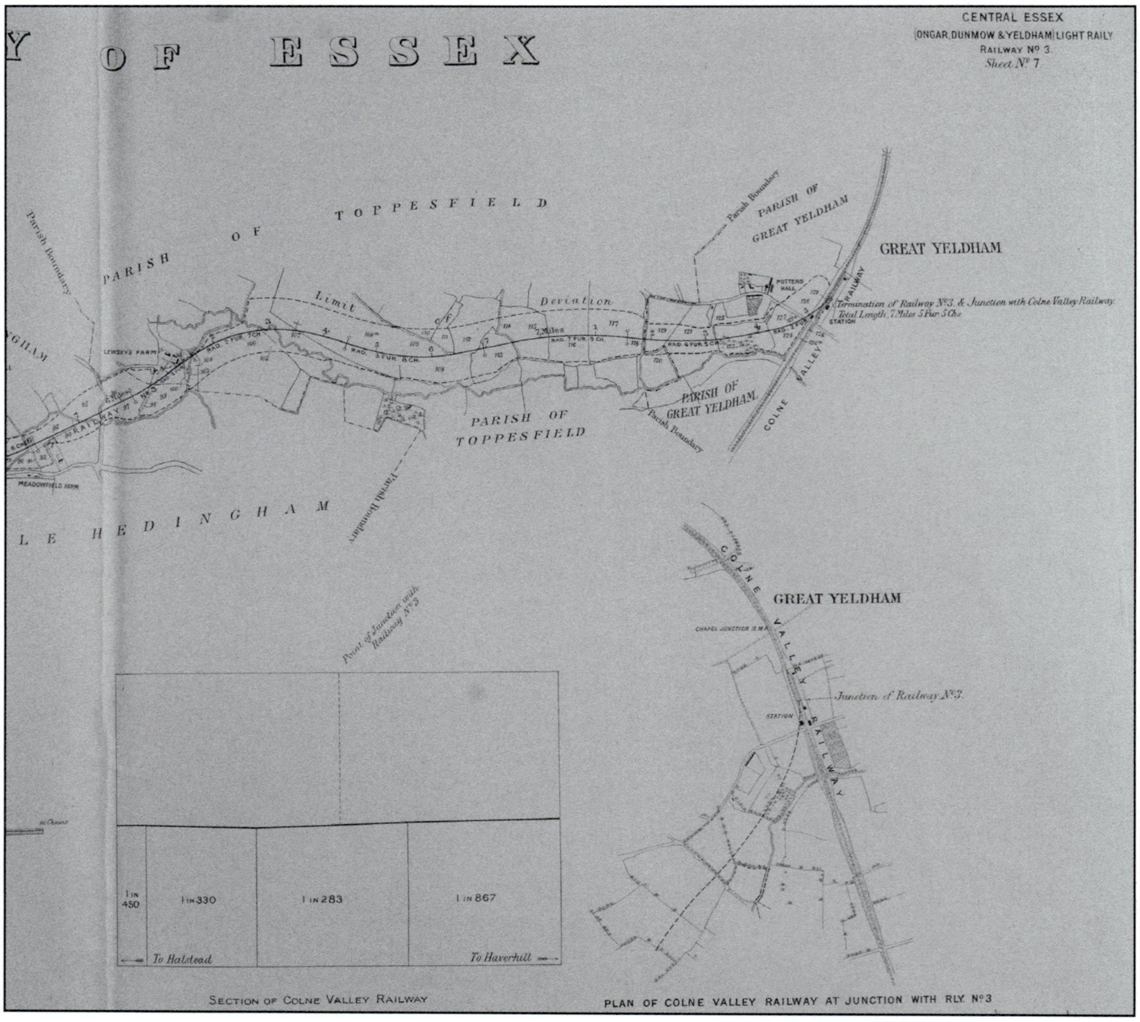

A plan of the Central Essex (Ongar Dunmow and Yeldham) Light Railway and its proposed junction with the CV&HR at Great Yeldham. Note the close proximity of both railways with Potters Hall Brick Works. (Reproduced courtesy of Essex Record Office ref: D/Dwv P21)

Mark Gentry took no end of trouble to get the Central Essex Light Railway into existence but it was never built. The original route surveyed circa 1896-97 was from Ongar, via Dunmow to Great Yeldham. This would have passed near two brickworks at Fyfield, one at Great Dunmow and one at Great Yeldham. The Fyfield brickworks were at Clatterford End of which Henry Lindus was proprietor and another north of Fyfield operated by the Bentley family. At Great Dunmow the line would have passed under the Dunmow viaduct, which carried the GER (Bishop's Stortford, Dunmow and Braintree Branch) over the River Chelmer. A link between the two railways was planned terminating with a junction 360 yards south east of the end of the up platform at Great Dunmow Station. This was very close to the Park Brick Works of Messrs. Hasler at Great Dunmow. At Great Yeldham the route was south of Potters Hall Brick Works, before its termination at a junction with the CV&HR about 150 yards to the north of the level crossing at Great Yeldham Station. When the route was surveyed the proprietor of Potters Hall Brick Works was William Corder and the land surrounding Potters Hall was farmed by Charles Bocking who later became proprietor of the brickworks. The railway would have passed through seven fields occupied by Charles Bocking of which one was owned by Edward Holmes, one by Sir Alfred Hughes, Bt., four by Charles Martin Wade and one jointly by Charles Martin Wade and Lewis John Way. (11)

On 13th,14th and 15th October 1898 a Public Inquiry was held in the Assembly Rooms, Swan Street, Sible Hedingham into the proposed building of three light railways. The three schemes were;

(i) A line from Ongar by way of Dunmow and Bardfield to Great Yeldham, to be known as the Central Essex Railway;

(ii) A continuation of the same from Sible Hedingham by way of Gestingthorpe, Belchamp and Long Melford;

(iii) The Bardfield and Sible Hedingham Light Railway, a projected continuation of the line which it was proposed to build from Elsenham to Great Bardfield.

The Commissioners appointed under the Light Railways Act to hear the evidence were the Earl of Jersey, G.C.M.G. (Chairman), Gerald A. R. Fitzgerald and Colonel Boughey, C.S.I. Many people in the Sible Hedingham area were witnesses, some of whom were represented by Counsel and Solicitors. The CV&HR and the GER were represented. One witness was Mark Gentry who gave evidence that since he had been in the district his business had been steadily growing and Hedingham bricks had made a reputation for themselves. When he first came to Hedingham the output was under 500,000 a year but had increased to between 10 and 12 millions, representing from 25,000 to 30,000 tons. He sent bricks all over England, also to Ireland and sometimes to Africa. He had recently sent bricks to Egypt by ship and had supplied all the facing bricks for Dublin Barracks. The majority of his bricks were sent to London and the suburban districts near Ongar.

Mark Gentry had originally favoured an extension to Hedingham of the Elsenham and Thaxted Railway but when the Central Essex Railway was planned he preferred that because of a more direct route with London and it would be more economical to build. He stated that if he had railway accommodation to his works he could double output in a year. If they had made double the quantity of bricks at Hedingham in 1898 they could have sold them. (12)

The Central Essex Railway would have been 27 miles long and cost an estimated £131,320 5s 0d. (13) It was promoted as a steam railway whereas some other light railways proposed in other parts of England were electric. (14) It was supported by Charles Wing Gray, former Member of Parliament for the Saffron Walden Constituency, which included Sible Hedingham. In fact Charles Wing Gray was occupier of about 300 acres of land in Sible Hedingham including a field owned by Mark Gentry, which was on the route of the proposed Hedingham to Long Melford Light Railway. This was field no. 36 on the railway plans. The route also passed through the Langthorne Brick Works and field no. 35 both owned and occupied by Mark Gentry. (15)

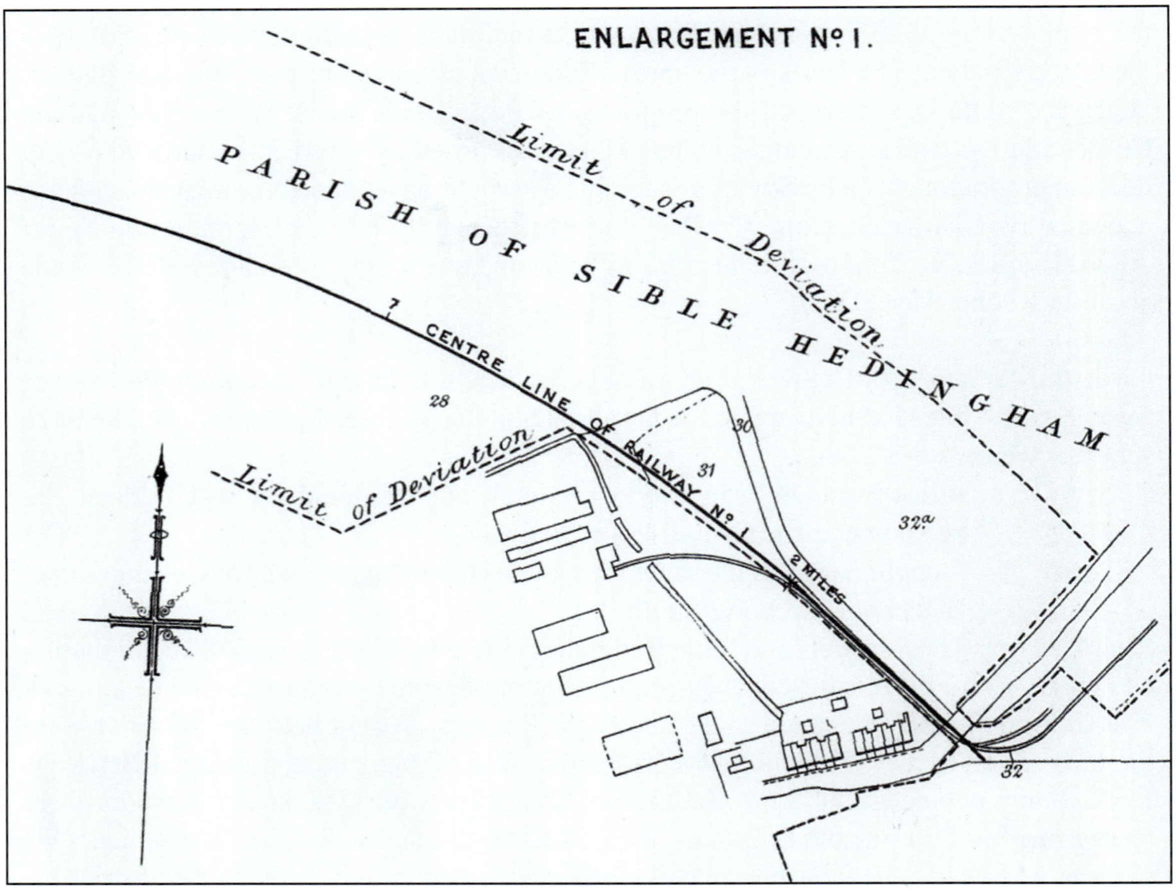

Plan showing the route of the railway through the Langthorne Brick Works

Evidence was later given in support of the line from Hedingham to Long Melford. This would start by branching off from the Central Essex Railway at a point near Bloys Farm, about two miles from Great Yeldham Station and sweep round by Sible Hedingham, cross the Colne Valley line along which it would run for half a mile and then proceed round by Castle Hedingham to Gestingthorpe, Belchamp and Long Melford where it would join with the GER. It was originally proposed to take the line from North End, Little Yeldham to Great Yeldham but this part was dropped so the line, could serve as many brickworks as possible. This reduced the total length from 15 to 12½ miles but the estimated cost was still £84,000. (16)

Robert Balls, F.A.I., a land agent, (17) was authorized to appear for various landowners who were all very much in favour of the line. He stated that, *"With regard to Gestingthorpe, the line could not fail to be of great assistance to it, for the brickfields there had gone down entirely for want of railway accommodation. The cartage was so heavy, the brickyards, where there was as good earth as could be found in Essex, being four miles from the station".*

The Rev. Crowder Thomas Bromwich of Gestingthorpe stated the population of the village had gone down about 100 since 1891 partly caused by the closing of the brickworks (which later re-opened). He had been told that flower pots could be sent into Sudbury from Staffordshire cheaper than they could be brought from Gestingthorpe simply on account of the heavy cartage.

Mark Gentry then gave evidence in support of the Castle Hedingham loop which he said was laid out chiefly to meet the requirements of the brickyards and it would give them a direct line to London. The accommodation provided by the CV&HR was very unsatisfactory. He stated that on the previous day he wanted to load eight trucks on the CV&HR but could only get two. The CV&HR was unable to cope with his business. Although it did its best, its resources did not meet his requirements. He could load 20 and sometimes 30 more trucks a week than the railway could give him.

With regard to Gestingthorpe, Mark Gentry went on to state, *"The Gestingthorpe earth was very different from that at Hedingham; they got into the gault there, and it was more suitable for pottery work."*

For the previous four or five years, Mark Gentry had kept the works at Gestingthorpe going by taking all the best they could make, but they had to stop because they could not sell their common bricks at prices, which would pay for the cartage. Mark Gentry added that he was prepared to take these works on, if the line runs through to them, because they have at Gestingthorpe a bed of earth equal in quality to that on the Great Northern where there was a great rush. If the line was built he offered to pay £100 an acre for the land which adjoined the works.

Other people who gave evidence and supported the scheme included William Corder, a miller, of Belchamp Walter, King Downs, an iron founder of Gestingthorpe, the Rev. Henry Foyster Bull, M.A., of Borley and Samuel John St. Clere Raymond, J.P., of Belchamp Hall. However there was also local opposition particularly from Lord Waldegrave of Borley and Colonel Burke of Bulmer. (18)

The inquiry took three days and resulted in the Central Essex Light Railway being supported as opposed to the other schemes. The Hedingham to Long Melford line was disallowed. The Commissioners decided to allow Swan Street to be crossed on the level instead of by a bridge as proposed in the plans. Gates, a gatekeeper and gatekeepers house were requested and the level crossing would allow an important flattening of the gradient on the approach to Hedingham Station.

In 1901 two Orders were confirmed by the Board of Trade namely The Central Essex Light Railway Order dated 3rd July 1901 and the Bardfield and Sible Hedingham Light Railway Order dated 18th November 1901. At this time it was proposed that the Central Essex

Light Railway would join the CV&HR at Great Yeldham. The route between Finchingfield and Great Yeldham passed south of Flowers Hall Toppesfield, north of Bloys Farm and Meadowfield Farm Sible Hedingham, south of Lewseys Farm Toppesfield and south of Potters Hall Great Yeldham. (19) The Hedingham to Long Melford Light Railway branch to Sible Hedingham was planned to commence at a junction with the Central Essex Light Railway west of Bird's Green Farm, Sible Hedingham and pass to the north of the Farm, through Meakley Wood, the Langthorne Brick Works, Church Street and Swan Street to join the CV&HR south of Castle and Sible Hedingham Station. (20)

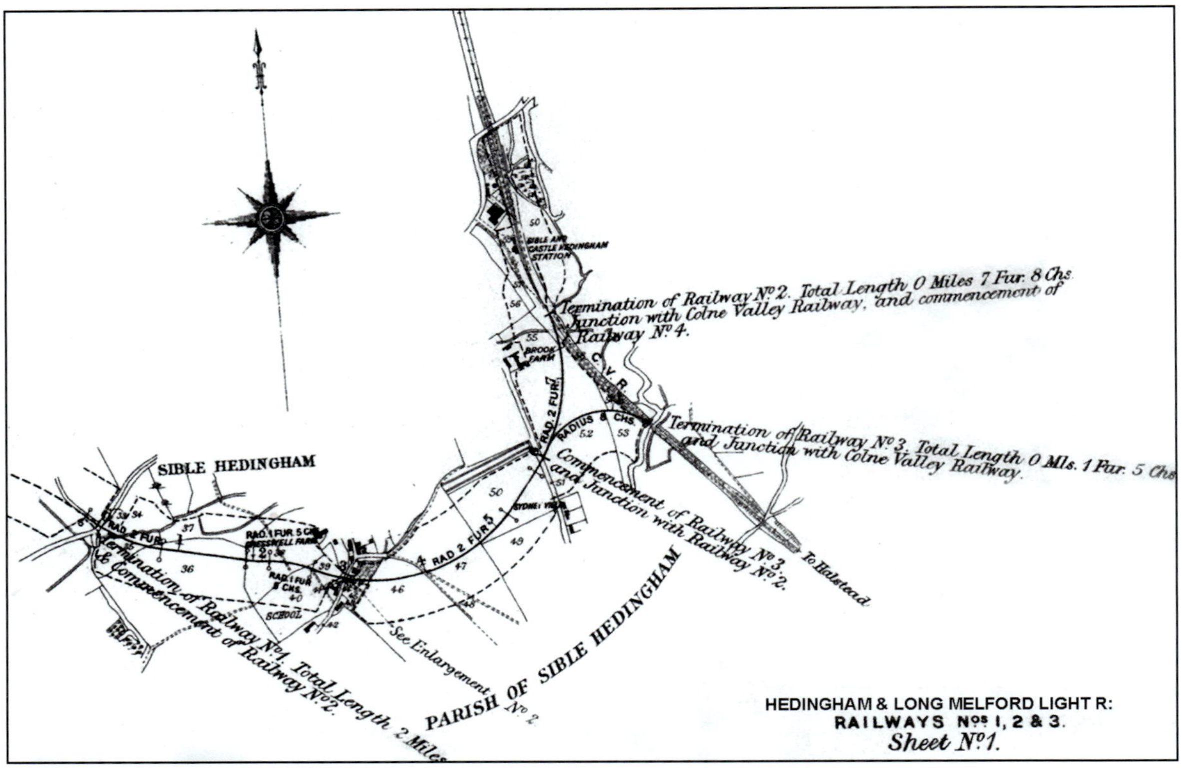

Plan showing the route of the Hedingham to Long Melford Light Railway branch through Sible Hedingham, which was disallowed. It was later decided not to extend the Central Essex Light Railway to Yeldham but to divert it to Sible Hedingham when the route shown on this plan was adopted by the Central Essex Light Railway

The former route terminated in Finchingfield where the new route diverted through Wethersfield and followed part of the route of the disallowed Hedingham to Long Melford Light Railway from near Birds Green Farm to the CV&HR. (21) An inquiry was held in 1901 when it was again suggested that a bridge be provided in Swan Street and a level crossing in Church Street, Sible Hedingham. Objections were raised to a bridge in Swan Street and a level crossing was again preferred. Unfortunately these issues delayed the scheme.

In June 1904 the Halstead Rural District Council received a request on behalf of the promoters of the Central Essex Light Railway to cross Church Street on the level. The Light Railway Commissioners approved a level crossing upon condition that a footbridge was provided for the use of the general public. Mark Gentry and Eli Cornish, both members of Halstead RDC, proposed and seconded respectively that the Council give its sanction, which was carried. The Council also gave its consent to extend the time granted in 1901 for the compulsory purchase of lands and other property and the completion of the railway and works. (22)

In May 1904 the Light Railway Commissioners decided that the Bardfield to Sible Hedingham Light Railway Company should be wound up and amalgamated with the Central Essex Light Railway Company. (23) When the 1901 Orders expired an extension of time was obtained under the Central Essex Light Railway (Amendment) Order 1905, which was confirmed by the Board of Trade on 4th September 1905. (24) In November 1906 another application and order was made namely the Central Essex Railway (Amendment Order) 1906, which amended the order of 1905 by extending the time for the compulsory purchase of lands and for completion of the railway. (25) When this expired in 1907 a further Order intituled Central Essex Light Railway (Extension of Time) Order 1907, confirmed by the Board of Trade on 5th June 1907, was granted. On 15th August 1908 the Board of Trade confirmed a new Order intituled Central Essex Light Railway (Amendment and Extension of Time) Order 1908 which granted an extension of time to purchase land to 31st December 1909 and for the completion of the works to 31st December 1911. (26)

In about January 1907 the Central Essex Light Railway book of reference (27) was amended, which gives details of property owned by Mark Gentry in the Wethersfield Road area of Sible Hedingham as follows:

No. on plan	*Description of property*	*Owner*	*Occupier*
25	*Field and footpath*	*Robert Balls and Mark Gentry*	*John Perrit*
27	*Field and footpath*	*Mark Gentry*	*John Perrit*
28	*Field*	*Mark Gentry*	*John Perrit*
30	*Field*	*Mark Gentry*	*John Perrit*
31	*Field*	*Mark Gentry*	*John Perrit*
32	*Occupation road*	*Mark Gentry*	*John Perrit*
33	*Field*	*Mark Gentry*	*John Perrit*
34	*Field and footpath*	*Mark Gentry and George Ruse*	*John Perrit*
36	*Field and footpath*	*Mark Gentry*	*John Perrit*

When the book of reference was revised to May 1908 (28) the majority of fields, which had previously been owned by Mark Gentry were owned by Robert Balls. There were only two references to Mark Gentry as follows:

34	*Field and footpath*	*Robert Balls and George Ruse*	*Mark Gentry and John Perrit*
36	*Field and footpath*	*Robert Balls and Mark Gentry*	*John Perrit*

It would therefore appear that sometime during or between January 1907 and May 1908 Mark Gentry sold much of his land around Wethersfield Road to Robert Balls. John Perrit or Perrett, was a farmer from Wincanton, Somerset who farmed Hostage Farm and lived in Hostage Farm House. George Ruse was a farmer from Helions Bumpstead. During 1908 Greville Montgomery sold some of his retained land along the route of the proposed railway from a point near Church Street to the north side of Sydney Villa and across to the CV&HR.

In August 1909 a prospectus (29) was published, which provided that the share capital of the Central Essex Light Railway Company was £178,000 divided into 8,900 ordinary shares of £10 each and 8,900 preference shares of £10 each. The railway was to be about 30 miles in length on the ordinary gauge (4 feet 8½ inches) and worked by steam or electric power. The line was to commence at the GER terminus at Ongar with stations at Fyfield, Beauchamp Roding, Leaden Roding, High Roding, Great Dunmow, Stebbing, Great Bardfield, Wethersfield, Runalong and join the CV&HR at Hedingham Station. Runalong Farm sometimes recorded as Rumalong Farm is just within the boundary of Sible Hedingham and was the site of a former brickworks belonging to Orbell Cornish. The prospectus stated, *"The manufacture of Bricks is carried on on a large scale in the district, and this Railway will connect one of the largest Red Facing Brickworks in the Eastern Counties with London"* Whilst not specifically named, this is a reference to Mark Gentry's Langthorne Brick Works. It also stated, *"Sidings will be provided for several Manufactories, Farms, & c., and with the increasing output of Bricks by the local Brickfields, advantage will be taken of the facilities offered by this Railway for still further increasing the same. A very considerable traffic in the carriage of Bricks is already assured. It will therefore be apparent that all the elements of a profitable carrying business exist in the district which the Railway will open up"*

PROOF.—PRIVATE AND CONFIDENTIAL.

The Lists will open on **and close for both Town and Country on**

Central Essex Light Railway Company.

Incorporated by Orders under the Light Railways Act, 1896, by which the liability of Shareholders is limited to the amount of their Shares.

SHARE CAPITAL - - - £178,000,

Divided into 8,900 Ordinary Shares of £10 each, and 8,900 Preference Shares of £10 each.

ISSUE OF 8,900 PREFERENCE SHARES OF £10 EACH

AND

6,900 ORDINARY SHARES OF £10 EACH.

PAYABLE AS FOLLOWS :—

£1 per Share on Application, £1 10s. per Share on Allotment;

and the balance in Calls not exceeding £2 10s. per Share each, at intervals of not less than three months.

The remaining 2,000 Ordinary Shares will be allotted in payment of the Purchase Consideration mentioned below.
The Company is also empowered to issue Debentures to the extent of £89,000,

The Company having powers under the Orders will pay interest out of capital during the period allowed for construction, at the rate of £3 per cent. per annum upon the amount from time to time paid up on the Shares, in accordance with the provisions of section 51 of the Central Essex Light Railway Order, 1901, and section 54 of the Bardfield and Sible Hedingham Light Railway Order, 1901. Payment in full may be made on Allotment, and interest at the rate of £3 per cent. per annum will be allowed on payments made in advance.

Part of the front page of the prospectus for the Central Essex Light Railway, 1909

The prospectus also quoted from a report of January 1905 by George Copus, C.E., Manager of the CV&HR as follows:

"The goods traffic will produce the larger amount of revenue; from the Hedingham Station alone the Colne Valley Railway has carried 30,000 tons of bricks in one year, and some 73,500 tons of coal have been carried chiefly from Haverhill for brick burning and other purposes. This district of Hedingham is extremely rich in clay for the manufacture of red-facing bricks, and doubtless many other brickyards will be opened west of Hedingham as the clay lies that way; indeed, one of the largest makers in the district will be connected by a siding with the Central Essex Line."

Although not named, this is another reference to the Langthorne Brick Works because this is the only brickworks into which the Light Railway plans show a siding. It is quite likely that new brickworks in the vicinity of Runalong Farm could have been established, where it is known that good brick earth existed.

Eventually by 1914 all preparations for the building of the Central Essex Light Railway had been completed and it was planned to commence building the railway later that year. Contracts were placed for the construction of the section from Ongar to Dunmow, but the First World War initially deferred and later prevented any construction from taking place and the railway was never built. If it had been it would have provided a more direct route to London than either the earlier Elsenham to Bardfield route or the CV&HR through the Colnes, Chappel and Marks Tey (30) The 1909 prospectus included a table of comparative distances and those for Hedingham only are as follows:

"Hedingham to London via Marks Tey 60 miles. Via Central Essex Railway 50 miles
Hedingham to Bishop's Stortford via Haverhill 33 miles. Via Central Essex 25 miles
Hedingham to Ilford via Marks Tey 54 miles. Via Central Essex Railway 45 miles
Hedingham to Sawbridgeworth via Marks Tey 36 miles. Via Central Essex 28 miles

Mark Gentry did not wait for the light railways to be constructed and in 1899 he purchased a new light road locomotive to transport his bricks. (See chapter 16). If the Central Essex Light Railway had been constructed in 1914-1915 it would have been too late to serve the Langthorne Brick Works, which had closed in 1911.

In October 1920 inquiries were made as to the amount of support likely for a scheme for the revival of the Central Essex Light Railway. The new proposed line was from Ongar to the Suffolk coast, through Dunmow, Sible Hedingham and Haughley, Suffolk. At Haughley there would have been a link with the Mid-Suffolk Light Railway and by changing at Halesworth for the Southwold Railway provided a route to the coast at Southwold. (31) This ambitious revival and considerably extended scheme did not materialise.

From the 1920s parts of the route of the proposed Central Essex Light Railway through Sible Hedingham was built over. This included the Post Office built in 1928, two houses opposite namely 115 and 117 Swan Street, which were built by Frank Gibson and Westcot and Westcroft, Recreation Ground. (A complete list of proposed light railways for north Essex is contained in appendix five).

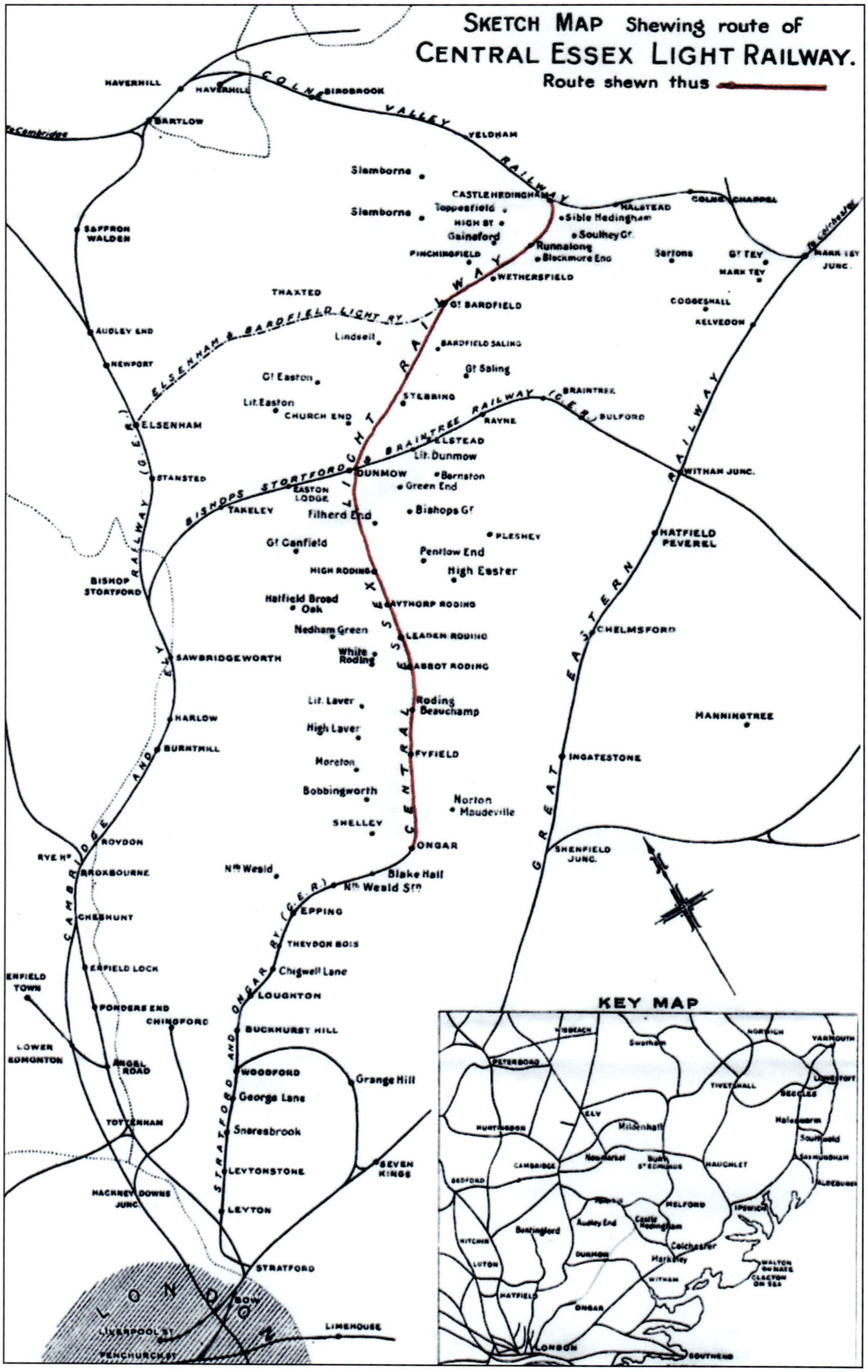

Map showing the proposed route of the Central Essex Light Railway highlighted in red

Chapter 16

THE BURRELL TRACTION ENGINE AND THE TIN POT

The Burrell Traction Engine

At a meeting of Essex County Council held on 3rd January 1899 a locomotive licence was granted to Mark Gentry for one traction engine. (1) In February 1899, Mark Gentry purchased a new Burrell 7 h.p. single crank compound traction engine No. 2163 from Charles Burrell & Sons Limited of St. Nicholas Works, Minstergate Street, Thetford, Norfolk. A plate on the side of the engine read, "MARK GENTRY, SIBLE HEDINGHAM, ESSEX". He also purchased two heavy traction trucks for the conveyance of bricks. (2)

The engine and trucks replaced eight strong mares and geldings and nine brick carts on springs, one of which was quite new. These carthorses and carts together with all the harnesses and feeding manger were sold by auction on 18th March 1899. (3)

ESSEX.

Sible Hedingham.

AT THE WETHERSFIELD ROAD BRICK WORKS.

SALE OF THE WHOLE of the CART HORSES, BRICK CARTS, HARNESS, TWO BOILERS, SAW BENCH, other MACHINERY, and Effects.

Messrs. BALLS

Have received instructions from Mr. Mark Gentry, to Sell by Auction, upon the premises, on SATURDAY, MARCH 18TH, 1899, at 11 for 12 o'clock (he having replaced same by acquiring a traction engine and trucks for conveyance of bricks, etc.), the above STOCK, including:—

8 Strong MARES and GELDINGS, as used in the business. 9 brick carts, on springs (one quite new), all the harness, also a larges quantity of suplus wood, iron, and various machines, comprising

TWO BOILERS, being

a 12 h.p. Vertical Boiler and fittings, insured up to 50lb. pressure, and a Cornish Boiler (8 h.p.) up to 50lb. pressure both being recently in use, but replaced by more powerful ones; iron-frame Saw Bench, for hand or steam power, with circular and band saw, about 200 assorted chimney pots, also 250 loads sharp builders' sand (which can be delivered on rail at a price to be arranged).

Loops of pales, old doors, gates, pieces stone and slate, about 300 old and new galvanised sheets, chiefly new (in convenient lots), firewood, broad-step ladders, iron tanks, feeding manger, and numerous effects, as described in catalogues, to be obtained of the Auctioneers, Castle Hedingham, Essex, and Haverhill, Suffolk.

Notice of auction in the Halstead Gazette on 2nd March 1899

A traction truck, similar to those hauled by Mark Gentry's Burrell traction engine, photographed by the author at the Chalk Pits Museum, Amberley, West Sussex.

The steel built traction trucks, which were very heavy even when empty, carried 2,500 bricks each. Initially, only one truck was used because of the state of the roads but later two trucks were employed making a total of 5,000 bricks per journey. The engine and trucks were usually engaged in transporting bricks from the Langthorne Brick Works to Hedingham Railway Station. Mark Gentry purchased four more traction trucks so that two could be loaded in the Brick Works, whilst two were being unloaded at the Railway Station and two were on the road. The engine carried out this journey eight times a day so 40,000 bricks a day were transported from the Brick Works to the Railway Station. (4) Fortunately Mark Gentry's Highfield Brick Works had a siding onto the CV&HR and therefore a traction engine was not necessary.

The traction trucks probably had no braking system of their own and controlling this heavy outfit was dependent upon the skill of the driver. He could screw on the engines one brake or put the engine slightly into reverse when descending a hill. This practise was not recommended as it could damage the piston and piston rods when the cylinder produced a pumping action against the direction of travel. (5) The brow of the hill outside Tortoise House, Wethersfield Road was removed at the expense of Mark Gentry to facilitate the work of his engine. He then supplied a large quantity of bricks to construct a retaining wall on the northwest side of Wethersfield Road opposite Tortoise House. At the same time another retaining wall was built further along Wethersfield Road opposite 1 and 2 Brick Cottages. The original name for this hill was *'Donkey Bob's Hill'*. Once the hill was significantly lowered it was easier for the traction engine towing two truck loads of bricks to climb it.

The north west side of Wethersfield Road where part of the hill was removed by Mark Gentry and a retaining wall erected by him.

Unfortunately the heavy engine and trucks loaded with bricks sometimes caused damage to road surfaces, bridges and culverts commonly referred to as *"culvert smashing"*. The first incident occurred within a few weeks of the acquisition of the engine when it broke a conduit under the road in Alderford Street, Sible Hedingham. During the ensuing debate at a meeting of Halstead RDC, Mark Gentry stated that his engine was 10¼ tons and it took four hours to remove it from the broken culvert. The Surveyor reported that the conduit was repaired by laying iron rails across as bearers and covering them with about nine inches of concrete, which cost £5. Although Mark Gentry disputed liability on the basis that there was no notice that it was dangerous for traction engines, he eventually met the Council with regard to payment. The Surveyor was requested to compile a list of bridges and culverts, which could carry ten ton engines and put up notices against those which could not. (6)

In June 1900 Essex County Council Highways Committee accepted £100 in settlement of its claim up to 31st March for damage to a road at Sible Hedingham caused by the engine when hauling bricks to the railway station. (7)

On 10th June 1905, the engine was towing a truck down Prayors Hill, Sible Hedingham when it was involved in a fatal accident. The driver was Harry Springett, Louis or Lewis Harrington was steersman and Maurice Springett was third hand. Violet Staines, a young girl, was playing with a box on wheels, which contained Frederick Joseph Elrington, aged 15 months. The engine was travelling at about 3½ to 4 miles an hour and went passed the girl, when she turned and the truck struck the box. The driver stopped the engine but the infant was dead. On 12th June 1905 an inquest was held in the house of Eli Cornish and the jury returned a verdict of *"Accidental Death"*. The Coroner said the driver had done all he could and there was no blame attached to him or anyone on the engine. The jury suggested that the police tell the parents of children living between the brickyard and railway station to keep them out of the road when the engine passes. (8)

In 1906 it was alleged that the engine had damaged two culverts in Petersfield Lane, Gosfield, whilst delivering bricks for a new house at Rayne Hatch. Harry Deal, a master builder of Gosfield quoted £12 10s 0d for repairs. Mark Gentry disputed his engine had caused the damage and having made enquiries ascertained that heavier engines had used the road. His driver said there were no weight notices near the culverts. However following a lengthy debate Mark Gentry agreed to pay £5 towards the cost of repairs. (9) Apparently, if horses pulling a 5 ton load damaged bridges or culverts the cost of repairs came out of public funds, but if a traction engine pulling the same load caused damage the owner paid! This indicates the attitude of highway authorities against engines during this transitional period. (10)

The last recorded incident occurred in May 1910 when the engine with two trucks of bricks was proceeding along Colchester Road, Coggeshall. One of the trucks suddenly dropped into a newly filled in trench opposite the home of Ernest Edward Surridge, a solicitor, where one of the mains for the new water works was laid. It was not possible to extricate the truck and therefore the bricks were unloaded by the side of the road. When empty the truck was lifted out, the bricks were reloaded and taken to the pumping station of the new water works. (11)

The Burrell traction engine hauling two trucks outside the former Red Lion Inn at Wethersfield. The men on the engine are Harry Springett and Ernest Wilding.

The official speed limit for steam traction engines hauling bricks was four miles an hour, but they could illegally reach twenty miles an hour. Improper speeds contributed to the breaking up of surfaces on un-metalled roads particularly with iron straked wheels. (12)

Mark Gentry sometimes hired out his Burrell traction engine to carry out haulage work. In 1904 it was used to collect a 30 ton steam boiler from Halstead Railway Station for delivery to Courtauld's Factory. The boiler was manufactured by J. Foster & Sons, Engineers of Preston, Lancashire. It took a whole day to transport the boiler the comparatively short distance from the Goods Sidings, along Kings Road and Trinity Street, over the level crossing into Bridge Street to the lower part of the High Street and right into Factory Lane East known as *'The Clippers'* (13) to Courtauld's Factory. The entrance into *'The Clippers'* was so narrow that it was necessary for some uncoupling and shunting. The trailer, with its wide load, had to be shifted into position to get it lined up to enter *'The Clippers'*, using powerful hydraulic jacks, which had to be repeatedly used along the narrow lane. It took another day to unload and manoeuvre the boiler into its final working position in the boiler house, which was part of a large new extension to the Halstead Mill built in 1904. The trailer weighed nearly 10 tons and with the boiler the total load was nearly 40 tons. The work was carried out under the direction of Mark Gentry junior and Mr. Claydon, Courtauld's engineer. (14) The bricks for the new buildings were supplied by Mark Gentry senior. (See chapter 11)

A SEQUENCE OF SIX VIEWS SHOWING DELIVERY OF THE NEW BOILER TO COURTAULD'S SILK FACTORY BY MARK GENTRY'S TRACTION ENGINE)

The traction engine and boiler leaving Kings Road and entering Trinity Street and Bridge Street. (Photograph courtesy of Braintree District Museum)

The Burrell towing the boiler in the High Street with Nathan William Pendle's furniture shop in the background. (Photograph courtesy of Kenneth Stanhope)

The boiler stationary in the High Street with the engine at right angles about to enter *"The Clippers"*. (Photograph courtesy of Kenneth Stanhope)

The boiler about to leave the High Street and enter *"The Clippers"* where the narrow entrance caused some uncoupling and shunting. The trailer had to be jacked over to get it lined up to enter with its wide load. (Photograph courtesy of Kenneth Stanhope)

The boiler stationary in the High Street with the engine at right angles about to enter *"The Clippers"*. (Photograph courtesy of Kenneth Stanhope)

The boiler entering the new boiler house at Courtauld's factory.
(Photograph courtesy of Malcolm Root)

It was an amazing feat to manoeuvre the boiler through the narrow lane and then turn it between the two terraces of Courtauld houses on the left before entering the boiler house on the right. The three storey Courtauld houses were designed by architect John Birch and built in 1872 of red brick with grey gault dressings. There were six houses in the first terrace and ten houses in the second, with a cart entrance between the two terraces. The drawings and plans by John Birch of 1871 describes, what is now known as Factory Lane East, by its old name of *"Quakers Lane"*. He was a well known architect of country architecture generally, including labourer's cottages and farm buildings. He also designed five pairs of two storey houses for Samuel Courtauld & Co., which were built at Church Street, Bocking in 1872. (15) The factory chimney was built opposite the boiler house, between and just to the rear of the two terraces of houses upon what was formerly the cart entrance. It was erected during 1904 by George Sudbury & Sons, builders, undertakers and insurance agents of Colchester Road, Halstead. It was 115 feet high and capped with an iron cornice, weighing 2½ tons, which was cast by The Tortoise Foundry Company Limited of Halstead. The chimney contained 50,000 bricks, weighed about 250 tons and stood on a concrete base 16ft x 16ft x 3ft, weighing 50 tons. The chimney was lined for 30ft inside with fire bricks. (16) It was a well known landmark in Halstead until it was demolished in 1969. The boiler house, which was later converted into a canteen and adjacent buildings were demolished circa 1985 but the entrance survives on the boundary of Solar Car Park and the year plaque *'1904'* is now in the collection of Halstead and District Local History Society and displayed in Halstead Museum.

The three employees of Mark Gentry who usually drove the engine between 1899 and 1911 were Harry Springett, Louis or Lewis Harrington and Ernie Wilding. (17)
Following the closure of the Langthorne Brick Works in 1911 the Burrell engine was sold to (Frederick) George Bishop of Alderford Water Mill, Alderford Street, Sible Hedingham. Interestingly, George Bishop, as he was known, had succeeded Mark Gentry as Chairman

of Sible Hedingham Parish Council in 1907. The Burrell was used for threshing purposes from 1911 until about 1921 when George Bishop sold it to Harold Orbell, an agricultural engineer, of Clare, Suffolk. (18)

Mark Gentry also owned a Marshall 16 h.p. semi portable engine, which he purchased second hand in February 1898 for £107 10s 0d. This was one of over two thousand lots in a five day auction of stock, plant and machinery of Harcourt Runnacles, a Halstead builder and contractor. The auctioneer was Stanley Moger and purchasers came from some distance including Reading, Swindon and London. Among the local purchasers of stone and bricks were George Sudbury & Sons of Halstead and Pudney & Son of Colne Engaine. Following the sale Charles Runnacles carried on his father's business from the same premises in Colchester Road, Halstead. (19) Harcourt Runnacles was also a master brickmaker owning a brickworks at Roydon, Essex. Mark Gentry probably purchased the Marshall portable to drive machinery such as pug mills in his brickworks.

The Tin Pot

When the clay around the Langthorne Brick Works was nearly exhausted a valuable field of brick earth was opened up on the opposite side of Wethersfield Road. A tramway was constructed to transport the clay from the new clay pits into the brickworks. The tramway initially crossed the road on a level crossing as shown on the 1897 Ordnance Survey map. However by 1903 as the pits became deeper it was necessary to construct a tunnel under the road. This was built in brick and of sufficient diameter to take an engine and loaded trucks. A description of February 1903 states that clay, *"is conveyed on a double line of metals and in small trucks, worked by a twenty-five horse power engine. The trucks were all built upon the premises. There are turn tables at each end of the line."* (20) The narrow gauge tramway was 2 feet wide, about a quarter of a mile in length and the rise averaged 1 in 10.

During the winter of 1904 to 1905 Mark Gentry and his son Mark Gentry junior built a home-made motor engine, which was nicknamed, *'The Tin Pot'* to replace the earlier engine. It was also used to haul the truck loads of clay from the clay pits into the Langthorne Brick Works. The new engine could haul four rather than two truck loads of clay. The vertical boiler and compound engine was purchased second-hand out of a small launch. It had been manufactured by A. G. Mumford Limited, marine and general engineers of Culver Street Iron Works, Colchester. The boiler was multi-tubular, 2ft 3in total height, by 2ft diameter at fire-box and 2ft 6in at top for extra steam space, with 170 steel tubes 1ft 6in long. The water was supplied by a three eighths inch Holden and Brookes injector. The engine was compound, with high pressure cylinder 3¾in by 3¾in and low pressure 7¼in by 3¾in. The power was transmitted from engine to countershaft by a 5in leather belt and from countershaft to road axles by Brampton's 1¾in pitch roller chain, the two axles being connected with similar chain. The road wheels and axles were made by Arthur Koppel, with roller bearings. The frame was made up of channel steel 6¼in by 2¼in by 5-16in riveted at angles. The weight of the motor was about one ton and it usually hauled two trucks of brick-earth weighing about two tons at a rate of six miles an hour. The cost of materials to build *'The Tin Pot'* was £50. (21) The engine was usually driven by *'Bunny'* Beadle.

The loco known as the *'Tin Pot'* with driver *'Bunny'* Beadle in 1905.

The *'Tin Pot'*, with trucks in the clay pits on the south east side of Wethersfield Road. The driver is *'Bunny'* Beadle and other men include William James *'Swagger'* Wiseman and Harry *'Higgler'* Broyd.

Chapter 17

MARK JOHN GLOVER GENTRY (1881-1918)

Mark John Glover Gentry was born 14th June 1881 at Stratford, the only son of Mark Gentry (1851-1912) and Jane Gentry formerly Glover (1852-1934). He moved with his parents from Stratford to Rookwoods in 1885 and then to Grove House, Sible Hedingham in 1894.

On 22nd January 1897 a smoking concert was held in the Assembly Rooms to celebrate his start in the brickmaking trade. (1) By 1901 he was a *"Clerk to Brick Manufacturer"* when he was employed by his father. (2) In circa 1902 Trooper M. J. Gentry was a member of B Squadron of the Essex Imperial Yeomanry under the command of Major Edmund Deacon of Sloe House, Halstead. (3) One of Mark's interests was cricket being a member of Sible Hedingham Cricket Club as evidenced by payment of a subscription of 5s 0d in 1904. (4) He was also Secretary of Hedingham Constitutional Club. (5)

Mark John Glover Gentry (1881-1918) on the forecourt of his garage in Swan Street with a car for public hire. Alexandra Road with its original red brick houses built during the early 1900s is in the background. This photograph was prior to 1915 because 'Downfield' at the junction of Alexandra Road and Swan Street had not been built.

By 1904 Mark Gentry junior established a motor and engineering works at Sible Hedingham. This was initially at his father's Langthorne Brick Works where a licence to store 80 gallons of petrol in a concrete shed was granted in June 1904. (6) Mark junior later moved his motor and engineering works to Swan Street, immediately opposite its junction with Alexandra Road. For a short time he was in partnership with a Mr. Perkins trading as Gentry and Perkins. In October 1908 they advertised for sale the stock, plant and garage at Swan Street, which had a 100 foot frontage and 250 foot depth. The description included business premises recently erected and used for the purpose of motor works. The sale by auction was fixed for 17th October 1908. (7) As there is no further reference to Perkins after October 1908 and as Mark junior clearly remained in business until 1917 it is assumed that he bought out his former partner and continued on his own account at the Swan Street site. Unfortunately the following year he was in financial difficulties and a meeting of creditors was held in July 1909. An auction of the motor works, stock and plant in August 1909 resulted in the property being withdrawn because the price bid was insufficient, although the stock and plant was sold. James Frederick Benson, an auctioneer, valuer, surveyor, land and estate agent of Toppesfield and Halstead was appointed trustee under a deed of arrangement and later declared a dividend to creditors. Notwithstanding Mark's financial problems the business continued and he was still listed as proprietor of Motor Cycle Works and as a haulier until 1917. (8) In that year he sold his Motor and Cycle Works in Swan Street to Lewis Wiseman. (9) This included some land at the rear of the Motor Works, which during the 1920s was excavated by Lewis Wiseman for use as a sand, gravel and stone pit. Among the local builders who purchased materials from this pit were Horace Palmer and Bert Corder trading as Palmer and Corder, builders and contractors.

Mark junior carried out a large amount of engineering and haulage work, sometimes using his father's traction engine. As an example, in June 1904 he directed the traction engine upon the removal of a large boiler from Halstead Railway Station to Courtauld's Factory. (See chapter 16). Mark continued to advertise as a haulage contractor until summer 1917. This included executing orders for the haulage of farmers produce to any part of the country. He charged per ton per mile for 4 or 5 ton lots. Mark also advertised buying all kinds of waste paper (10) and was proprietor of a newsagents business. Another business interest was as a coal merchant in Sible Hedingham, which traded for a number of years. (11)

Telephone: 10 Sible Hedingham. Telegrams: Gentry, Sible Hedingham.

MARK J. GENTRY,

Coal Merchant,

Sible Hedingham, 'Essex

Can supply coal, house or steam, on the best possible terms

Advertisement from the Halstead Gazette, August 1915

In August 1907 Mark junior purchased a motor bus which he ran to Braintree, Sudbury and Haverhill on the respective market days of those towns. Seats could be booked on receipt of a postcard but provision was made for emergencies. (12) He owned cars for hire and sold petrol, oil and accessories. His motor works also included a cycle works and he was a motor and cycle agent. He sold all makes of ploughshares and fittings. In 1917 he was advertising tractors for farm work. He held the agency for the Eros Ford Tractor Attachment which converted any Ford motor car into a farm tractor for ploughing (two furrows) or haulage work up to ten tons. (13)

Motor & Cycle Works,

TELEPHONE:
No. 10, SIBLE HEDINGHAM.

SIBLE HEDINGHAM.

Dr. to MARK J. GENTRY.

In 1911, Mark was living at Kennington Park Road, London and was employed as a *'shipping clerk'*. (14) His various business interests in Sible Hedingham continued in his absence. He returned to Sible Hedingham the following year as his father's health deteriorated.

Following the death of Mark senior in 1912, Mark junior managed the Highfields Brick Works. At the Building Trades Exhibition held at Olympia in 1913 *'red Essex facings'* made by him were exhibited with goods made by other firms represented by W. T. Lamb & Sons of 21 Essex Street, Strand, London WC1. (15) As a result of his poor health he was not able to join the forces on the outbreak of war in 1914 but was sworn in as a special constable at Hedingham Petty Sessions on 24th November 1914. At this time he was living at Kimberley Lodge, Sible Hedingham. (16)

MICHAELMAS, 1917.

Messrs. BALLS & BALLS

BEG to announce the following fixtures for their forthcoming Michaelmas Sales :—

HIGHFIELDS BRICKYARD, SIBLE HEDINGHAM.
On FRIDAY, September 7th, 1917.
THE STOCK-IN-TRADE and PLANT of a BRICKMAKER.

Messrs. BALLS and BALLS.

NOTICE.

Messrs. BALLS and BALLS

BEG to announce the Sale advertised for FRIDAY, September 7th, 1917, at Highfields Brickworks, Sible Hedingham,

WILL NOT TAKE PLACE.

Auction Offices: Castle Hedingham and Braintree, Essex; and Haverhill, Suffolk.

Notices in Halstead Gazette of August 1917

During March 1915 Mark junior advertised for sale two Harris' horizontal pug mills 4ft 6in by 2ft 10in, complete with 18in rollers and all gearing, in good condition, £16 each. (17) In June 1915 Mark advertised for a mechanic at his Motor and Engineering Works offering good wages and permanency for the right man. (18) On 17th June 1916 Jane Gentry conveyed the Highfields Brick Works to her son. On 24th August 1917, the stock in trade and plant of *'Highfields Brickyard'* was advertised for sale on 7th September 1917. However on 31st August 1917 it was announced that the sale would not take place. (19) At about this time Mark agreed to sell the Highfields Brick Works to Charles William Crawley of Great Maplestead and completion took place on 25th October 1917. He purchased the stock in trade and plant as well as the freehold. (See chapter 7)

Charles William Crawley (1864-1917) was born at Sutton, Cambridgeshire and educated at College School, Peterborough. He married Jane Charlotte Bellairs and they had six sons and two daughters. In 1917 he purchased Highfields Brick Works from Mark Gentry junior.

At about the same time Mark also relinquished his tractor business and garage in Swan Street on the advice of his doctor, Dr. Henry Joseph Twamley, in consequence of his state of health, which had never been robust. He subsequently accepted a position in the Braintree branch of the London, County and Westminster Bank. (20) Mark died at his mother's home, Nelson House, Church Road, Clacton-on-Sea on 9th January 1918 at the comparatively young age of 36 years having suffered from valvular heart disease. He was buried with his father in Sible Hedingham Churchyard on 14th January 1918. On 4th March 1918 administration of his estate was granted to his sister, Jennie Eleanor Gentry and he left £1,027 6s 5d. Thus father and son who had so many interests in Sible Hedingham died within six years of each other.

Chapter 18

THE GLOVER FAMILY

The Glover family was related to Mark Gentry through his marriage to Jane Glover in 1875. Jane was born on 14th February 1852 a daughter of Richard Glover (1813-1873) and Jane Glover nee Clark (1816-1893). Jane Glover lived latterly with her daughter and son in law, Jane and Mark Gentry at Rookwoods, (1) where she died. She was buried on 11th March 1893 in St. John's Churchyard, Stratford aged 76 years. (2)

Richard was an omnibus and coach proprietor at Stratford and married Jane Clark on 20th December 1842 at St. George Hanover Square, London. Their children were Richard, Frederick, Nathaniel, Jane, Elizabeth and John Christopher. The two elder sons were born at Pimlico and the four younger children were born at Stratford and baptised on 31st October 1860 at St. John's Church, Stratford. (3) Upon Richard's death in 1873, his widow continued the business of omnibus and coach proprietor until she moved to Sible Hedingham.

Richard junior (1844-1913) was initially a coach builder, who later became a veterinary surgeon and resided in Stratford. He married Clara Augusta White (1858-1940) and they had five children, Daisy Blanche Clara, Gladys White, Richard Clark, Leonard Talbot and Lilian Clara. Major Richard Clark Glover (1883-1957) became an army veterinary surgeon in the RAVC serving in India and Burma.

Descendants of Richard Glover

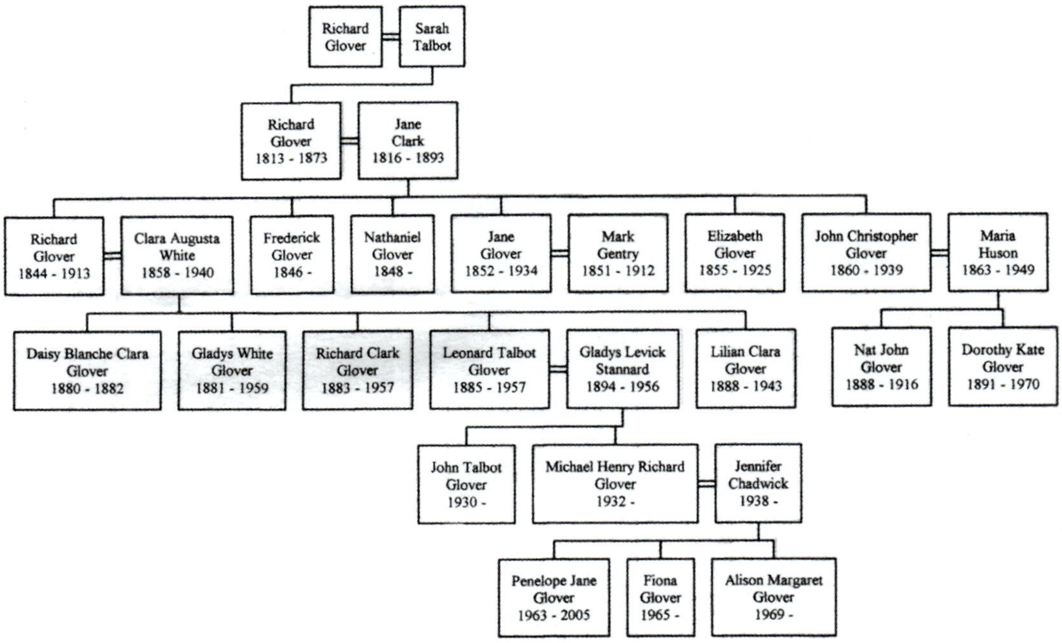

Leonard Talbot Glover (1885-1957) was an accountant and married Gladys Levick Stannard (1894-1956) in 1929. They moved to Hilton House, Sible Hedingham, which was purchased from Fannie Dowson as the executrix of Henriettta Frances Capes on 4th October 1930. They had two sons, John Talbot Glover and Michael Henry Richard

Glover who were born in 1930 and 1932 respectively. Miss. Gladys White Glover (1881-1959) also moved to Sible Hedingham where she lived at 4 Hilton Cottages, opposite Hilton House. 1 to 4 Hilton Cottages were purchased by Mrs. Gladys Levick Glover in December 1951 from the personal representatives of Miss. Emily May Kendall for £625 0s 0d. Following the deaths of Gladys and Leonard Glover in 1956 and 1957 respectively their sons sold Hilton House together with just over 3 acres of land to Stephen Leonard Taplin Crawford, F.C.A., on 27th November 1957. Stephen Crawford was a chartered accountant who continued the practise of Leonard Glover at Hilton House as Crawford & Co.

The rear of Hilton House c1947 when owned and occupied by the Glover family.

John Christopher Glover (1860-1939) was born at Stratford and married Maria Huson in 1887 at West Ham. In 1881 he was a builder's assistant living at West Ham with his widowed mother, Jane Glover, an omnibus proprietor. (4) In 1891 John was a clerk of works in the building trade living at Wanstead. (5) In 1901 he was described as a builder's foreman when living at Hornsey (6) and by 1911 he was a building contractor's agent residing at Wimbledon Park, London SW. (7) By 1916 John and Maria were living at Harefield Road, Uxbridge when their only son, Nat John Glover, who was serving in the London Regiment (Queen's Westminster Rifles) was killed in action aged 28 years. (8) John died in 1939 at Hove, Sussex aged 79 years and Maria died in 1949 at Chelsea aged 86 years. It is possible that during the 1880s John Glover was employed by his brother in law, Mark Gentry, in his building business at Stratford. John may have managed it from 1884, when Mark moved to Sible Hedingham, until its closure in 1892. Thereafter John clearly worked for other employers in the building industry in London. (9)

Chapter 19

THE HILTON FAMILY AND BRICK WORKS

John Hilton (1777-1835) a native of Middleton cum Cottingham, Northamptonshire married Hannah Jewitt (1784-1855) of Scarborough, Yorkshire on 8th April 1805 in Sible Hedingham Church. Their six children were born and baptized in Sible Hedingham between 1805 and 1824 as follows:

1. John Hilton, F.R.S., M.R.C.S., (1805-1878), was an anatomist and surgeon who became a distinguished doctor, surgeon-extraordinary to Queen Victoria, author of medical text books and a lecturer. He lived at Hedingham House, 53 South Side, Clapham Common, London. (1)

Dr. John Hilton (1805-1878)

Descendants of John Hilton

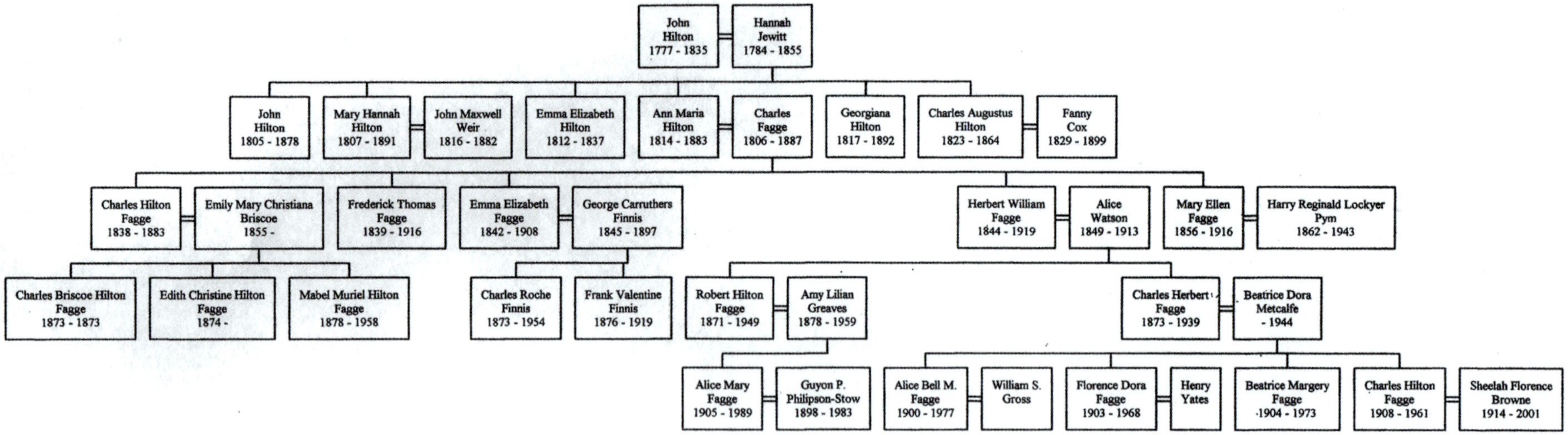

2. Mary Hannah Hilton (1807-1891) who married the Rev. John Maxwell Weir (c1816-1882) on 16th August 1853 at Sible Hedingham Church.
3. Emma Elizabeth Hilton (1812-1837)
4. Ann Maria Hilton (1814-1883) married Charles Fagge (c1806-1887), a surgeon. They had five children including Dr. Charles Hilton Fagge, M.D., (1838-1883), Frederick Thomas Fagge (1839-1916), a general practitioner and Herbert William Fagge, (1844-1919), a surgeon. Herbert's elder son Robert Hilton Fagge (1871-1949) was a physician and surgeon and younger son Charles Herbert Fagge (1873-1939) was a consulting surgeon.
5. Georgiana Hilton (1817-1892)
6. Charles Augustus Hilton (1823-1864)

John Hilton senior became a farmer and master brickmaker being proprietor of two brickworks in Sible Hedingham, one at Southey Green and the other at Alderford Farm. The manorial records of the Manor of Prayors record that John Hilton occupied the copyhold Brick Kiln at Southey Green, which had previously been in the occupation of Thomas Osborne. Daniel Smith, a bricklayer, had been admitted to the premises upon the surrender of William Bridges of Bures St. Mary, Suffolk on 25th March 1783. On 3rd June 1784 it was recorded that Daniel Smith *"....shall and do erect a tenement or dwelling house upon the said granted piece of ground and repair the brick kiln there...."* It appears that John Hilton became the tenant of Daniel Smith circa 1802 when it was stated that the property was for *".... the only proper use and behoof of John Hilton of Sible Hedingham aforesaid Brick Maker his heirs and assigns forever...."* (2)

John Hilton occupied the Brick Kiln at Southey Green until 1833 when on 30th September, Savill & Son advertised it for sale by auction at the Swan Inn, Sible Hedingham when it was described as follows: *"A LARGE and Capacious BRICK-KILN, substantial Brick-built COTTAGE, in Three Tenements, tiled shed, 63 feet long, about five roods of excellent Garden Ground, planted with young and thrifty fruit trees, advantageously situate on Southey Green in the parish of Sible Hedingham, copyhold of the manor of Prayors, subject to the usual fines on death or alienation, are in an excellent state of repair, and offer a desirable investment for a small capital."* (3)

John Parish became tenant of the Brick Kiln until 1858 when it was advertised as follows: *"TO BE SOLD BY AUCTION By John Savill, on Tuesday, 1st June 50,000 KILN- BURNT & STOCK BRICKS and a few Plain and Pan Tiles, Southey Green, Sible Hedingham. Sale to commence at One o'clock. TO LET, BRICK KILN, with 3½ acres of land and 3 tenements - Enquire of the Auctioneer.* (4) William Corder (1835-1903) then became proprietor of the Brick Kiln, land and tenements. The Southey Green Brick, Tile and Pottery Works remained in the Corder family until 1942.

John Hilton's other brickworks was freehold and located at Watermill Lane on what is now Alderford Farm, Alderford Street, just within the parish boundary of Sible Hedingham, with Great Maplestead. It was known variously as The Brick Kiln, Watermill Lane or Mill Lane and as Alder Hall Brick Kiln. (5) This property is shown as field numbers 1181 Brick Kiln Garden, 1182 Kiln Pasture and 1183 Kiln House and Yard on a map surveyed by Thomas Savill in 1834 (6) and on the tithe map for Sible Hedingham of 1840. (7) These maps also show field number 1118, which was a copyhold meadow. On 2nd November

1832 John Hilton paid £170 to Samuel Cowell, a shopkeeper of Gosfield for the purchase of this meadow, which was formerly a hop ground. It was named *'Bondmans Meadow'* in the manorial records and *'Bond Meadow'* in the tithe records. Samuel Cowell had inherited this meadow in 1815 upon the death of his brother Joseph Cowell, a butcher of Sible Hedingham. (8)

Extract from a map of Sible Hedingham surveyed by Thomas Savill in 1834 (courtesy of ERO., ref: D/DSm P8) **showing field numbers 1118 Bond Meadow, 1182 Kiln Pasture and 1183 Brick Kiln. The 1840 tithe map has the same boundaries and field numbers.**

By 1832 John Hilton was recorded in a trade directory as a brick and tile maker at Sible Hedingham (9) The Churchwardens Accounts for Sible Hedingham Church 1833-34 (10) records: *"Hiltons bill for Bricks and Tiles used at the Church by Brett and Smith £1 6s 6d"*

The Hilton family lived at Hilton House, Swan Street now a general-practice doctor's surgery. It is highly likely that the bricks for encasing the timber framed building of Hilton House, during the early nineteenth century were made at one or both of John Hilton's two Brick Works. It is a large house in Flemish bond, which still survives, although the rear of the house has been altered and extended. The majority of the former three acres of grounds and gardens has disappeared with recent developments, including the appropriately named Hilton Way and Hilton Walk.

Hilton House during the early 1900s when occupied by Miss Henrietta Capes.

John Hilton died at Cheltenham, where he had gone for the benefit of his health, on 23rd June 1835 aged 58 (11) and was buried in Sible Hedingham Churchyard. In his will dated 14th January 1835 he made the following provision:

"In respect to my son Charles Augustus Hilton who is not more than twelve years of age and I am undetermined what he shall be brought up to my will is that he may be clothed and educated from the profits of all my other property situate in this Parish of Sible Hedingham and Maplestead (part of the Brick Kiln Field is in Maplestead Parish) and the surplus arising from the Farms and Brick Kiln and all my land or lands tenement or tenements cottage or cottages let or in my possession (not herein before mentioned) over and above what is necessary for Charles Augustus Hiltons clothing education and pocket money my will is that such surplus money be carefully invested by my Wife in Charles Augustus Hiltons name in the Public Funds to accumulate until he Charles Augustus Hilton arrives at twenty one years of age when he shall take all sums of money as may have so accumulated in the

public securities in his name and all the Lands Tenements Cottages Brick Kiln farming live and dead stock and stock of bricks to his own use and profit and shall pay to his brother John or his heir or heirs seven hundred pounds; if John should be dead and left no issue then Charles shall pay the seven hundred pounds to his four …… sisters or the survivor or survivors of them." (12)

His widow, Hannah, was appointed guardian of Charles and administered the properties, which were held in trust until he became of age at twenty one on 11th May 1844 and inherited them. These properties are shown on the tithe map and award of 1840 (13) as follows:

Plot No	**Name and Description**	**Cultivation**	**Quantity A R P**	**Landowner**	**Occupier**
605	Stanment Croft	Arable	6 3 0	Sarah Hopkins	Hannah Hilton
615	Bishops	Arable	7 3 0	Sarah Hopkins	Hannah Hilton
616	Forrey Field	Arable	8 2 26	Sarah Hopkins	Hannah Hilton
617	Homestead		0 2 11	Sarah Hopkins	Hannah Hilton
618	Homefield	Arable	7 1 0	Sarah Hopkins	Hannah Hilton
619	Cails Close	Arable	11 0 30	Sarah Hopkins	Hannah Hilton
648	Homestead	Pasture	0 3 20	Hannah Hilton	Hannah Hilton
649	Home Field	Pasture	7 1 31	Hannah Hilton	Hannah Hilton
654	Chaseway	Pasture	0 3 31	Hannah Hilton	Hannah Hilton
655	Three Quarter Field	Pasture	8 2 30	Hannah Hilton	Hannah Hilton
656	Fenners Chaseway	Chaseway	1 3 18	Sarah Hopkins	Hannah Hilton
658	Pound Field	Arable	8 1 0	Hannah Hilton	Hannah Hilton
659	Pond Field	Arable	6 1 20	Hannah Hilton	Hannah Hilton
660	Monkhurst Field	Arable	14 3 7	Hannah Hilton	Hannah Hilton
661	Timber Field	Arable	7 2 20	Hannah Hilton	Hannah Hilton
662	Moat Field	Arable	11 2 30	Hannah Hilton	Hannah Hilton
663	Peppers Wood	Woodland	5 1 15	Hannah Hilton	Hannah Hilton
664	First Wood Field	Arable	8 2 24	Hannah Hilton	Hannah Hilton
665	Further Wood Field	Arable	9 1 4	Hannah Hilton	Hannah Hilton
691	Eleys Ley	Arable	2 2 19	Hannah Hilton	Hannah Hilton
710	Great Stubbing	Arable	8 3 22	Sarah Hopkins	Hannah Hilton
711	Little Stubbing	Arable	6 1 18	Sarah Hopkins	Hannah Hilton
712	Gobbards	Pasture	7 1 20	Sarah Hopkins	Hannah Hilton
716	Pightle	Pasture	1 0 18	Sarah Hopkins	Hannah Hilton
719	Great Grigs	Arable	8 0 25	Hannah Hilton	Hannah Hilton
720	Five Acres	Arable	5 1 11	Hannah Hilton	Hannah Hilton
722	Cottage and Ground		0 1 3	Hannah Hilton	James Elsdon
723	Acre Piece	Arable	1 1 32	Hannah Hilton	Hannah Hilton
724	Collis Wood	Woodland	2 0 34	Hannah Hilton	Hannah Hilton
735	Lodge Croft	Arable	5 1 20	Hannah Hilton	Hannah Hilton
741	Plantations	Woodland	1 1 5	Hannah Hilton	Hannah Hilton
743	Cobs Plantation	Woodland	2 3 16	Hannah Hilton	Hannah Hilton
744	Cobs Field	Arable	3 22 7	Hannah Hilton	Hannah Hilton
748	Garden Field	Arable	1 2 5	Hannah Hilton	Ann Flack

760	Cottage & Ground		0	0	30	Hannah Hilton	Edward Wiseman
812	The Down	Pasture	5	2	35	Hannah Hilton	Hannah Hilton
819	Home Field	Arable	2	2	4	Hannah Hilton	Hannah Hilton
822	Cottage & Garden		0	2	3	Hannah Hilton	Sarah Green
845	Elys Grove	Woodland	2	2	30	Hannah Hilton	Hannah Hilton
846	Buets	Arable	9	1	8	Hannah Hilton	Hannah Hilton
847	Goles	Arable	6	1	13	Hannah Hilton	Hannah Hilton
849	A Garden		0	1	15	Hannah Hilton	Hannah Hilton
850	Farm Yard	Yard	0	0	39	Hannah Hilton	Hannah Hilton
851	Cottages & Ground		0	2	25	Hannah Hilton	Sam Toby Susan Harrod
865	Cottage & Garden		0	0	35	Hannah Hilton	William Boreham
866	West Chandlers	Arable	3	1	37	Hannah Hilton	Hannah Hilton
867	Middle Chandlers	Arable	2	2	10	Hannah Hilton	Hannah Hilton
868	North Chandlers	Arable	3	0	34	Hannah Hilton	Hannah Hilton
		Pasture	0	1	28	Hannah Hilton	Hannah Hilton
895	Perry Field	Arable	6	0	9	Hannah Hilton	Hannah Hilton
896	Homestead	Yard	0	1	11	Hannah Hilton	Hannah Hilton
902	Hook Field	Arable	1	2	30	Hannah Hilton	Ann Flack
903	Five Acre Field	Arable	5	1	30	Hannah Hilton	Hannah Hilton
1011	Cottages & Ground		0	3	27	Hannah Hilton	Sam Pamplin Wil Osborne Ann Smith William Smith
1118	Bond Meadow	Pasture	1	1	20	Hannah Hilton	Ann Flack
1151	Cottage & Ground		0	1	13	Hannah Hilton	Joseph Curtis
1171	Bond Meadow	Pasture	2	1	21	Hannah Hilton	Ann Flack
1181	Brick Kiln Garden	Garden	5	0	30	Hannah Hilton	Ann Flack
1182	Kiln Pasture (part of)	Pasture	1	2	4	Hannah Hilton	Hannah Hilton
1183	Kiln House & Yard (part of)		1	1	19	Hannah Hilton	Hannah Hilton
1202	Cottages & Ground		0	0	31	Hannah Hilton	Robert Young Isaac Plumb Mary Plumb William Reuton
1203	Tenements & Ground		0	0	24	Hannah Hilton	R. Harrington G. Redgewell W. Gibbons J. Ward
1215	House and Garden		0	1	22	Hannah Hilton	Hannah Hilton

John and Hannah's eldest daughter, Mary Hilton, also owned the following property:

790	Cottages & Ground	0	0	26	Mary Hilton	Thomas Kendal Edward Watkinson William Kendall Thomas Underwood

The Tithe Map of Great Maplestead for 1840 records Hannah Hilton as owner and occupier of 'Kiln Pasture Field', being field number 92 in Great Maplestead. (14) This field was adjacent to the Brick Kiln House and Yard in Sible Hedingham.
John and Hannah Hilton's eldest son, John, was pursuing a successful medical career, in London. The youngest son, Charles Augustus, therefore inherited the brickworks and farm land in Sible Hedingham when he became of age. By 1851 (15) Charles, aged 26 years, was described as a farmer of 320 acres. Hannah died May 1855 at Sible Hedingham aged 71 years and was buried in the village churchyard. In 1861 (16) Charles was recorded as a farmer of 500 acres employing 27 men and 7 boys and a brickmaker employing 3 men and 2 boys.

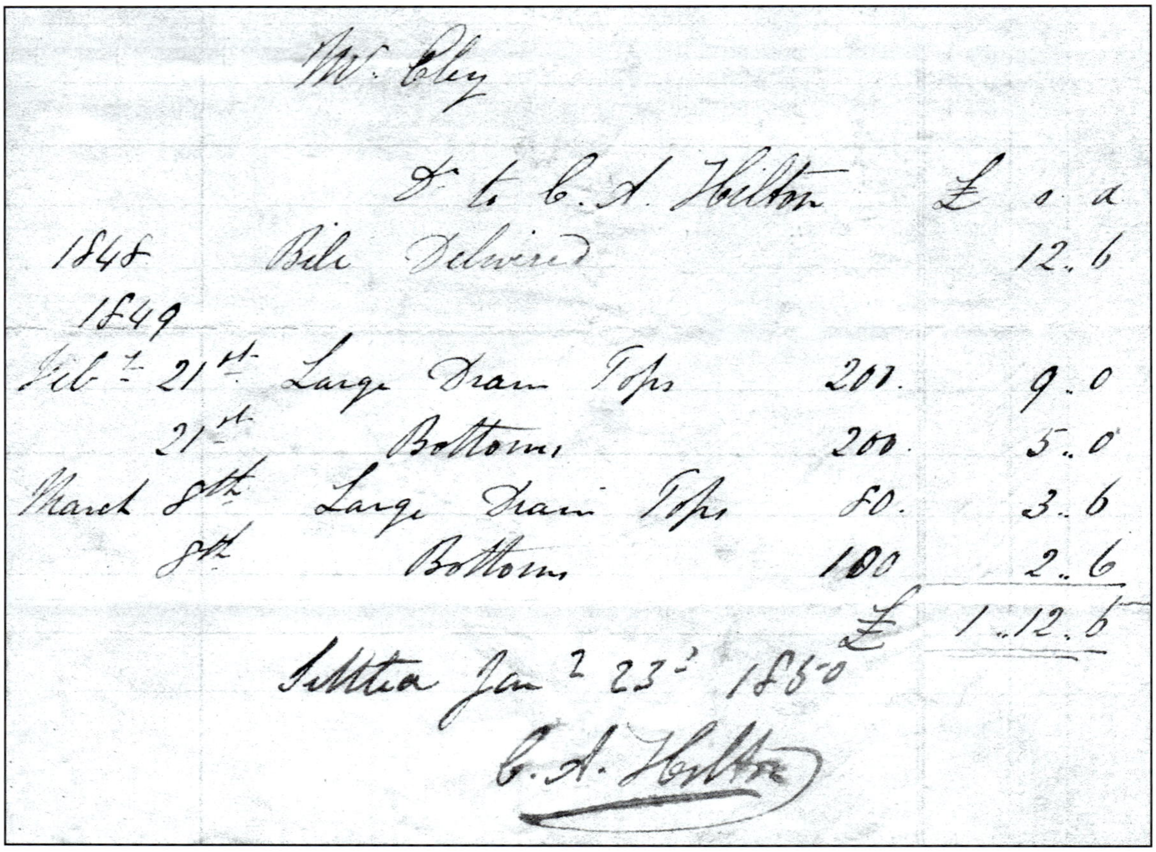

Mr. Eley

	Dr to C. A. Hilton		£ s d
1848	Bill Delivered		12.6
1849			
Feby 21st	Large Drain Tops	201.	9.0
21st	Bottoms	200.	5.0
March 8th	Large Drain Tops	80.	3.6
8th	Bottoms	100	2.6
		£	1.12.6

Settled Jany 23d 1850
C. A. Hilton

An account from Charles Hilton to John Eley for the supply of drain tiles in 1849.

During the late 1850s and early 1860s Charles was tenant of Hawkwood's Farm of 59a. 2r. 14p. of arable and pasture land and a farmhouse, now known as Hawkwood Manor in Potter Street. The agricultural buildings included stables, gig house, bullock shed, cart lodge, cattle shed and piggeries. At an auction held on 30th May 1860 at the White Hart Hotel, Braintree, the personal representatives of Edward Clark Eley sold the freehold. The particulars stated, *"The whole is in the occupation of Mr. C. A. Hilton, a most respectable tenant, at the moderate rent of £105 per annum. .... The Lands are of most productive quality and are exceedingly well farmed."* (17) Until his death he was the tenant of Pevors Farm of 97 acres leased to him by the owner Ashurst Majendie of Hedingham Castle. (18)

On 28th April 1859 Charles Hilton married Fanny Cox (1829-1899) at the Old Church, Brighton, Sussex. She was the youngest daughter of Thomas Evans of Crescent House,

Taunton and widow of Henry Morrell Cox of Westbourne Park. They had no children. Charles took an active part in the affairs of Sible Hedingham. As early as 1843 when he was only 20 years old, he was one of seven prominent residents in the village appointed to examine the Churchwarden's Accounts at the Vestry Meetings. When the CV&HR was opened to Sible Hedingham in 1861 he decorated the bridge at Alderford Hill at his expense and arranged for the Band of the 12th Essex Rifles to play. (19) When The Hedinghams' Gas Company Limited was incorporated in 1862 Charles Hilton became a director and was elected the first chairman. Its first half yearly meeting was held in September 1862 when it was reported that 4,862 yards of main pipes had been laid through the streets of Castle and Sible Hedingham. The gasometer, works and buildings were complete and had drawn commendation for the simplicity and durability of their construction. (20)

Among his employees at The Brick Kiln, Watermill Lane was the Bareham family who originated from Great Cornard, Suffolk including William Bareham and his four sons, Henry, Charles, William and George. They were all described as brickmakers including the youngest son, George, who was only 8 years old. (21) Later employees were the brothers Orbell Cornish (1832-1923) and William Cornish (1842-1931) from Woolpit, Suffolk. (22) In September 1861 Charles Hilton placed the following advertisement in the Halstead Gazette: *"To be sold 200,000 of good red bricks to be delivered to any station on the Colne Valley Railway. For price apply to Mr. Hilton, Sible Hedingham."* (23)

Charles Augustus Hilton died on 28th January 1864 aged 40 years and was buried in Sible Hedingham Churchyard on 4th February 1864. In his Will dated 25th January 1864 (witnessed by Sidney Thorp, surgeon of Sible Hedingham and Philip Martin, coachman to Mr. C. A. Hilton) he directed that his properties be sold, the proceeds of sale invested and the income paid to his widow, Fanny Hilton, during her life or until her remarriage. Thereafter the income was to be shared equally between his surviving siblings, Dr. John Hilton, Hannah Weir, Anne Maria Fagge and Georgiana Hilton. Probate was granted on 10th May 1864 and the value of the effects was under £7,000. His farms, land and the brickworks were advertised for sale by auction at the Horn Inn, Braintree on 6th July 1864. Lot 19 was the brickworks, comprising of tenement, brick kiln, sheds, cottage called Kiln House and adjacent arable, meadow land and hop ground in Sible Hedingham and Great Maplestead extending to 13a 3r 15p with timber valued at £34. This lot was purchased by John Cutts for £700. (24)

On 12th September 1864 the tools, equipment and remaining products and stock of the brickworks was sold by auction by Messrs. Newman and Savill on premises near the old water mill at Sible Hedingham. (25) The items for sale included:

"Pan tile, ridge tile and plain tile moulds and board
Brick tables, moulds and boards
One mill for grinding earth
Pipe engine with pipe discs
Eight and ten tier pipe and tile stages (19½ to 41 feet long)
200 strikes
Brickbarrow with iron wheels, brick setting barrow
Brick carrying off barrow and kiln barrow
Various quantities of red, white, splay drain, coping, gutter, paving white, culvert

and sink bricks
Ridge, plain and pan tiles
3" and 4" flat bottom pipes and 1½" & 2" drain pipes."

Among the purchasers at the auction were Orbell Cornish, Edward Bingham of the Pottery Castle Hedingham, William Corder of the Southey Green Brick, Tile and Pottery Works, Sible Hedingham and George English, master brickmaker of Bulmer. The brick barrow with iron wheels was sold to William Corder for 7/- and 4,050 red building bricks were sold to Edward Bingham for £3 12s 10d. Other bricks were sold as follows:

5,200 - £4 3s 2d   7,100 - £5 17s 2d   9,100 - £6 16s 6d

and 6,000 2 inch pipes were sold for £5 18s 4d

LOT 19.

A BRICK-BUILT AND TILED MESSUAGE OR TENEMENT,

With Two lower Rooms and Two Chambers, Brick-kiln, Stable, and Three Sheds, Kiln-house, and several Enclosures of excellent first-class Arable, Meadow, and Pasture Land, and Hop-ground, situate in the Parishes of Sible Hedingham and Great Maplestead, and containing altogether 13*a*. 3*r*. 15*p*.

No.			A.	R.	P.
1181	Brick-kiln Field	Arable	3	1	15
1182 1183	Brick-kiln, Sheds, Cottage Brick-yard and Pasture	Grass	3	1	19
	Ditto, in Maplestead	Do.	1	1	7
1179	Meadow, late King	Do.	0	3	30
	Other part Ditto in Maplestead	Do.	0	0	10
1118 1171	Bond Meadow	Do.	3	3	1
1182ᵃ	Hop-ground in Maplestead	Do.	1	0	13
			13	3	15

There is an abundant supply of Brick-Earth on this Property, and a Well of excellent Water.

Bond Meadow is Copyhold of the Manor of Hedingham Upland—Quit-rent, 3s. 8d.; and the remainder of this Lot is Freehold.

The Land in Great Maplestead pays a Free-rent of 14s. 7d. to the Lord of the Manor of Dynes Hall. Land-tax in Sible Hedingham, 12s. 10d. Ditto, in Great Maplestead, 12s.

Possession at Michaelmas next.

N.B.—There is a Siding from the Railway to the Brickyard, of which the Purchaser will have the benefit, subject to the conditions of an agreement for the use thereof about to be entered into between the Vendors and the Colne Valley and Halstead Railway Company.

The Purchaser of this Lot will be at liberty to take the Stock-in-Trade in and about the Brickyard, at a valuation to be made by two referees, or their umpire, in the usual way. The valuation-money to be paid at the time of completing the purchase; but should the Purchaser neglect to signify in writing, to the Vendor's Solicitors, within Fourteen days from the day of Sale, his intention of taking the same as aforesaid, he will thenceforth be precluded.

An extract from the sale particulars of Charles Hilton's properties in Sible Hedingham (Courtesy of Essex Record Office, ref: B 2570)

The sale particulars for the auction on 6th July 1864 and the catalogue for the sale of the contents of the brickworks, both record that there was a siding from the Colne Valley and Halstead Railway to the brickyard. The sale particulars additionally state that *"the purchaser will have the benefit* (of the siding) *subject to the conditions of an agreement for the use thereof about to be entered into between the Vendors and the Colne Valley and Halstead Railway Company."* No maps have been found showing this siding but judging by the width of the cutting on the north east side of the railway immediately adjacent to the brickworks it is possible that the siding was located in this cutting between the main line and the brickworks. If so it had been removed by the time the 1876 Ordnance Survey map was surveyed.

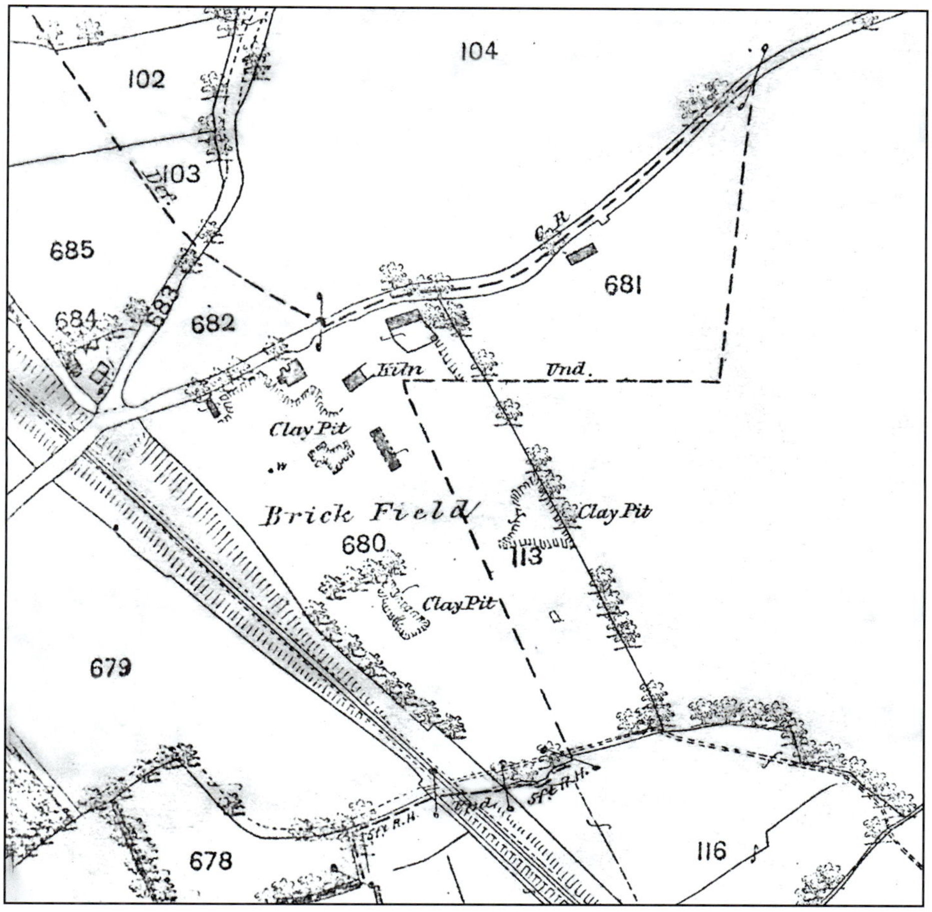

Alderhall Brick Works from the 25inch to one mile Ordnance Survey map of 1876

Quite apart from being a master brickmaker and farming over 500 acres, Charles Hilton also carried on an extensive steam plant business comprising of threshing, chaff-cutting, seed drawing and timber-sawing. In May 1864 this business was taken over by John Savill, land surveyor and auctioneer, of Orange Hall, Gosfield and managed for him by John Shepherd Eley and Alfred Cooke of Sible Hedingham. John Savill advertised corn being threshed by the quarter and corn ground by the day as well as seed drawing, chaff cutting and timber-sawing. (26) Samuel Newman of Rayne and John Savill were the joint auctioneers of Hilton's property. John Eley was a miller and maltster and Alfred Cooke a traction engine proprietor, who later carried on business from Marshey Farm (now Mashey Hall) Little Yeldham.

Towards the end of 1864 Fanny Hilton sold her household goods at Hilton House and *"left the county"*. She died at Paddington, London in 1899. On 29th September 1865 the trustees and executors of Charles Hilton conveyed the freehold of Alderhall Farm and Brick Field to John Cutts who let it to Orbell Cornish who was proprietor from 1865 until c1880. The copyhold of Bond or Bondsmans Meadow was transferred to Samuel Goodchild of Bloys, Sible Hedingham with an admittance in fee, dated 30th August 1867 pursuant to an indenture of bargain and sale by the executors also dated 29th September 1865. Upon the absolute surrender of Samuel Goodchild on 27th January 1885, Henrietta Frances Capes was admitted to Bond or Bondsmans Meadow, which was enfranchised on 11th March 1885. (27)

Orbell Cornish, (28) was succeeded by John Taylor (c1833-1910) as proprietor of Alderhall Farm and Brick Works. He was the last master brickmaker to operate from this site, where the brickworks were active throughout the 1880s. (29) John Taylor, who was born at Castle Hedingham c1833, was son of William and Mary Taylor. He was an agricultural labourer living in Watermill Lane, Sible Hedingham and married Emma Byford in 1857. They later lived at Sheepcote Road and then at Hosdens Lane both in Castle Hedingham.

The freehold of Alderhall Farm and Brick Works was owned by John Cutts until his death on 21st July 1882. John Taylor was the tenant paying £50 a year for a brick and tile cottage, brick kiln, sheds, stable and just over 13 acres of land. Following litigation in the High Court a sale of this and other properties was ordered, with the consent of the Mortgagee, John Evans. The sale took place on 24th April 1883 when the cottage, brick kiln, other buildings and the freehold arable and grass land extending to 13a. 3r. 15p. was sold to John Taylor as agent for Mrs. Fanny Capes for £550. (30) Mrs. Capes was the wife of George Augustus Harrison Capes, a surgeon who lived at Hilton House, the former home of the Hilton family. George Capes originated from Croydon and purchased Hilton House and 3¼ acres of arable land, which was leasehold with 722 years unexpired, for £700. Alderford Farm was later inherited by their daughter, Henrietta Frances Capes who sold it to (Arthur) Frank Gibson on 24th December 1914. (See chapter 20) Henrietta Capes continued to live at Hilton House until her death in 1930 aged 75 years, following which her executrix sold it to Leonard Glover. (See chapter 18).

John Taylor employed Joseph Gepp, who lived at Alderford Hall and William Elsden of New England as brickmakers. Joseph Gepp (1850-1930) was also a maltster during the winter months until his retirement from both occupations in 1918, having worked latterly for other brickmakers. John Taylor ceased brick manufacture circa 1890. The Land Tax Assessment records for Sible Hedingham up to 1890 describe the property owned by Henrietta Capes and occupied by John Taylor as *"House, Brick Kiln and Sheds, Brick Kiln Yard and Meadow land"* and from 1891 as *"House, Buildings Field and Meadow"* with no reference to Brick Kiln or Yard. (31)

John Taylor farmed the land belonging to *'Alderhall Farm'* from c1880 until he vacated the farm at Michaelmas 1899. Upon leaving Alderhall Farm, John Taylor became caretaker at the Infectious Diseases Hospital at Castle Hedingham (32) where his wife, Emma, was the Matron. By 1907 they were living at Hosdens Farm, Great Maplestead and in 1909 at New England, Sible Hedingham. John and Emma both died in 1910 at the ages of 76 and 75 years respectively.

After John Taylor the next tenant of Alderford Farm was Joshua Fenner. (33) In 1901 Edward Corder (1868-1940) lodged at Alderford Farm when he was foreman at the Hedingham Brick and Tile Works for Mark Gentry. (34) By 1906 George Westrop occupied Alderford Farm followed in 1907 by Charles Rulton, 1909 by A. Lewis and from 1910 Frederick and Frank Gatward. When Alderford Farm was owned by (Arthur) Frank Gibson it was let to John Thomas Goodwin, who also farmed Hopwells Farm at Great Maplestead. He continued to occupy Alderford Farm when it was owned by Rippers Limited and later by The Sible Hedingham Red Brick Company Limited but by 1922 William Harry Chapman was the tenant. (35) The farm remained in the ownership of SHRBC until 1960 when it reverted to Rippers Limited. (See chapter 20).

Chapter 20

THE SIBLE HEDINGHAM RED BRICK COMPANY LIMITED

The Sible Hedingham Red Brick Company Limited, (SHRBC) being company no. 161961, was incorporated on 22nd December 1919 under the provisions of the Companies Acts 1908 to 1917. It was a private company limited by shares with a capital of £15,000 in £1 shares made up as to 7,500 preference shares and 7,500 ordinary shares. The objects for which the company was established included:
"……. to carry on, develop, extend and turn to account the business of brick manufacturers …….. formerly carried on by Eli Cornish ……. and also the business formerly carried on by Mark Gentry, now deceased, at Highfield, Sible Hedingham ……… particularly the business of brick, tile or drain-pipe manufacturers and dealers in all kinds of drain-pipe, terra cotta and pottery, stone, marble, sand, gravel, slate, cement, lime, clay, lead and glass."

The subscribers of this new company who took one share each were Harry Tucker Ripper of Nunnery Street, Castle Hedingham and William Charlton Ripper of Willowbrooke, Sible Hedingham. They were both described in the Memorandum and Articles of Association as Manufacturing Joiners and were also directors of Rippers Limited which effectively owned SHRBC. The first directors and shareholders of SHRBC were Reuben Hunt, J.P., (1836-1927), Eli Cornish, J.P., (1860-1939), Harry Tucker Ripper (1868-1953) and William Charlton Ripper (1871-1947). The qualification was 100 shares and the registered office was Purls Hill Brick Works, Sible Hedingham. (1)

Harry Tucker Ripper (1868-1953) a director and shareholder of The Sible Hedingham Red Brick Company Limited. He was also a director of Rippers Limited and Evans Bellhouse Limited.

No. 161961.

Certificate of Incorporation

OF

THE SIBLE HEDINGHAM RED BRICK COMPANY

LIMITED.

I hereby Certify that THE SIBLE HEDINGHAM RED BRICK COMPANY LIMITED is this day Incorporated under the Companies Acts 1908 to 1917, and that the Company is Limited.

Given under my hand, at London, this Twenty-second day of December One thousand nine hundred and nineteen.

H. BIRTLES,

Registrar of Joint Stock Companies.

Fees and Deed Stamps, £9 : 0 : 0.

Stamp Duty on Capital, £37 : 10 : 0.

C T 15

Certificate of Incorporation from the Memorandum and Articles of Association of The Sible Hedingham Red Brick Company Limited, dated 22nd December 1919.

William Charlton Ripper (1871-1947)

John Wilkin Porkess (1879-1963)

Charlton Ripper, as he was known, was a director and John Wilkin Porkess, the company secretary of The Sible Hedingham Red Brick Company Limited. Charlton Ripper was also a director of Rippers Limited and Evans Bellhouse Limited.

Reuben Hunt J.P., was the managing director of R. Hunt & Co. Limited, agricultural engineers of Atlas Works, Earls Colne and the father of Sir Reuben James Hunt, Kt., (1886-1970). The Hunt family and in particular Reuben Hunt senior was responsible for building extensive industrial housing in Earls Colne over many years. Many of these houses were constructed with Hedingham bricks, which were easily transported along the CV&HR. He commenced building houses in Earls Colne for his employees in 1872 and in 1909 built almshouses for retired workmen. He believed that good housing was the root of all social progress and by the time of his death in 1927 had built 150 houses. One of many handsome gifts from him was Earls Colne Village Hall built with red brick in 1913. (2)

Eli Cornish was appointed managing director of the new company a position he held for three years. The remuneration of the directors (except the managing director) was initially fixed at £150 per annum. (3) Provision was made for the remuneration of the managing director to be by way of salary or commission or participation in profits or by any or all of those modes. (4) When Eli Cornish left in 1922, William Meadowcroft was appointed as manager but not a director. He was a son in law of Orbell Tom Cornish (1859-1939) one of Eli's brothers.

With the departure of Eli Cornish in 1922 and the death of Reuben Hunt in 1927 the company continued under the control of the Ripper family. Ashley Edward Ripper, J.P., (1898-1966) became a director and latterly chairman. Stanley Keith Finch (1900-1982) a nephew of Tucker and Charlton Ripper was also appointed a director and became responsible for the day to day running of the brick company. The long serving company secretary from incorporation was John Wilkin Porkess (1879-1963) who was the brother in law of Charlton Ripper. John Wilkin Porkess, who lived at Brook House, Sible Hedingham, was also company secretary for Rippers Limited, the position latterly held by Maurice Nash.

Eli Cornish, J.P., (1860-1939)

Reuben Hunt, J.P., (1836-1927)

Eli Cornish was managing director and Reuben Hunt a director of The Sible Hedingham Red Brick Company Limited

Ashley Edward Ripper, J.P., (1898-1966)

Stanley Keith Finch (1900-1982)

Ashley Ripper and Stanley Finch, were later directors of The Sible Hedingham Red Brick Company Limited and directors of Rippers Limited and Evans Bellhouse Limited

Alderford Farm of just over 20 acres of land was purchased by Rippers Limited from (Arthur) Frank Gibson for £500 on 10th July 1918. This included the site of the earlier brickworks owned by Charles Augustus Hilton. On 23rd March 1920, Rippers Limited sold Alderford Farm and the site of Highfield Brick Works to SHRBC. Eli Cornish as vendor and his mortgagee namely Samuel Fennell Hurnard of Lexden, Essex simultaneously sold 41a. 3r. 33p. of land including the Purls Hill Brick Works to Rippers Limited and SHRBC for £2,000. This was the amount which Eli Cornish owed under the mortgage of 1909 to Samuel Hurnard, with all interest having been paid. In effect the brick company paid Samuel Hurnard £2,000 to discharge the mortgage and purchase the property. However Eli Cornish held one thousand of six pounds per cent preference shares in the new brick company, which covenanted with him not to sell or let the property without his consent whilst he or his heirs still held any of those shares or any other shares or debentures in substitution. Quite apart from Purls Hill Brick Works, the 41 acres purchased from Eli Cornish included Purls Hill Grove also known as Purls Hill Plantation containing sand pits, Shuttleton Plantation and some agricultural fields nearby known as Lower Field and Snails Croft.

On 29th September 1921 the brick company conveyed to William Henry Chapman the majority of the freehold of Alderford Farm except for part of plot no. 183 on the O.S. map. The company also let other land to him including part of 'Lower Field', 'Snails Croft' and 'High Field' extending to about 32 acres. The company retained the right to all trees and timber on the land and to all minerals under the land and to carry them away. William Chapman, formerly of High House, Sible Hedingham established a dairy at Alderford Farm, which was taken over by George Roy Tanner in 1941. Whilst Roy Tanner, as he was known, served in the Royal Air Force during the Second World War, his wife Margaret continued running the dairy. In 1946 it relocated to Prayors Hill where it remained until closure by Milk Link in January 2006. William Chapman died on 1st October 1953 and in 1954 George Albert Page purchased Alderford Farm and also rented other land from Rippers Limited. In 1976 he purchased 48.5 acres of freehold land at Purls Hill from Rippers Limited. Later the same year a further 12.23 acres was purchased by Peter Henry Gagen of Hulls Mill Farm. (5)

On 29th September 1928 an extraordinary general meeting of members of SHRBC was held at the registered office of Rippers Limited at Station Road, Sible Hedingham when special resolutions were passed (a) that as from 31st March 1928, the 4,500 preference shares issued and the 3,000 preference shares not issued be converted into ordinary shares and rank equally in all respects with the 7,500 ordinary shares and (b) that the existing certificates relating to the preference shares be called in by the directors and new certificates be issued in exchange. These resolutions were confirmed by the members of the company at a subsequent extraordinary general meeting held on 15th October 1928. The special resolutions were signed by J. Wilkin Porkess (secretary) and filed with the Registrar of Companies on 23rd October 1928. (6)

SHRBC became commonly known as *"the New Yard"*, *"the Red Brickyard"* or *"Rippers Brick Works"*. It was called *"the New Yard"* because the new down draught kilns and drying sheds were built there mainly on the site of Mark Gentry's former Highfield Brick Works. This distinguished it from the adjacent Purls Hill Brick Works of the former Hedingham Brick Company, which became known as *"the Old Yard"*.

A Berry brickmaking machine was used, which was manipulated by seven men and made about 16,000 to 17,000 bricks a week. (7) Repairs to machinery until 1933 were carried out by Frederick George Bishop, miller, agricultural and electrical engineer at Alderford Water Mill. A few entries from his account book (8) for work carried out are as follows:

		£	s	d
"27th April 1925	*Mans time taking down bearings relining with white metal boring, turning and fitting same*	*8*	*11*	*9*
	Use of engine and man 10 days	*7*	*10*	*0*
30th March to 27th April 1929	*Taking down engine, re-metalling bearings, boring scraping and fitting same, drilling out broken screws to oil ring and fitting new ones, erecting and testing engine, mans time and materials*	*4*	*0*	*0*
	Making new pair of bearings for spare	*1*	*15*	*0*
21st May 1929	*New rivets in brick mould*	*0*	*1*	*0*
1st September 1930	*Lamps repaired and one new burner*		*10*	*6*

There were also many entries for oil supplied and the following are examples:

		£	s	d
3rd September 1924	*1 Barrel Gas Oil*	*1*	*10*	*0*
	5 Gallons Diesel Oil		*4*	*7*
	1 Barrel Diesel Oil	*1*	*10*	*0*
	1 Barrel Gas Engine Oil	*5*	*0*	*0*
	5 Gallons paraffin		*4*	*7*

From 1933 until closure the machinery, including the Berry brickmaking machine and a Ruston's engine, were maintained by Bertram Hogarth. He was also works manager for Rippers Limited of which he later became a director until his retirement in 1972.

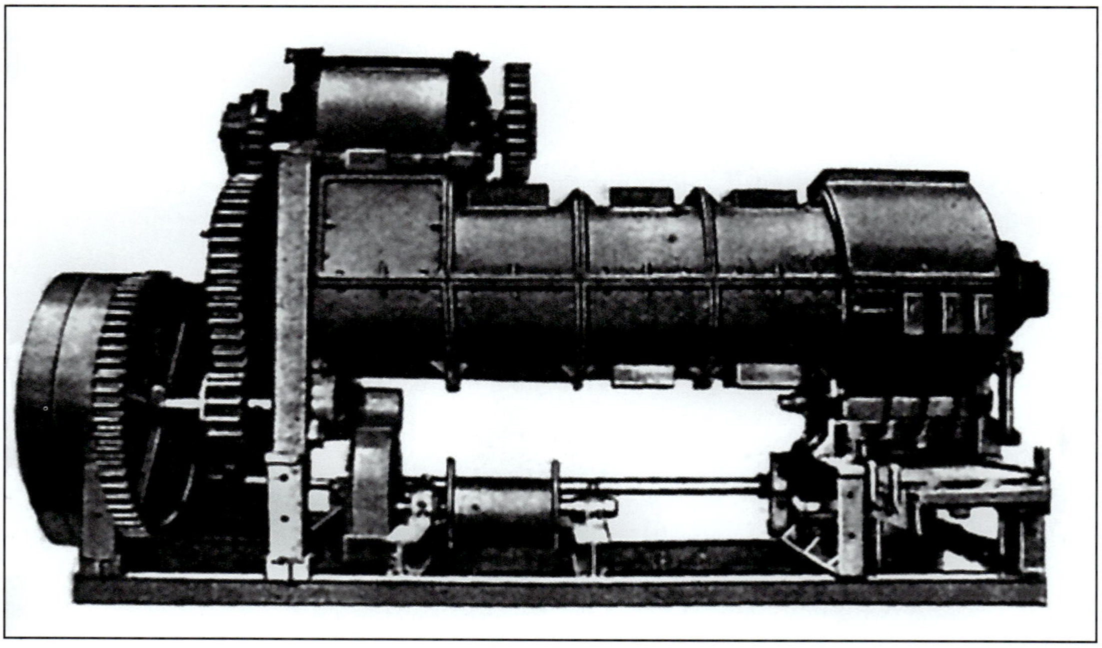

A Berry brickmaking machine made by Berry & Son, Metal Works, St. Helen's Road, Westcliff, Southend and used by The Sible Hedingham Red Brick Company Limited.

The Sible Hedingham Red Brick Works with a downdraught kiln being fired by Albert Redgewell (1880-1968) who succeeded John Corder as burner in 1938.

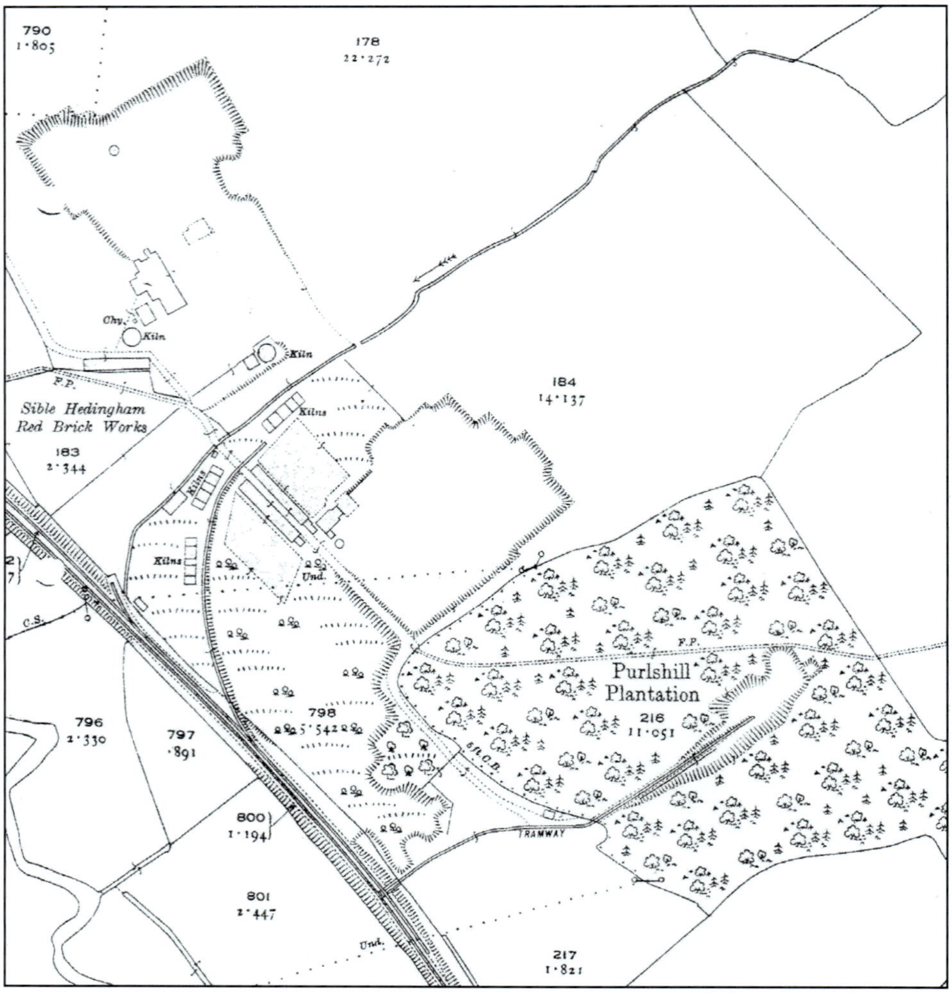

The Sible Hedingham Red Brick Works from the 25 inch to one mile Ordnance Survey map of 1922 showing the siding from the Colne Valley and Halstead Railway and the tramway into the sand pits in Purls Hill Plantation known as The Grove. This was the siding which had served the former Hedingham Brick Company at the Purls Hill and Sidings Brick Works. The siding into the former Highfields Brick Works (see map in chapter 7) had been removed by 1922.

The brickworks was served by a standard gauge siding from the CV&HR, which in 1923 became part of LNER. This was the same siding, which had previously served Mark Gentry's Highfield Brick Works and later the Hedingham Brick Company, which each had a different branch from the siding. Sometime prior to 1922 the branch into the former Highfield Brick Works was removed leaving the almost parallel branch to the south east into the former Purls Hill Brick Works. This branch was constructed circa 1900 after which the works became known as the Purls Hill and Sidings Brick Works. The main siding was extended towards the Halstead direction to also serve a narrow gauge tramway in Purls Hill Grove, which was used to convey sand to a tipping dock on the siding. LNER was responsible for maintenance of the whole siding and also part of the branch for a distance of 2 chains and 34 links and thereafter the maintenance of the branch was the responsibility of SHRBC. (9) This branch was eventually replaced with another branch, which ran diagonally across the site towards the downdraught kilns. This route is shown on the 1953 O.S. map.

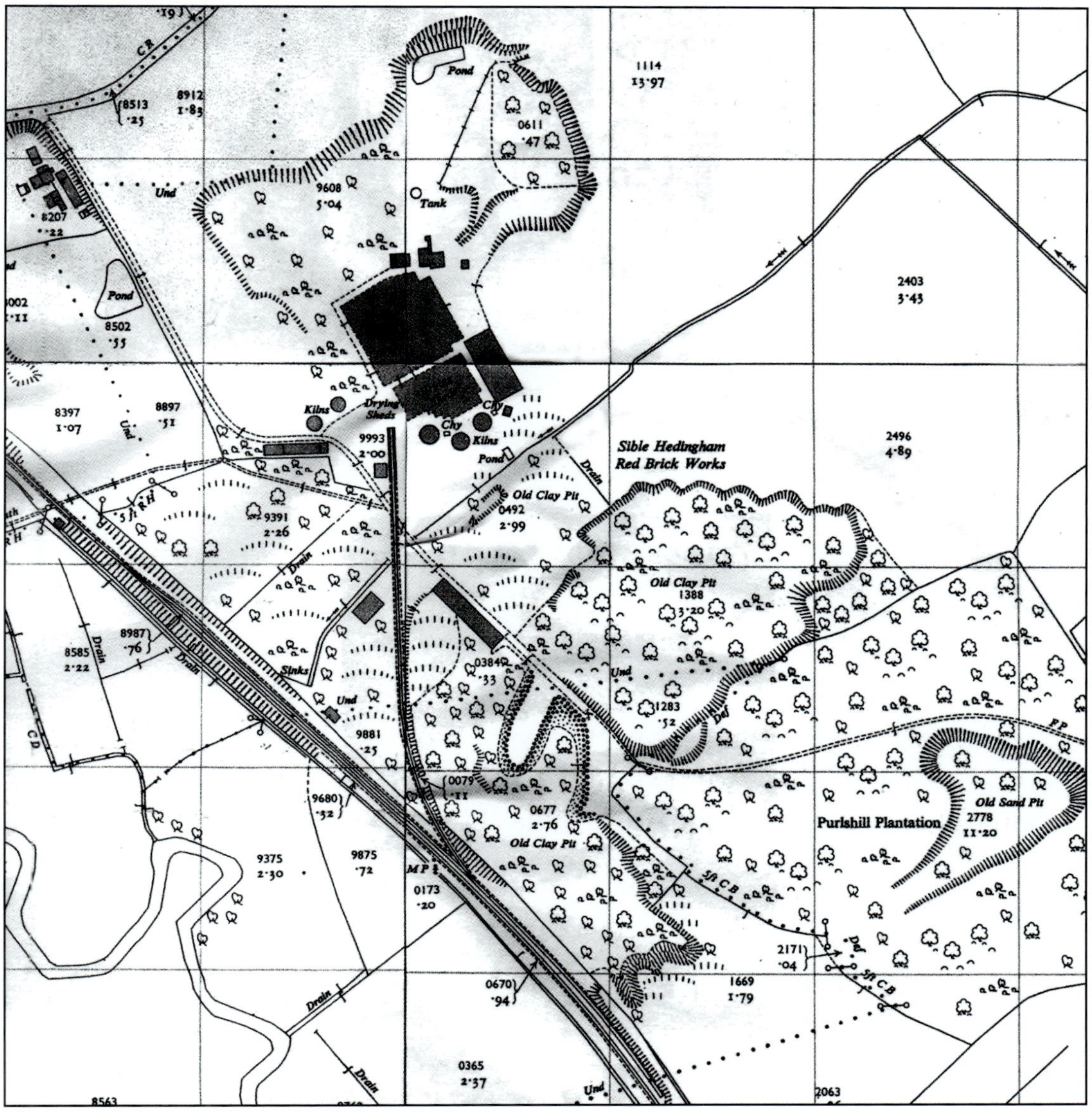

The Sible Hedingham Red Brick Works from the 25 inch to one mile Ordnance Survey map of 1953. Upon comparison with the map opposite it can be seen that the brickworks expanded on the Highfields part of the site with the Purls Hill site becoming mainly disused and the majority of buildings removed. The siding was realigned into the main manufacturing area, which was the third siding on the site. The tramway into the sand pit had been removed and a small tramway constructed into the clay pits north of the drying sheds.

Station : Sible & Castle Hedingham.	THE SIBLE HEDINGHAM RED BRICK CO., LTD. Sible Hedingham, Essex.	Telephone : Hedingham 39 2 lines.

Letter heading from the 1930s including the name of the local railway station

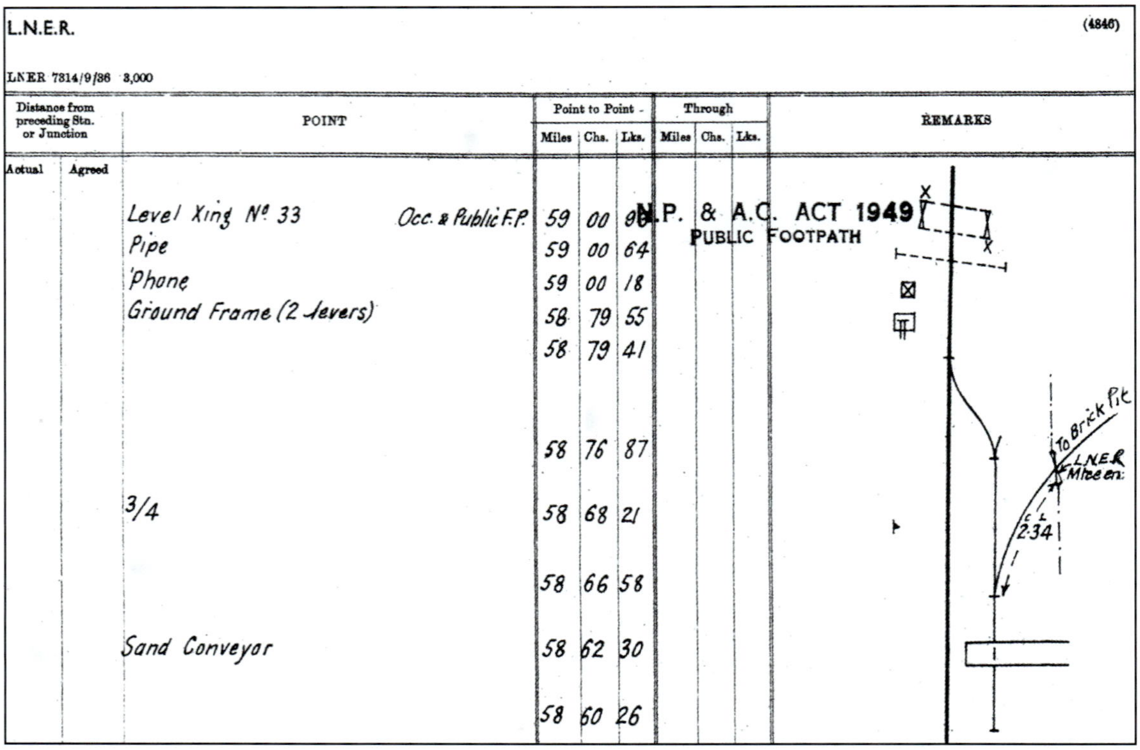

L.N.E.R. (4846)

LNER 7814/9/86 3,000

Distance from preceding Stn. or Junction		POINT		Point to Point -			Through			REMARKS
Actual	Agreed			Miles	Chs.	Lks.	Miles	Chs.	Lks.	
		Level Xing No 33	Occ. & Public F.P.	59	00	9[illegible]				N.P. & A.C. ACT 1949 PUBLIC FOOTPATH
		Pipe		59	00	64				
		Phone		59	00	18				
		Ground Frame (2 levers)		58	79	55				
				58	79	41				
				58	76	87				
		3/4		58	68	21				
				58	66	58				
		Sand Conveyor		58	62	30				
				58	60	26				

Extract and plan from the records of the London and North Eastern Railway relating to the siding from the Colne Valley Railway into The Sible Hedingham Red Brick Works. (NAO ref: RAIL 798/263)

The brickworks had five circular *'beehive'* downdraught kilns. The furnaces could be sufficiently covered so that during the Second World War production continued without any risk of the pilots of enemy aircraft seeing the fires. This did not apply to the updraught kilns in other brickworks, which could not be used for the duration of the war. There were large drying sheds where coke was burnt to dry the bricks but they were also dried in hacks in the conventional way. SHRBC generated its own electricity on site.

The former drying sheds during the 1960s when they were used as piggeries and which remain as the only surviving buildings on the site.

Albert Redgewell stoking a furnace with coke in a drying shed

Interior of a drying shed with 'green' bricks drying

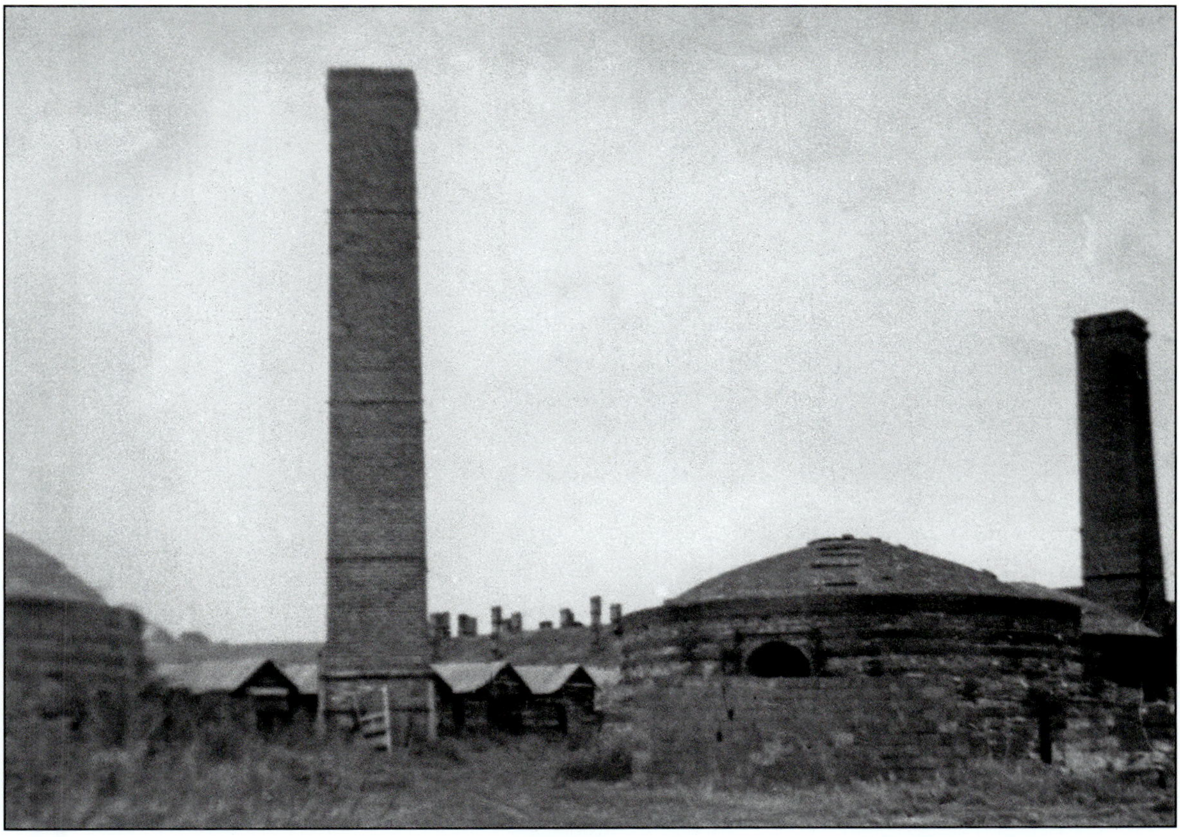

The Sible Hedingham Red Brick Works with down draught kilns, chimneys, hacks and the roof of a drying shed in the centre background.

At a meeting of Castle Hedingham Parish Council held 25th March 1929, Harry Ripper informed the Council that a hole was available at Highfield Brick Works large enough for depositing 100 tons of refuse. At that time the carting of refuse was at peoples own expense. (10) On 2nd September 1940 a fire broke out on the refuse dump and because of blackout regulations the local fire brigade extinguished the fire. From the end of the war in 1945 some of the former clay and sand pits in Purls Hill Grove were used for dumping rubbish in. They were used by Rippers Limited, local builders and dustcarts belonging to Halstead RDC. There was dumping and continuous fires for about thirty years. In September 1947 it was reported that a child had fallen into the burning saw dust at Purls Hill and was badly burnt about the feet and legs. Sible Hedingham Parish Council asked SHRBC to erect a fence or alternative protection as the fire was very near the footpath. The company replied that they were moving the fires further away from the public footpath. (11) During the 1960s the area known as The Grove, including the former sand pits, was used for motor bike scrambling. Over the years the area used for dumping refuse extended towards the former railway line. Earth was placed over this area but it still remains contaminated today.

A former sand pit in The Grove during the 1960s.

On 7th February 1947 the Tenants' Selection Committee of Halstead RDC reported to the full Council meeting the receipt of a letter from the Regional Office of the Ministry of Health stating that the Minister, in connection with his consideration of the national housing programme, had been conscious of the limitations imposed by the acute shortage of basic building materials. In order to increase the output of bricks and other materials for houses it would be necessary to transfer workers, who required housing accommodation. The Minister therefore requested Halstead RDC to allocate up to 12 houses at Sible Hedingham for employees of SHRBC. The Tenants' Selection Committee recommended to the full Council that it is suggested to the Minister that the best method for providing houses for brickmakers would be to authorise the Brick Company to build houses for its employees, which was agreed. The Chairman, Harold Henry King, J.P., (12) thought that in view of the shortage of houses it would be unfair to allocate 12 Council Houses to workers from out of the area. (13) The Brick Company did not apply for permission to build any houses for its employees. However Rippers Limited owned over one hundred houses in Sible Hedingham and it is possible that some may have been allocated to brickmakers.

In 1950 SHRBC applied for permission to dig clay from 7.624 acres of land owned by it in Great Maplestead, which was northeast of and adjoining their existing clay pits and brick works. The application revealed that the company intended to excavate 5,000 cubic yards of clay per annum from 1st July 1951 until 1973. It was estimated that there was sufficient clay available to last for 22 years. The earlier excavation figures were as follows:

1938-1939	3,750 cubic yards
1939-1946	nil (closed as a result of the Second World War)
1947-1948	625 cubic yards
1948-1949	625 cubic yards
1949-1950	625 cubic yards
1950-1951	625 cubic yards

The above figures were from 1st July one year to 30th June the following year. It is curious that no clay was excavated during the Second World War when some bricks were made. One explanation could be that sufficient clay was dug before the war to last for the duration. In February 1950 there were three men employed by the company who were removing over- burden from the clay beds. In July 1950 permission was granted to dig clay until 1957 only. (14) At a meeting of Halstead RDC held 5th January 1951 it recommended that the extraction of clay for brickmaking at Sible Hedingham be included in the list of mineral workings in the County Development Plan and Essex County Council was notified of this observation. (15)

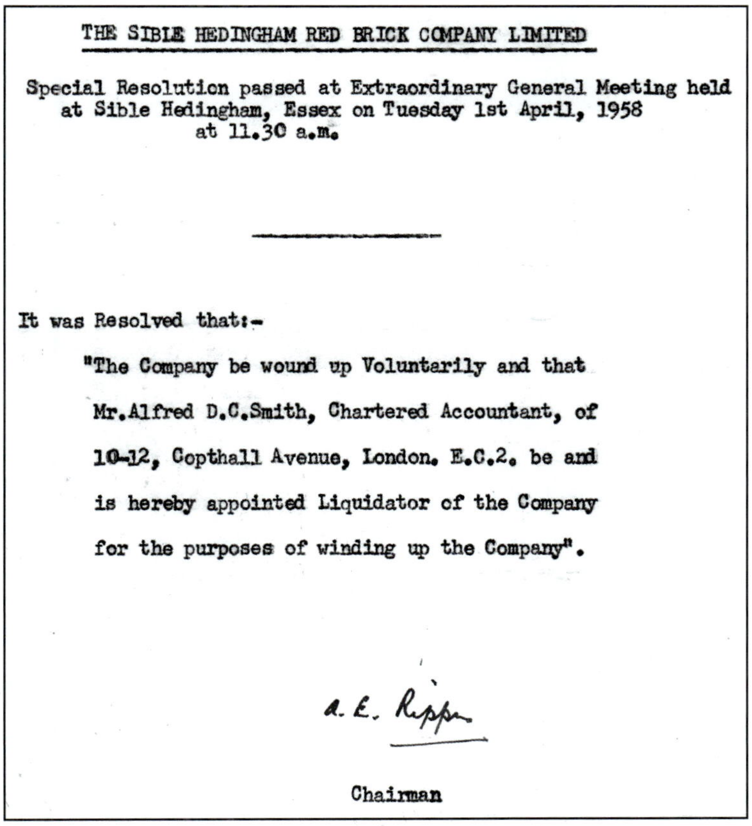

THE SIBLE HEDINGHAM RED BRICK COMPANY LIMITED

Special Resolution passed at Extraordinary General Meeting held at Sible Hedingham, Essex on Tuesday 1st April, 1958 at 11.30 a.m.

It was Resolved that:-

"The Company be wound up Voluntarily and that Mr.Alfred D.C.Smith, Chartered Accountant, of 10-12, Copthall Avenue, London. E.C.2. be and is hereby appointed Liquidator of the Company for the purposes of winding up the Company".

A. E. Ripper

Chairman

The Voluntary Winding Up Order of The Sible Hedingham Red Brick Company Limited signed by Ashley Ripper on 1st April 1958.

The brickworks unfortunately closed in 1954 and was the last of the many brickworks, which once existed in Sible and Castle Hedingham to close. Although production ceased in 1954 stocks of bricks continued to be sold until 1956 or later. The company continued to exist until 1958 when at an Extraordinary General Meeting held at Sible Hedingham on 1st April a special resolution was passed that:
"The Company be wound up Voluntarily and that Alfred D. C. Smith, Chartered Accountant, of 10-12 Copthall Avenue, London EC2 be and is hereby appointed Liquidator of the Company for the purposes of winding up the company."
This was signed by Ashley Edward Ripper, Chairman. (16) On 28th March 1960 The Sible Hedingham Red Brick Company Limited in liquidation and Alfred David Crawford Smith its liquidator sold the property of the company extending to nearly 69 acres to Rippers Limited.

It is appropriate to record, that as the various brickworks in the Hedinghams gradually declined and closed during the fifty year period from about 1905 when there was a building depression, many of the unemployed brickmakers found employment with Rippers Limited at its nearby joinery works, which gradually increased in size over the years. It was thanks to Rippers Limited that there was never any large scale unemployment amongst the brickmakers in the Hedinghams. In fact some employees of brickworks voluntarily left their work to join Rippers Limited, in order to secure full time employment during the winter months, bearing in mind that brickmaking was largely a seasonal occupation. It must be remembered that when brickmakers were out of work during the winter months, there was no unemployment benefits and conditions were very hard. In addition Rippers Limited had the advantage that their employees could work inside the factory and not out in all the elements as at brickworks.

Employees of SHRBC, whose timekeeping was based on passing trains include the following:

Bareham Bertie Albert or Alfred (1879-1950), previously worked for Mark Gentry at his Langthorne Brick Works.
Boreham Bert, who lived at Church Street was a brickmaker.
Brett Leslie Verdun (1916-1941), was employed by SHRBC and afterwards by Rippers Limited. He joined the Essex Regiment in April 1940 and died in the Middle East in August 1941 when he was believed to be the first native of Sible Hedingham to die on active service during the Second World War.
Corder John (1863-1957), who fired the kilns until his retirement aged 75 years in 1938.
Corder Walter Edward (1896-1983), who was employed here for a short time between the closure of the Southey Green Brick, Tile and Pottery Works in 1939 and later working for Rippers Limited until his retirement in 1961.
Drury Bertie Henry (1899-1958) who lived at Alderford Street was a brickmaker.
Heavingham Frederick Henry (1892-1976) of Chapel Hill, Halstead was a brickmaker c 1933.
Letch Walter Edward (1878-1961), previously worked for Mark Gentry and later for Rippers Limited.
Mansfield Tim, brickmaker.
Pilgrim Percy, who was employed by SHRBC during the 1920s and 1930s.

Pilgrim Victor, who lived at New England and later worked for Bert Corder, a master builder.
Redgewell Albert (1880-1968), previously worked at Rayners Brick Works, Maiden Ley, Castle Hedingham and succeeded John Corder firing the kilns from 1938 until closure.
Steward Harry (1875-1953), who also worked for Rippers Limited.
Wiseman William James (1882-1959) known as "Swagger" Wiseman, who married Margaret Corder (1879-1940), a daughter of Alfred Corder (1845-1898).

In March 1920, SHRBC was included amongst a list of employers who had either completed undertakings for training or employing men under the National Scheme for Disabled men or had notified vacancies to the Local Employment Exchange for Disabled men. These included ex-servicemen, some of whom had lost limbs or suffered some form of ill health and it was claimed, that although disabled they were quite able to do a good days work if only the right job could be found or made for them. No other brick manufacturers were on the list of employers, which also included the CV&HR and A. Birkin & Sons, builders of Coggeshall (who later became brickmakers). (17)

Bricks made by SHRBC were used on the following buildings:

Various buildings at Rippers Joinery Works including a Goodall Drying Kiln built circa 1934. The bricks cost £66 5s 0d. The builder was (Arthur) Frank Gibson who provided labour and materials (excluding bricks) for £172 17s 6d.

Hedingham Secondary School, was built between 1937 and 1939 with Hedingham Reds.

A house in Thistley Green Road, Bocking built for Dixon Smith.

274 and 276 Broad Road, Bocking, two bungalows, which were built by Clarence Birch on land originally owned by his mother, Daisy Pretoria Birch. Clarence initially occupied 274 Broad Road and his sister and brother in law, Iris and George Alen occupied 276 Broad Road.

Some of the last bricks to be sold in May, 1956 were 3,500 Tudor Red Bricks purchased by Bertram Hogarth for £42 0s 0d as facing bricks for Rustlings, Howe Drive, Halstead.

933

All Orders are booked subject to Strike, Lock-out and Accident Clauses as in the Coal Trade

Date May 29th 195

Telegrams:
SIBLE HEDINGHAM BRICK CO.
SIBLE HEDINGHAM
Station:
CASTLE & SIBLE HEDINGHAM

Mr. B H Hogarth
Station Road
Sible Hedingham

PLEASE RECEIVE FROM:

THE SIBLE HEDINGHAM RED BRICK COMPANY, LTD.

SIBLE HEDINGHAM, Essex

Consigned to Collected from Works

Quantity	*No. of Truck*			£	s.	d.
3.500 Tudor Red Bricks @ £12-0-0 per 1.000				£42	-	-
~~Received~~						

Order No. Verbal....

Carriage... Forward.

No Complaint will be recognised by us unless made within 3 days after delivery

Chapter 21

ARCHAEOLOGICAL EXCAVATIONS ON THE SITE OF THE LANGTHORNE BRICK WORKS

Following the closure of the Langthorne Brick Works in 1911, the site was purchased by (Arthur) Frank Gibson, a builder. Although some sources indicate that he established a builders yard here, this is unlikely because he already had a large yard in Swan Street. This was near his home, Oakdene where the yard remained in existence until his retirement as a builder in 1943. Frank Gibson removed the former brickworks buildings and presumably sold the materials or reused them in other buildings elsewhere. The 1922 Ordnance Survey map does not show any buildings whatsoever on the site of the former brickworks, which appears to have returned to agricultural use.

By the mid 1920s a poultry farm was established on the site, known as Langthorne Poultry Farm, owned by Harry Henderson Nathan. He later became a poultry food specialist and by the mid 1930s a poultry food manufacturer. (1) He lived in Langthorne House with his wife Winifred Downs Nathan and in 1932 Laurence King, an architect, successfully applied for additions to the house. (2) The following year permission was granted to Harry Nathan for a warehouse in association with the poultry farm and food manufacture. (3) Part of the former brickworks site later became the omnibus depot for Aubrey Letch and remains a depot for Hedingham and District Omnibuses.

During January and February 2006, the north west corner of the former Langthorne Brick Works was excavated by archaeologists in advance of the construction of a lagoon for a flood alleviation scheme for Sible Hedingham. Three lagoons were later constructed of which part of lagoon number two covered the area of the archaeological excavations. Lagoon number one is north of lagoon two and lagoon three is on the opposite side of Wethersfield Road to the west of the driveway to Hostage Farm. The author attended the official opening of the lagoons, in his capacity as Clerk to Sible Hedingham Parish Council, on 18th June 2008 (his birthday!).

The archaeological trial trenching and excavation only uncovered the small area of the former brickworks, which was required for lagoon two. The remainder of the site is undisturbed. A detailed report of the excavation and finds is contained in a report published by Essex County Council Field Archaeology Unit in July 2006. (4) Therefore only a brief outline is given here. Whilst the excavation was in progress, the author visited the site and shared with the archaeologists documents, maps and information about the history of the former brickworks. He helped to identify some of the buildings and structures, which were revealed, as did Adam Garwood, Peter and Tony Minter and Pat Ryan who also catalogued the bricks. The project manager was Mark Atkinson and project officer Mark Germany, who carried out fieldwork with Chris Down, Andy Lewsey (who also made illustrations), Matt Pocock, Dave Smith and Adrian Turner. The project was monitored by Vanessa Clarke and finds were processed and reported on by Phil McMichael and Joyce Compton respectively. Access to the site was facilitated by the Mynott family of Hostage Farm and Mick Everitt of Essex County Council Highways and Transportation Department.

The main building excavated was an engine house, including stoker's pit and furnace, iron grill and plate, boiler support and supports for what the archaeologists described as a brick mill. In Essex, Suffolk and elsewhere a brick mill is more usually called a pug mill. It is clear from the surviving brick supports that the pug mill was installed horizontally, whereas some in other brickworks were erected vertically. It is equally possible that the brick supports were for a horizontal brick machine, many of which were combined with pug mills. It is known that Mark Gentry experimented with brick machines including wire cut brick machines but these were not successful owing to the nature of the clay in Sible Hedingham.

Very small sections of three other buildings were also excavated of which one was clearly a drying shed. The other two buildings were not positively identified but one of them, with the base for a brick chimney was possibly a drying shed as well, although it could have been a workshop. The three latter buildings appear and correspond with the 1898 Ordnance Survey map but not the engine house. This indicates that it was probably built after 1898.

Quite apart from the above buildings, the remains of parts of other ancillary structures were also found. In the area between the engine house and drying shed an iron sleeper and the impression of a track were found from a tramway of 2' 2" gauge. Amongst the finds were a number of red bricks impressed with *"M.G."* If the remainder of this area is excavated in the future it is highly likely that more artefacts and evidence will be found to increase our knowledge of this interesting site.

In conclusion the following paragraph is quoted courtesy of the Archaeological Report:

> *"The results of the archaeological investigation give an indication of the complexity of the development of the brickworks, not all of which can be ascertained or appreciated from the documentary and cartographic evidence alone. It is now known that the focal point of the brickworks was moved at least once within the overall brickmaking site, and that only a proportion of the buildings and structures that were once present appear on the 1898 map. Some of the developments uncovered by the archaeological investigation reflect increasing mechanisation and industrialisation in the brickmaking process. The introduction of the engine house and brick mill, and the probable replacement of its original steam engine and boiler are the clearest indication of this. It is probable that behind most of the developments lay Gentry's known liking for improvements and innovation, and the expansion in the capacity of the brickworks that is known from the documentary evidence to have taken place from 1887 onwards."* (5)

The following photographs of the excavations were taken by the author.

A typical Mark Gentry red brick with the brickmark *"M.G."* in the frog.

An early general view of the excavation area looking north west

The engine house looking north

The south west end of the engine house viewed from the north west looking towards the south east showing the remains of the brick steps on the right leading down to the stoker's pit on the left.

Part of the engine house looking north east showing furnace and boiler/engine support in the background constructed of ordinary red bricks.

Appendix One

PUBLICATIONS BY H. GREVILLE MONTGOMERY AND THE CLAYWORKER PRESS

H. Greville Montgomery was proprietor of The Clayworker Press and the following books were either published by him personally or by The Clayworker Press.

The Science of Brickmaking with some account of the Structure and Physical Properties of Brick, by George Frederick Harris, 1897

The Manufacture of Glazed Bricks and Glazed Sanitary Ware, by H. Ansell, 1898

Brick Drying. A Handbook for Clayworkers. A Practical Treatise on the Drying of Bricks and similar Clay Products, by Arthur E. Brown, B.Sc., 1902

The Science and Practice of Drying. A Handbook for Clayworkers. A Scientific and Practical Treatise on the Drying of Clay and Clay Products on Modern Principles, by Arthur E. Brown, B.Sc., (undated)

Hand Brickmaking, by Arthur E. Brown, B.Sc.,

Practical Clayworking, by Arthur E. Brown, B.Sc.,

The Design and Burning of Kilns, by Arthur E. Brown, B.Sc.,

Arthur Edward Brown, B.Sc., (1864-1939) was the son of James Brown (1834-1921) who owned brickworks at Boreham, Braintree, Brentwood, Chelmsford, Hatfield Peverel, Upminster and Writtle. The Brown's London Office was shared with George Sherrin (1843-1909), the architect who designed Halstead Hospital, the Workmen's Club at Bocking and many major private houses in Essex notably at Ingatestone. Arthur Brown designed a continuous kiln which was patented in 1889 and called *'Brown's Patent Kiln'* and he formed Brown's Patent Kiln Limited. He also invented a tunnel dryer. One was built and used at W. H. Collier's Brick Works at Marks Tey, which was later used as a shed for storage of bricquettes. In 1900 Arthur Brown applied for a patent for drying bricks, tiles, pipes, pottery, etc., (Patent No. 21,226) (1). From 1924 he was Secretary of the British Paving Brick Association. A copy of James Brown's catalogue, "*Brick Ornament and Its Application*", 1900 edition, which contains drawings by George Sherrin is held at the ERO. (2)

'A History of English Brickwork', by Nathaniel Lloyd, 1925. This is a massive and well illustrated volume of 450 pages with an introduction by Sir Edwin Lutyens. In his Preface, Nathaniel Lloyd includes,

> *"..... To Mr. H. Greville Montgomery, Hon. A.R.I.B.A., I am also much indebted for the interest he has shown and for the assistance afforded in arranging the production of this volume to exhibit the greatest advantage the materials I have gathered. I do*

not think any author or any book can have been more fortunate in a publisher."

Nathaniel Lloyd, O.B.E., F.S.A., F.R.I.B.A., (1867-1933) lived at Great Dixter, Northiam, Sussex, which later became the home of his son Christopher Lloyd. The mid 15th century house was restored and enlarged by Sir Edwin Lutyens who was commissioned by Nathaniel Lloyd in 1910. The house and well known gardens remain open to the public. The celebrated, *'A History of English Brickwork'* has remained the great standard work on the subject ever since it was published in 1925.

Directories of British Clayworkers, 1931, 1938.

In 1948 a new company namely *'Clay and Brick Publications Limited'* was incorporated to take over the goodwill and copyright of the *'British Clayworker'*, the *'Brickbuilder'* and the *'Directory of British Clayworkers'*. It had a nominal capital of £32,000 and its objects included, *'Proprietors and publishers of newspapers, journals, etc.,'* (3) The *'British Clayworker'* or the *'Clayworker'* as it became known was published latterly by the Turret Press Group, which was also the publisher of *'Ceramics'*. In 1974 it was decided to incorporate *'Clayworker'* with *'Ceramics'* resulting in one publication, the *'Ceramics Industries Journal'*, which provided combined coverage of the whiteware, heavy clay and refractory manufacturing industries. It was circulated to over one hundred countries. (4)

The *'British Clayworker'* and the *'Brickbuilder'* sometimes contained articles about Mark Gentry, his brickworks and buildings for which he supplied bricks. He also advertised his bricks in many other Journals and Newspapers.

An early advertisement of Mark Gentry trading as Hedingham Brick, Tile and Terra Cotta Works, which appeared in *'The Architect'* of 16th July 1886 and included his well known *'MG'* trade mark

Appendix Two

A HISTORY OF THE TRADE EXHIBITIONS ARRANGED BY THE MONTGOMERY FAMILY AND COMPANIES

The Montgomery Worldwide companies trace their origin to 1895 when Greville Montgomery organised the first building exhibition in London, perceiving a demand for the manufacturers of bricks and other building materials to meet architects and builders merchants in order to display and sell their products. Exhibitions of the 'industrial arts' not least the Great Exhibition of 1851, had become a feature of Britain's business scene. Trade exhibitions were to become increasingly popular and effective and the Montgomery family business was in the vanguard, producing a popular 'Building Trades Exhibition' that grew to the extent that by the 1970s, as 'Interbuild', it became the largest specialised industrial trade show in Britain.

From the 1960s, with Mrs. Molly A. Montgomery as Chairman and her son Bryan Montgomery, grandson of the founder, leading the development of the business, the group began to internationalise. The experiment was based first on the management of British groups of exhibitors at building exhibitions in export markets in Europe and then, in the late 1960s, on the formation of Specialised Exhibitions (Pty) Limited to stage a Building Exhibition and other events in South Africa. With the economic take-off in the Arabian Gulf and the 'Tiger' countries of Asia in the 1970s, Montgomery was quick to move using their management team's rapidly accumulating expertise to pioneer ventures in Bahrain, Singapore, Malaysia and several other countries. Successful exhibition programmes in these emerging economies boosted their economic growth and helped to establish their host cities as modern business destinations.

Through Exhibition Consultants Limited a number of challenging but successful special projects were carried out, including the establishment of the International Fair of Khartoum in 1978 and the management services for the first Lagos International Fair in 1977. Such major projects added to the group's prestige and world-wide reputation, setting Montgomery apart from other 'trade show only' organisers.

Exhibition Consultants Limited provided the operations and marketing services for the Liverpool International Garden Festival in 1984. The largest public event to be held in the UK since the 1951 Festival of Britain set new standards and expectations for British visitor attractions and drew 3.4 million visits – more per day than the 'Dome' in 2000.

In the UK the first International Food Exhibition (IFE) was launched in 1979, and in the 1980s the Irish market developed through Irish Exhibition Services Limited.

In the late 1990s it was decided to withdraw Montgomery interests from a number of overseas ventures and the decline and unpredictability of the construction industry lead to the eventual loss of 'Interbuild'. The company restructured to consolidate UK and European exhibition organising and the parent company was rebranded Andry Montgomery Limited (AML). AML established new operations in territories such as Europe, Africa and Asia, more recently launching new events such as Hong Kong Art Fair,

World Photography Awards and buying new business in South Africa called Exhibitions for Africa (Pty) Limited.

The Montgomery Group brand under the chairmanship of Christopher Newton also launched new shows in markets as diverse as Hungary and Poland through Montgomery Exhibitions Limited. The company also continues to grow Irish Exhibitions Services Limited and its new business in India.

AML was rebranded Montgomery Worldwide in October 2008. The company expects to remain in the front rank of producers of specialist exhibitions and business events, alert to the ever-changing dynamics of the global events industry. It is open to proposals for new ideas, new projects and new markets. (1)

An ornamental brick made by Mark Gentry known as the '*Dragon's Head*'. These bricks were later made by The Sible Hedingham Red Brick Company Limited using Mark Gentry's mould. They were among popular Hedingham red bricks exhibited at successive Building Trades Exhibitions and are in two photographs in chapter 12.

Appendix Three

A HISTORY OF THE TRADE EXHIBITIONS ARRANGED BY THE MONTGOMERY FAMILY AND COMPANIES

The British Clayworkers' Mutual Insurance Corporation Limited (1) was incorporated on 21st June 1898. Its first directors were: John Horton Blades (West Bromwich), Edward Philip Collier (Reading), John Cathles Hill (Highgate, London), William Barnsley Hughes (Tunbridge Wells, Kent) and Henry Greville Montgomery. With the exception of Greville Montgomery, they were all master brickmakers, although William Hughes was also a surveyor as well as being a brick manufacturer. Edward Collier was related to William Homan Collier of Marks Tey, Essex who became a director by 1904. John Hill was proprietor of the London Brick Company, which then owned a brickworks at Great Bentley, Essex. When Edward Collier died on 12th October 1919 the two remaining directors were William H. Collier and H. Greville Montgomery. By 1921 William Anderson Collier, a brick manufacturer of Reading was appointed as a director.

The nominal capital was £100,000 divided into ten thousand shares of ten pounds each. Among the large number of initial shareholders in 1898 throughout the British Isles were the following Essex master brickmakers:

No of shares	Name	Address
5	Alfred Blomfield	Orange Hall, Gosfield, Halstead
3	Thomas Cloughton	Felsted
50	William Homan Collier	Marks Tey
50	Mark Gentry	Sible Hedingham
10	Eli Plowman	Stanpit, Shefford, Bedfordshire
3	George S. Plowman	Gamlingay, Cambridgeshire
4	Richard Rushbrook & Sons	Corringham Brickfields Stanford le Hope
1	Thomas H. Webster	Ingatestone

(Note: Thomas Sneeds Eli Plowman purchased Hambro Hill Brick Works, Rayleigh from the Executors of William Clover in 1901 and later owned the New Manor Brick Works, Thundersley. The Plowman family who originated from Woolpit, Suffolk also owned brickworks in Bedfordshire and Hampshire).

1899		
2	Daniel Cornish	Oaklands, Shenfield

1900		
10	James Brown	Essex Wharf, Whitechapel
3	Walter Pudney	Colne Engaine

(Note: James Brown owned brickworks in Boreham, Braintree, Brentwood, Chelmsford, Hatfield Peverel, Upminster and Writtle but gave the address of his London depot and office).

Appendix Four

EARLY OCCUPIERS OF HOUSES IN ALEXANDRA ROAD, SIBLE HEDINGHAM

A list of the remaining early occupiers of houses in Alexandra Road, Sible Hedingham (1) in addition to those detailed in chapter 14.

1904

William Bareham
Charles Carter (from Wethersfield Road)
Charles William Everitt
John Lock (from Great Maplestead)
Henry Palmer

1905

William Gibbons, junior

1906

William Calver (from Castle Hedingham)
Percy Carter (from Alderford Street and in 1908 moved to Queen Street, Castle Hedingham)
John William Coates (from Swan Street)
James Parr (from near Rookwoods)
Harry Springett (from Swan Street – a different Harry Springett lived in Wethersfield Road)
Albert George Tokely (from Castle Hedingham)
Joseph John Vale (from Swan Street – stationmaster at Hedingham Railway Station)

1908

Weston Chilvers Cobb
Robert Drury
Harry Faiers (tenant of John Corder)
Thomas Garwood
Albert Edward Hunt
Frederick Taylor
William Bailey Theobald

1910

Edward Farrow
Annie Moon
Charles Rulton (from Alderford Street)
Harry Sandford (from Swan Street)

1911

Ernest Reginald Bayley (from Church Street)
Frederick Henry Bryant (from cottage at Maiden Ley)
Rev. James Grinnell (Minister of Sible Hedingham Baptist Church)
Frank Metson
Alfred Mulley
Thomas Saunders
Alfred Scott

1912

Lewis Wiseman (who moved to Swan Street in 1913)

1913

Herbert Partridge

1914

Ashley Adkins
Arthur Bareham

Appendix Five

PROPOSED LIGHT RAILWAYS IN NORTH ESSEX

The following is a list of proposed light railways in north Essex:

1893 Colne Valley Haverhill – Takeley line
1896 Elsenham – Thaxted – Hedingham
1897 Central Essex Light Railway (Ongar – Dunmow – Yeldham)
1898 Hedingham – Bardfield Light Railway
1898 Kelvedon – Halstead via Coggeshall and Colne, known as the Coggeshall Light Railway.
1898 Hedingham to Long Melford Light Railway
1898 Central Essex Light Railway (Ongar to Sible Hedingham)
1900 Braintree – Halstead Light Railway

The above light railways, if built, would have connected with or run close to the CV&HR, which ran from Haverhill, Birdbrook, Great Yeldham, Sible and Castle Hedingham, Halstead, Earls Colne, White Colne, Wakes Colne and Chappel.

Coggeshall, where a couple of small brickworks were located, was the only town in Essex not to be connected to a railway. The Coggeshall Light Railway, from Kelvedon to Halstead, which was proposed in 1898, did not proceed (1) although some preliminary surveying was carried out and it would have passed through Pattiswick, Burton's Green and followed the course of Bourne Brook. It would have had junctions with GER at Kelvedon and with CV&HR near Colne Station. A station was planned at Coggeshall and the total length was about ten miles

1898 Great Bentley, Thorington and St.Osyth – The London Brick Company, which owned brickworks at Great Bentley sought powers for the construction of this proposed light railway. (2)
1919 Braintree, Bardfield and Finchingfield Light Railway or Tramway – This line was proposed by the Braintree Chamber of Commerce from a junction with the GER near Clapbridge Farm between Braintree and Rayne to Bocking and following the River Pant to Panfield, Shalford, Wethersfield, Bardfield and then a branch to Finchingfield. (3)
1919 Manningtree to Bures Light Railway (4)
1919 A Light Railway to Mersea Island (5)
1919 Coggeshall to Kelvedon Light Railway (6)
1919 Coggeshall and Marks Tey Light Railway (from Witham through Cressing, Stisted, Bradwell, Feering, Pattiswick and Great Coggeshall terminating at Marks Tey. (7)
1919 Braintree to Marks Tey (through Cressing, Stisted, Coggeshall to Marks Tey – later varied to start at Bocking Church Street, which received the support of Courtaulds Limited. (8)
1920 Central Essex Light Railway – Ongar to Dunmow, Sible Hedingham, Haughley and the Suffolk Coast. (See chapter 15)

GLOSSARY

A glossary of brickmaking terms used in north Essex Brickworks is detailed on pages 147 to 149 of, *'Our Ancestors Were Brickmakers and Potters - A history of the Corder and related families in the clay working industries'*, by Adrian Corder-Birch, 2010. Many of those terms appear in this book and although the glossary is not repeated, a few additions are as follows:

Arch bricks	Special bricks tapered to the shape of an arch
Arris	The edge formed by the intersection of two surfaces.
Journeyman	Someone who has completed his apprenticeship and is a qualified brickmaker but remaining as an employee and not a master.
Overburden	Earth removed to expose the deposit (clay for brickmaking) sought
Pressed bricks	Bricks moulded under great pressure in metal moulds (including hand-pressed and machine-pressed) (See chapter 8).
Rubbers	Bricks suitable for cutting and carving
Terracotta	Ornamental building blocks, statues or garden ornaments made from fine brick-earth and moulded to almost any shape prior to firing. In common with bricks, the colour of terracotta varies according to the composition of the brick-earth.
Wire-cut bricks	Taut wires cutting extruded clay into brick shapes.

ABBREVIATIONS

ARP	Acres Roods Perches (40 perches made one rood, a quarter of an acre)
CV&HR	Colne Valley and Halstead Railway
ERO	Essex Record Office
GER	Great Eastern Railway
HBC	Hedingham Brick Company
LNER	London and North Eastern Railway
NAO	National Archive Office
RDC	Rural District Council
SHRBC	The Sible Hedingham Red Brick Company Limited

BIBLIOGRAPHY, SOURCES, NOTES AND REFERENCES

Chapter 1 The Gentry family

1. Baptism Register for Bocking Church: ERO., T/R 111/2-5
2. Marriage Register for Upminster Church: ERO., D/P 117/1/4
3. Baptism Register for Rainham Church: ERO., D/P 202
4. Burial Register for Rainham Church: ERO., D/P 202
5. Census Return 1851: HO107/1772
6. Marriage Register for St. Botolph's Without, Aldgate, City of London
7. Census Return 1851: HO107/1768
8. Census Return 1871: RG10/1624
9. Probate of John Gentry dated 16th February 1886
10. Marriage Register for St. Paul's Church, Stratford: ERO., D/P 627/1/11
11. Baptism Register for St. Paul's Church, Stratford: ERO., D/P 627/1/5
12. Halstead Gazette, 9th December 1960
13. Baptism Register for St. John's Church, Stratford: ERO., D/P 601/1/3

Chapter 2 Mark Gentry, his life and public positions

1. NAO., BT 31/3383/20225
2. NAO., BT 31/3910/24707
3. Chelmsford Chronicle, 12th February 1892 and Essex Newsman, 13th February 1892
4. Newham Library, Stratford; List of Councillors 1886 to 1889
5. Essex Standard, 30th March 1889
6. Essex Newsman, 2nd August 1902
7. The British Clayworker, April 1908 p. 11 and Halstead Gazette, 6th June 1912
8. Essex Standard, 3rd November 1888
9. The Colne Valley Chapter No. 2154, attached to the Joshua Nunn Lodge, A Centenary History 1891-1991 by R.W.G. Simmons, C.W.M. Harvey and N.H. Williams, 1991.
10. Essex Standard, 10th November 1888
11. For further information about the Assembly Rooms see, Our Ancestors were Brickmakers and Potters, by Adrian Corder-Birch 2010 pp. 139, 140 & 161
12. Essex Newsman, 17th November 1888
13. Sible Hedingham Land Tax Assessment records, 1866-1922, ERO., D/Z 2/18/24
14. Essex Newsman, 27th October 1888
15. Essex Standard, 5th January 1889
16. Hunt for Machinery – The Rise, Success and Demise of R. Hunt and Company Limited of Earls Colne, 1825-1988, by P. J. Burton-Hopkins, Halstead and District Local History Society, 1995 p. 93
17. Essex Newsman, 30th March 1907
18. Essex Newsman, 4th April 1896
19. Henry Ranger, F.R.H.S., (1858-1937) was Master of the British School at Castle Hedingham and author of the book, 'Castle Hedingham its History and Associations' published 1887. He later wrote 'A Century of Work for the Young' commemorating the work of the Sunday School Union.
20. Essex Newsman, 1st May 1886
21. Halstead Gazette, 16th January 1890
22. Essex Standard, 18th January 1890
23. Our Ancestors were Brickmakers and Potters, A History of the Corder and related families in the clayworking industries, by Adrian Corder-Birch, 2010, pp. 139 & 140
24. Essex Standard, 23rd February 1889
25. NAO., BT 31/35978/57861
26. Essex Standard, 27th April 1889
27. Chelmsford Chronicle, 16th January 1891
28. Viscount Deerhurst (1865-1927) was son and heir of the 9th Earl of Coventry who survived him and the Earldom therefore passed to his eldest son the Hon. George W.R.V. Coventry who had lived at Dynes Hall, Great Maplestead as a young boy.

29. Halstead Gazette, 12th August 1927
30. East Essex and Halstead Times, 12th February 1898
31. The Essex Almanac, 1899 p. 198
32. Chelmsford Chronicle, 12th October 1900
33. Essex Newsman, 15th December 1900
34. Kelly's Directory of Essex, 1899
35. East Essex and Halstead Times, 29th January 1910
36. Sible Hedingham Church Magazines 1904
37. The British Clayworker, April 1898 p. 11
38. Halstead Gazette, 6th June 1912

Chapter 3 Properties owned and occupied by Mark Gentry

1. Census Return 1881: RG11/1705
2. Halstead Gazette, 21st January 1892 and Essex Newsman, 23rd January 1892
3. Ulick John Burke, who was born 29th July 1843, was the third surviving son of James St. George Burke, Q.C., of the Auberies, Bulmer, who died 25th February 1881. Ulick was called to the bar on 30th April 1867 and practiced at 3 Essex Court, Temple, London EC. He married Edith Charlotte, a daughter of Nathaniel Clarke Barnardiston of The Ryes, Great Henny on 5th August 1869. They had a son, Ulick Roland and three daughters, Violet, Kathleen Laura and Dorothy. The family resided at 14 Clarendon Road, South Kensington prior to Rookwoods and later lived at Broxhead Warren, Alton, and The Manor House, Newton Valance, Alton, Hampshire. Ulick was formerly a Captain in the Suffolk Yeomanry Cavalry and later a JP for Essex and Hampshire. He died 12th March 1913.
   Men at the Bar, by Joseph Foster, 1885
   Burke's Landed Gentry, 1894 and 1937
4. Information from the deeds of Rookwoods courtesy of Peter and Sandra Robinson
5. Sale particulars, ERO., B655
6. Essex Standard, 10th November 1894
7. Florence Ellen Sparrow (1855-1937) and Ethel Bertha Sparrow (1862-1943) died on 3rd May 1937 and 28th October 1943 respectively. Another sister, Serena Elizabeth Sparrow (1852-1920) became the third wife of George Courtauld, M.P., J.P., (1830-1920) in 1888. (See, A Centenary History of Halstead Hospital 1884-1984, by Adrian Corder-Birch, Halstead and District Local History Society, 1984 pp. 22 & 76) Their father Basil Sparrow, D.L., J.P., (1820-1880) married Julia Scratton (1826-1897) in 1846 He was a banker with the family bank of Sparrow Tuffnell & Co., a well known Essex bank. He owned the Gosfield Place Estate, which was later inherited by his eldest son Rev. Basil James Harold Sparrow-Beridge, M.A. (1854-1929). Between 1900 and 1908 there was a brickworks, on the estate at Grange Field, Russells Road, Halstead. The Misses Sparrow's youngest brother was Col. Richard Sparrow, C.M.G., D.S.O., F.R.G.S., F.Z.S., M.B.O.U., J.P., (1871-1953) who lived at Rookwoods for some twenty years before moving to Colne Engaine in 1926. For further information and photograph see, A Pictorial History of Sible Hedingham, by Adrian Corder-Birch, Halstead and District Local History Society, 1988, second edition 1996 p. 115.
8. Sale particulars, ERO., B655
9. Kelly's Directories of Essex, 1886 and 1890
10. Robert Hanbury of Poles, Thundridge, Hertfordshire and of The Brewery, Brick Lane, Middlesex was one of the principal landowners in Sible Hedingham.
11. Sale particulars, ERO., B641
12. ERO., D/F 35/7/589
13. Sible Hedingham Land Tax Assessment records 1866-1922, ERO., D/Z 2/18/24
14. Court Books of the Manor of Prayors, Sible Hedingham, 4 vols. 1733-1935, ERO., D/DSm. M17-20 and NAO., MAF 9/90
15. Kelly's Directories of Essex, 1890, 1899, 1902, 1906, 1908, 1910 and 1912.
16. Census Return 1891: RG12/1420
17. NAO., MAF 9/81
18. Essex Standard, 4th May 1889
19. Court Books of the Manor of Prayors, Sible Hedingham, 4 vols. 1733-1935, ERO., D/DSm. M17-20
20. NAO., MAF 9/90

21. Sible Hedingham Land Tax Assessment records, 1866-1922, ERO., D/Z 2/18/24
22. Essex Standard, 28th September 1889
23 Chelmsford Chronicle, 31st January 1890
24. Halstead Gazette, 22nd May 1890
25. East Essex and Halstead Times, 3rd September 1898
26. Land Tax Assessment records for Sible Hedingham 1866-1922, ERO., D/Z 2/18/24
27. Kelly's Directory of Essex, 1895
28. Robert Leabon Curtis (1842-1918), who was born at West Ham, became a surveyor at 8 Union Court, Old Broad Street, London. He was the largest shareholder of the West Ham and Barking Brickfield Company Limited, which was incorporated on 8th March 1875 and voluntarily wound up on 29th March 1882. He later owned two brickworks at Vange, having purchased Vange Hall and some 350 acres of land in 1880. In 1887 he became Master of the Worshipful Company of Tylers and Bricklayers. He was a Director of The Brickmasters Employers' Liability Association Limited and a member of West Ham Borough Council, becoming Mayor in 1888-89. Curtis and Gentry knew each other from the 1870s when they were both associated with the building industry and the municipal affairs of West Ham. In the 1890s they both had offices at London Wall. During the 1890s Curtis owned land at the rear of Hill House, Sible Hedingham, which he sold on 30th June 1897 to Samuel Edgar Van of Hill House and Robert Sargent Carter, grocer and draper of Swan Street and Church Street. This land later became part of six acres belonging to Alderford Grange, when it was sold in July 1950. Curtis designed the Catholic Church, Presbytery and Convent at Dock Road, Tilbury for which Gentry supplied the red facing bricks (See chapter 11)
29. Deeds of Hostage Farm, Sible Hedingham, 1887-1925, ERO., D/DSf/T43
30. Essex Newsman, 23rd January 1892
31. Chelmsford Chronicle, 3rd and 10th June 1892
32. ERO., 35/2/423
33. Essex Standard, 8th October 1892
34. Halstead Gazette, 21st January 1892 and Essex Newsman, 23rd January 1892
35. Chelmsford Chronicle, 4th March 1892
36. Essex Newsman, 13th February 1892
37. Essex Newsman, 20th February 1892
38. Essex Newsman, 21st May 1892
39. The London Gazette, 15th July 1892 p. 4113
40. ERO., D/D5f/T43
41. Essex Standard, 2nd December 1893
42. London Standard, 18th June 1892, Illustrated Police News, 25th June 1892 and Lloyd's Weekly Newspaper, 26th June 1892
43. Lloyd's Weekly Newspaper, 12th February 1893
44. Surrey Mirror, 2nd December 1893
45. Sale particulars ERO., D/DHi T77
46. Information from the deeds of Grove House, courtesy of Andrew Putnam, William Heffernan and the late (Tim) Mortimer William Wakefield Heffernan.
47. The British Clayworker, November 1937 p. xvi
48. Sale particulars of Brook Farm in the possession of the author.

Chapter 4 Mark Gentry, Master Builder, Contractor and Timber Merchant

1. Census Return 1871: RG10/1624
2. Essex Newsman, 13th February 1892
3. Census Return 1881: RG11/1705
4. Stratford, West Ham and The Royal Docks, by Stephen Pewsey, Sutton Publishing Limited, 1996 p. 8.
5. London Land Tax Records 1885-89: LMA/MS/11316/475-478 & TCMR 11316/479
6. Halstead Gazette, 10th June 1909
7. Corporation of London ref: COL/SVD/PL/06/0212, 0213 & 0215
8. The Builder, 21st January 1882 p. 89
9. London Standard, 24th January 1884
10. Morning Post, 27th January 1885.

11. Corporation of London ref: COL/PLD/PL/02/LCM/GM/193 & 196
12. Survey of London: Vol 26: Lambeth: Southern area, by F. H. W. Sheppard (General Editor) 1956
13. The Brick and Tile Gazettes, October 1885 and November, 1885, p. 130
14. The Brick and Tile Gazette, 12th January 1886 p. 216
15. The Builder, Vol. 163, pp. 123, 171 and 486
16. Survey of London, Vols. 31 & 32, St. James, Westminster
17. Corporation of London ref: COL/PL/01/101/C/002, 003 & 006
18. The Brick and Tile Gazette, May 1886 p. 350
19. Corporation of London ref: COL/PLD/PL/02/LCM/ANX/067, 068 & 069
20. The Brick and Tile Gazette, March 1888 p. 276
21. Reynolds Newspaper, 11th November 1888
22. Corporation of London ref: COL/PL/01/194/D/014, 015 & 016
23. City of London Cemetery and Crematorium at Aldersbrook, booklet 2011.
24. Corporation of London ref: COL/PL/01/194/D/014,015 & 016
25. English Heritage Listed Buildings, Newham, Greater London, building ID: 204914 listed 25th October 1984
26. Bill of Quantities for work done by Mark Gentry in erecting artisans' dwellings at Spitalfields, London, 1891, NAO ref: RAIL 227/292
27. British Railways (Eastern Region), GER deeds at Marylebone Station S2/98BA – Misc M. 279
28. Ibid., Misc M. 285
29. Ibid., Misc M. 279
30. Ibid., Misc M. 285
31. Bill of Quantities for work done by Mark Gentry in erecting artisans' dwellings at Spitalfields, London, 1891, NAO ref: RAIL 227/292 (Also see Survey of London, Vol. 27, Spitalfields and Mile End New Town).
32. Essex Newsman, 20th February 1892
33. The Builder, 4th February 1882 p. 149
34. The Builder, 1st April 1882 p. 407
35. The Brick and Tile Gazette, September 1886
36. Halstead Gazette, 21st January 1892 and Essex Newsman, 23rd January 1892
37. London Daily News, 17th March 1892
38. Census Return 1871: RG10/1700
39. Census Return 1881: RG11/1723
40. The Victoria History of the County of Essex, Vol. V1 p. 89.
41. Kelly's Directory of Essex, 1886
42. Kelly's Directory of Essex, 1890
43. London Gazette, 20th October 1896
44. Census Return 1891: RG12/1312. Census Return 1901: RG13/1564. Census Return 1911: RG14/9356 West Ham Schedule No. 321
45. Stratford, West Ham and The Royal Docks, by Stephen Pewsey, Sutton Publishing Limited, 1996 p. 97

Chapter 5 Mark Gentry, master brickmaker

1. Halstead Gazette, 23rd March 1893
2. The British Clayworker, May 1893 p. 40
3. Halstead Gazette, 16th January 1896 and Chelmsford Chronicle 17th January 1896
4. Essex Newsman, 4th August 1906
5. The Brickbuilder, April 1898
6. Advertisements in Kelly's Directories of Essex, 1895, 1899, 1902 and 1906
7. The Brickbuilder, April 1898 p. xiii and May 1899 p. xxviii
8. The Brickbuilder and Cement Maker, April 1907 p. viii
9. The Brick and Tile Makers Directories, 1903 to 1905
10. The Brickbuilder and Cement Maker, May 1903 pp. ix to xii
11. The British Clayworker, June 1912 p. 83

Chapter 6 The Langthorne Brick Works, Sible Hedingham

1. East Essex and Halstead Times, 7th February 1885
2. The name of Langthorne originated from Stratford where the railway station was built on the site of the former Langthorne Abbey. Mark Gentry's builder's yard at West Ham Lane, Stratford was named the Langthorne Works and he clearly used the same name for his brickworks in Sible Hedingham.
3. Henry Ranger the headmaster of Castle Hedingham British School.
4. See A Centenary History of Halstead Hospital, by Adrian Corder-Birch, Halstead and District Local History Society, 1984
5. East Essex and Halstead Times, 19th December 1885
6. Halstead Gazette, 28th July 1887 and Essex Standard, 30th July 1887
7. Halstead Gazette, 24th July 1890
8. Daniel Cornish, C.C., J.P., (1861-1943) later became a master brickmaker at Shenfield, Hutton, Cranham and Wickford, Essex. He was the 'governing' director of Daniel Cornish Limited, brickmakers and gravel merchants, which owned land and a stone pit on part of Sparrows Farm, Sible Hedingham. In 1899 he succeeded in patenting a tool to make a frog in a wire cut brick.
9. Halstead Gazette, 8th January 1891
10. The Brickbuilder, April 1898 pp. ii to iv
11. The British Clayworker, April 1894 p. vi
12. The British Clayworker, August 1894 p. xxv
13. The Brickbuilder, April 1898
14. The British Clayworker, October 1899 p. 225
15. Robert Balls, F.A.I. was a partner in the firm of Balls & Balls, Auctioneers and Estate Agents of Castle Hedingham. He held the appointment of Lords Valuer to several manors including Hedingham Castle, Gosfield Place and Belchamp Hall.
16. William Radley later succeeded Robert Balls as captain of The Joint Castle and Sible Hedingham Fire Brigade. Radley was landlord of the Three Crowns Public House, Forge Green and later of the Bell, St. James's Street, Castle Hedingham.
17. The British Clayworker, April 1908 p. 11

Chapter 7 The Highfield Brick Works, Sible Hedingham

1. The Place Names of Essex, by P. H. Reaney, Cambridge University Press, 1969 p. 446 (Great Maplestead)
2. Court Books for the Manor of Hedingham Upland, ERO., D/DSm M16
3. NAO., RAIL 798/263
4. Memorandum and Articles of Association of the Purl's Hill Brick, Tile and Terra Cotta Company Limited dated 12th April 1898
5. The British Clayworker, June 1899 p. 87
6. Memorandum and Articles of Association of SHRBC dated 22nd December 1919
7. Halstead Gazette, 24th March 1906
8. Halstead Gazette, 23rd February 1911
9. The Brick and Pottery Trades Journal, April 1913
10. The Brick and Pottery Trades Journal, February 1914 p. 79
11. East Anglia in the Twentieth Century, Contemporary Biographies, by W. T. Pike, 1912 p. 603
12. Vintage Steam Owners and Operators of the Colne Valley Area, by Robin A. Harding, Halstead and District Local History Society, 1985 p. 71
13. Deeds of Alderford Farm, Purls Hill and The Grove.
14. Memorandum and Articles of Association of SHRBC dated 22nd December 1919

Chapter 8 Inventions and patents

1. Halstead Gazette, 6th June 1912
2. The Brickbuilder, April 1898 p. iii
3. The British Clayworker, April 1908 p. 11
4. The British Clayworker, July 1893

5. The British Clayworker, May 1894 p. 45
6. The British Clayworker, August 1894 p. 112
7. The British Clayworker, September 1897
8. The British Clayworker, April 1900
9. The British Clayworker, May 1901, p 49
10. Ibid, p 50
11. The British Clayworker, January 1903, p 350
12. The British Clayworker, January 1911, p 241
13. The British Clayworker, November 1907, p xix

Chapter 9 Mark Gentry's employees

1. Our Ancestors Were Brickmakers and Potters, A history of the Corder and related families in the clayworking industries, by Adrian Corder-Birch, 2010, pp 68, 70-74 & 139
2. East Essex and Halstead Times, 17th April 1913 and The British Clayworker, May 1913 p. 80
3. Chelmsford Chronicle, 4th July 1890
4. Halstead Gazette and Times, 25th April 1947
5. Our Ancestors Were Brickmakers and Potters, A history of the Corder and related families in the clayworking industries, by Adrian Corder-Birch, 2010, p 124
6. Halstead Gazette, 14th July 1950
7. Halstead Gazette, 30th May 1952
8. Our Ancestors Were Brickmakers and Potters, A history of the Corder and related families in the clayworking industries, by Adrian Corder-Birch, 2010, pp. 119 & 120
9. Ibid., pp. 94 & 105-108
10. Ibid., pp. 93-98
11. A Pictorial History of Sible Hedingham, by Adrian Corder-Birch, Halstead and District Local History Society, 1988, pp. 113 & 114
12. Halstead Gazette, 30th October 1914
13. Halstead Gazette, October 1953
14. Chelmsford Chronicle, 17th January 1896
15. Essex Newsman, 15th April 1905
16. Essex Standard, 14th March 1891

Chapter 10 Houses and buildings constructed by Mark Gentry at Rookwoods, Hostage Farm and Wethersfield Road, Sible Hedingham and at Nunnery Street, Castle Hedingham

1. Industrial Housing in Essex, by Tony Crosby, Adam Garwood and Adrian Corder-Birch, Essex County Council, 2006
2. Charles Wash (1838-1924) was the sanitary inspector to the rural authority of Halstead Union. He was a builder, contractor and undertaker at Earls Colne where he was assistant overseer and clerk to the Parish Council. He also became inspector of nuisances to Halstead RDC. His elder brother Walter Wash (1837-1924) was the father of Annie Louise Wash (1876-1907) the first wife of Ernest Frederic Corder (1877-1925). See Our Ancestors were Brickmakers and Potters – A History of the Corder and related families in the clayworking industries, by Adrian Corder-Birch, 2010 p. 112.
3. Essex Standard, 2nd April 1887.
4. Land Value Duty Survey 1910: ERO., A/R 2/2/18
5. Department of the Environment List of Buildings of Special Architectural or Historic Interest, District of Braintree, Sible Hedingham, 1984 p. 106
6. Ibid, p. 106
7. Ibid, p. 105
8. Ibid, p. 105
9. Industrial Housing in Essex, by Tony Crosby, Adam Garwood and Adrian Corder-Birch, Essex County Council, 2006
10. Chelmsford Chronicle, 24th April 1891
11. Halstead Gazette, 14th April 1922
12. Halstead Gazette, 25th April 1903

Chapter 11 Buildings constructed with Mark Gentry's bricks

1. The Brickbuilder, April 1900 p. vi
2. The Brickbuilder, April 1898 p. iii
3. The Brickbuilder, April 1900 p. vi
4. The Brickbuilder, April 1898 p. iii
5. The Brickbuilder and Cement Maker, April 1907 p. ix
6. The British Clayworker, April 1908 p. 11
7. Who's Who of British Members of Parliament, Vol. II, 1886-1918
8. Col. Robert W. Edis, C.B., D.L., J.P., F.S.A., F.R.I.B.A., (1839-1927) was a prominent London architect and was President of the Architectural Association for two years. He was a strong advocate of the extended use of terra-cotta for building purposes. His other work included a Ball-room and additions at Sandringham for King Edward VII, alterations and additions at York Cottage for the Prince of Wales later King George V, the Inner Temple Library and the Badminton Club, London and the Conservative Club, Glasgow. Col. Edis was also a traveller, author and artist; many of his sketches of old buildings in Germany, France and Italy were published. The Brickbuilder and Cement Maker, May 1904 p. xiii
9. The British Clayworker, April 1908 p. 11
10. The Brickbuilder, April 1898 pp. iii & iv
11. The British Clayworker, April 1908 p. 11
12. The Brickbuilder, April 1898 p. iii & iv
13. The Victoria History of the County of Cambridgeshire, Vol. 10, 2002, p. 40
14. Kelly's Directory for Cambridgeshire 1929
15. Additional notes: Col. McCalmont revived Cheveley Park Stud in the 1890s. It was nationally famous mainly because of the successes of his horse Isinglass, which has been called 'perhaps the greatest racehorse that ever ran'. He was Patron of the Living, Lord of the Manor and chief landowner of Cheveley. He restored Cheveley Church in 1902 at a cost of about £3,000 and an alabaster tablet in his memory, to which all parishioners contributed, was erected in 1903.
16. Chelmsford Chronicle, 16th September 1898
17. Earls Colne Grammar School Essex A History, by A. D. Merson, M.B.E., M.A., 1975 p. 114
18. Information courtesy of the late Bill Blowers
19. The British Clayworker, June 1897 pp. 57 & 58
20. The Buildings of England, LONDON Vol. One: The Cities of London and Westminster, by Nikolaus Pevsner and Judy Nairn, Third Edition revised by Bridget Cherry, 1981, p. 565
21. 'Brook Street: South Side', Survey of London: Vol. 40: The Grosvenor Estate in Mayfair, Part 2 (The Buildings), 1980, pp. 21-32. (I am grateful to Angela Weatherley for alerting me to this reference).
22. Information courtesy of Tony Minter of Bulmer Brick and Tile Company Limited
23. The Brickbuilder and Cement Maker, August 1907 p. li
24. Essex Newsman, 14th February 1903
25. The Buildings of England LONDON Volume One, The Cities of London and Westminster, by Nikolaus Pevsner revised by Bridget Cherry, Penguin Books Limited, 1973 p. 498
26. During the Second World War, W. H. Gaze & Sons Limited, built over 150 assault craft including some which took part in the D-Day landing.
27. Information courtesy of Peter Minter of Bulmer Brick and Tile Company Limited
28. The Brickbuilder and Cement Maker, January 1903 pp. lxxiv & lxxv
29. The Brickbuilder, April 1900 p. vi
30. The British Clayworker, April 1908 p. 11
31. The Buildings of England ESSEX, by James Bettley and Nikolaus Pevsner, Yale University Press, 2007 p. 783

Chapter 12 The Institute of Clayworkers and Building Trades Exhibitions

1. The British Clayworker, October 1897 p. 163
2. The British Clayworker, May 1898 p. 43
3. The British Clayworker, November 1901 p. 293
4. The British Clayworker, April 1908 p. 11
5. The British Clayworker, May 1899 pp. 45 & 46

6. The British Clayworker, February 1898 p. 263
7. The British Clayworker, October 1898 pp. 186,193 & 194
8. The British Clayworker, December 1900 pp. 338-340
9. The British Clayworker, November 1900
10. The British Clayworker, March 1903 p. 418
11. The British Clayworker, May 1936 p. 60
12. The Brickbuilder, April 1900 pp. ix & x
13. Horace Rendall Mansfield, M.P., J.P., (1863-1914) was MP for Spalding from 1900 to 1910.
14. The British Clayworker, April 1897
15. Ibid, p. 12
16. The British Clayworker, May 1899
17. The British Clayworker, June 1901 p. 103
18. Halstead Gazette, 2nd May 1901
19. The Brickbuilder and Cement Maker, July 1903 p. xxix
20. The Brickbuilder and Cement Maker, April 1907 p. ix
21. The Brick and Pottery Trades Journal, 1st May 1907 p. 251
22. The British Clayworker, May 1910 p. 36
23. The Brickbuilder and Cement Maker, April 1907, p. viii
24. Census Return 1891: RG12/419 folio 26 p. 10
25. Census Return 1901: RG13/1620 folio 53 p. 16
26. Census Return 1891: RG12/1339 folio 60 p. 29
27. Census Return 1901: RG13/1595 folio 19 p. 30
28. The British Clayworker, November 1910 p. 203
29. The Brickbuilder and Cement Maker, April 1907 p. viii
30. NAO., BT 31/19791/113413
31. Post Office London Directory 1913
32. NAO., BT 31/19791/113413
33. Chelmsford Chronicle, 4th December 1903

Chapter 13 H. Greville Montgomery, M.P., J.P., Hon. A.R.I.B.A., (1863-1951)

1. Kelly's Directories of Essex, 1899 and 1902
2. Bakers in Greville Montgomery's time, is now known as Baykers. The name was changed by George Jonah Howell, the owner from 1921 to 1947, to try and stop millers and others sending samples of flour and yeast addressed to G. J. Howell, Bakers, Sible Hedingham, so he put a 'Y' in the name.
3. Sible Hedingham Land Tax Assessment records 1866-1922, ERO., D/Z 2/18/24
4. Sible Hedingham Parish Magazine, January 1905
5. London Land Tax Records 1897 to 1909 ref: LMA/4263/01/0213-0220
6. NAO., BT 31/35978/57861
7. Who's Who 1952, Who Was Who 1951-1960 and Who's Who of British Members of Parliament Vol. II, 1886-1918 p. 253
8. The Times, 4th December 1951
9. The British Clayworker, August 1896 p. 128
10. The British Clayworker, November 1934 p. 233
11. The British Clayworker, February 1918 p. xli
12. The British Clayworker, August 1904 p. 138
13. The Brickbuilder, February 1918, p. xli
15. The British Clayworker, October 1948 p. 162
16. The British Clayworker, December 1948 p. 242
16. The Times, 4th December 1951, The British Clayworker, December 1951 p. 231 and Claycraft, December 1951 p. 190 and April 1952 p. 413
17. The British Clayworker, January 1906 p. 311
18. The British Clayworker, February 1906 p. 349
19. The British Clayworker, April 1906 p. 12
20. The British Clayworker, July 1907 p. 110
21. The British Clayworker, March 1909 p. 346

22. The British Clayworker, October 1909 p. 191
23. The British Clayworker, May 1909 p. 36

Chapter 14 The Alexandra Building Estate at Sible Hedingham

1. Halstead Gazette, 26th July 1902
2. J. Deeks & Son were builders and contractors at Castle Hedingham. John Thomas Deeks was a builder at 72 North Street (now Hedingham Road), Halstead. – Kelly's Directory of Essex, 1902
3. Harry Gooch was a joiner and builder operating from a yard at the rear of his house, Zeerust, Swan Street, Sible Hedingham – For further information see: Our Ancestors were Brickmakers and Potters – A History of the Corder and related families in the clayworking industries, by Adrian Corder-Birch, 2010 p. 74
4. Deeds, ERO., A 9704
5. For further information see: Our Ancestors Were Brickmakers and Potters – A History of the Corder and related families in the clayworking industries, by Adrian Corder-Birch, 2010 p. 42
6. The Altered Apportionment of Tithe Rentcharge under the Tithe Acts 1836 to 1918 dated 18th May 1921
7. Plans, ERO., D/RH Pb 1/18
8. Plans, ERO., D/RH Pb 1/33
9. Plans, ERO., D/RH Pb 1/12
10. Oliver Wallace continued to own the remaining land belonging to Brook Farm and also farmed Cresswells Farm. In addition he hired other land exceeding 33 acres which was part of the Glebe Lands of Sible Hedingham. On 27th July 1915 the Rev. Welby Russell Warburton sold the Glebe Lands covering an area of 62 acres. The majority was purchased by Arthur Frank Gibson, which included 28 of the 33 acres occupied by Oliver Wallace. By the 1920s he had left Brook Farm and moved to Grays Hall. During the early 1900s Oliver Wallace employed Herbert Charles Corder (1888-1970) for a few years at Brook Farm.
11. Deeds – Indenture Henry Greville Montgomery to Jane Gentry 6th November 1908 and Indenture Jane Gentry to Alice Springett 1st December 1908.
12. Central Essex Light Railway Book of Reference revised to May 1908, ERO., C/PP 205
13. The Brickbuilder, December 1926 p. xxxv

Chapter 15 Proposed Central Essex, the Hedingham to Long Melford and other Light Railways

1. East Essex and Halstead Times, 3rd September 1898
2. The Hedingham Brick Industry and the Colne Valley and Halstead Railway, by Adrian Corder-Birch, Colne Valley Newsline, Number 1, Spring 1985
3. Ibid.
4. Proposed Light Railways for North Essex, by Adrian Corder-Birch, Colne Valley Newsline, Number 5, Spring/Summer 1986
5. The British Clayworker, September 1896 p. 152
6. The British Clayworker, August 1896 p. 128
7. Halstead Gazette, 13th August 1896
8. East Essex and Halstead Times, 6th August 1896
9. Chelmsford Chronicle, 31st July 1896
10. Correspondence in the possession of Gestingthorpe Parish Council
11. Central Essex (Ongar, Dunmow and Yeldham) Light Railway, book of reference, plans and Light Railway Order 1897, ERO., D/DWv P21
12. East Essex and Halstead Times, 15th October, 1898
13. Central Essex (Ongar, Dunmow and Yeldham) Light Railway estimate dated 30th November 1897, ERO., D/DWv P21
14. The British Clayworker, December 1897 p. 216
15. Hedingham to Long Melford Light Railway plans, c1898
16. East Essex and Halstead Times, 15th October 1898
17. Robert Balls was a partner of Balls & Balls, Estate Agents and Auctioneers of Castle Hedingham. He was a great nephew of William Mayhew who was Member of Parliament for Colchester in 1831. Robert

Balls was elected Chairman of the East Anglian Branch of the Auctioneers Institute in 1910.
18. East Essex and Halstead Times, 15th October 1898
19. Central Essex (Ongar, Dunmow and Yeldham) Light Railway, plans 1897, ERO., D/DWv P21
20. Hedingham to Long Melford Light Railway plans, c1898
21. Central Essex Light Railway, amended book of reference January 1907, ERO., C/PP197
22. Halstead Gazette, 4th June 1904
23. Central Essex Light Railway (Amendment) Order 1904, ERO., C/PP160
24. Central Essex Light Railway Company, prospectus, August 1909
25. Central Essex Light Railway (Amendment) Order 1906, ERO., C/PP191
26. Central Essex Light Railway Company, prospectus, August 1909
27. Central Essex Light Railway Company, amended book of reference, January 1907, ERO., C/PP197
28. Central Essex Light Railway Company, book of reference revised to May 1908, ERO., C/PP205
29. Central Essex Light Railway Company, prospectus, August 1909
30. Proposed Light Railways for North Essex, by Adrian Corder-Birch, Colne Valley Newsline, Number 5, Spring/Summer 1986
31. Halstead Gazette, 22nd October 1920

Chapter 16 The Burrell Traction Engine and the 'Tin Pot'

1. The Essex County Standard, West Suffolk Gazette and Eastern Counties Advertiser, 7th January 1899
2. Vintage Steam Owners and Operators of the Colne Valley Area, by Robin A. Harding, Halstead & District Local History Society, 1985 p. 74
3. Halstead Gazette, 2nd March 1899.
4. Halstead Gazette, 16th February 1899.
5. Vintage Steam Owners and Operators of the Colne Valley Area, by Robin A. Harding, Halstead & District Local History Society, 1985 pp. 74 & 75
6. Halstead Gazettes, 18th May 1899 and 12th October 1899.
7. Chelmsford Chronicle 29th June 1900 and East Essex and Halstead Times, 30th June 1900.
8. Essex Newsman, 17th June 1905.
9. Halstead Gazettes, 7th and 21st April 1906.
10. Vintage Steam Owners and Operators of the Colne Valley Area, by Robin A. Harding, Halstead & District Local History Society, 1985 p. 75
11. Halstead Gazette, 26th May 1910.
12. Vintage Steam Owners and Operators of the Colne Valley Area, by Robin A. Harding, Halstead & District Local History Society, 1985 p. 75
13. The Clippers is a corruption of the name of Clipt Hedges. It was formerly Quakers Lane and is now Factory Lane East.
14. East Essex and Halstead Times, 4th June 1904 and Vintage Steam Owners and Operators of the Colne Valley Area, by Robin A. Harding, Halstead & District Local History Society, 1985 pp. 48, 49 & 75.
15. Country Architecture, by John Birch, Architect, 1874 pp. 30 & 31 and plates 13, 13A, 14 and 14A. Examples of Cottages, by John Birch, Architect, 1892, pp. 31 & 55 and plate 17
16. Chelmsford Chronicle, 3rd June 1904 and information courtesy of Major Michael Portway, T.D.,
17. Information courtesy of the late Stanley Springett, a son of Harry Springett.
18. Vintage Steam Owners and Operators of the Colne Valley Area, by Robin A. Harding, Halstead & District Local History Society, 1985 p 22
19. Halstead Gazette, 12th February 1898
20. Essex Newsman, 14th February 1903.
21. The British Clayworker, February 1905 p. 351 and Industrial Locomotives of Essex, by Robin Waywell & Frank Jux, Industrial Railway Society 2011, pp. 93 & 94

Chapter 17 Mark John Glover Gentry (1881-1918)

1. Chelmsford Chronicle, 29th January 1897
2. Census Return 1901: RG13/1721
3. Essex Newsman, 22nd November 1902
4. Sible Hedingham Parish Magazine, 1905

5. Kelly's Directory of Essex, 1906
6. Halstead Gazette, 4th June 1904.
7. East Essex and Halstead Times, 17th October 1908.
8. Kelly's Directory of Essex, 1917.
9. A Pictorial History of Sible Hedingham, by Adrian Corder-Birch, Halstead & District Local History Society, 1988, second edition 1996, p. 72.
10. Halstead Gazettes, Summer 1917
11. Halstead Gazette, August 1915.
12. East Essex and Halstead Times, 10th August 1907 and 21st December 1907.
13. Halstead Times and Haverhill Express, 21st April 1917.
14. Census Return 1911: Kennington Schedule No: 184.
15. The British Clayworker, July 1913.
16. Kimberley Lodge was the home of the Stuart family. John Sidey Stuart and Mark Gentry senior were both Churchwardens at Sible Hedingham. Following the death of Mark senior in 1912, his widow later moved to Clacton on Sea. It would appear that Mark junior then lodged with the Stuart family.
17. The British Clayworker, March 1915, p. xiii.
18. Essex Newsman, 12th June 1915
19. Halstead Gazettes, 24th and 31st August 1917.
20. The British Clayworker, January 1918, p. 157

Chapter 18 The Glover family

1. Census Return 1891: RG12/1420
2. Burial Register for St. John's Church, Stratford: ERO., D/P 601/1/40
3. Baptism Register for St. John's Church, Stratford: ERO., D/P 601/1/1
4. Census Return 1881: RG11/1705
5. Census Return 1891: RG12/1350
6. Census Return 1901: RG13/1242
7. Census Return 1911: RG14/2402 Wandsworth Schedule No: 244.
8. Commonwealth War Graves Commission records.
9. The remaining information in this chapter was kindly provided by Michael Glover.

Chapter 19 The Hilton family and Brick Works

1. For further information see Oxford Dictionary of National Biography, Oxford University Press, 2004.
2. Court Books for the Manor of Prayors, Sible Hedingham – 4 vols. 1733-1935, ERO., D/DSm. M 17-20
3. Chelmsford Chronicle, 27th September 1833
4. Chelmsford Chronicle, 21st May 1858
5. Census Returns 1861: RG09/1112 and 1871: RG10/1699
6. Map of Sible Hedingham surveyed by Thomas Savill in 1834, ERO., D/DSm P8
7. Tithe Map and Award for Sible Hedingham 1840 ERO., D/CT 174
8. Court Books for the Manor of Hedingham Upland, ERO., D/DSm M16
9. Directory of Essex 1832
10. Sible Hedingham Churchwarden's Accounts, ERO., D/P 93
11. London Standard, 10th July 1835
12. Court Books for the Manor of Manor of Hedingham Upland, ERO., D/DSm M14
13. Tithe Map and Award for Sible Hedingham, ERO., D/CT 174A
14. Tithe Map and Award for Great Maplestead, ERO., D/CT 231
15. Census Return 1851: HO 107/1784
16. Census Return 1861: RG9/1112
17. Sale particulars of Hawkwood's Farm, Sible Hedingham, 1860 and Ipswich Journal 19th May 1860
18. ERO., D/DSf T35
19. The Story of the Colne Valley, by R. A. Whitehead and F. D. Simpson, Francis Ridgway Limited, 1951, p. 10
20. Halstead Gazette, 18th September 1862. Other directors of The Hedinghams' Gas Company Limited

included Vero William Taylor of Rookwoods, William Munro of Stratford St. Mary who was the contractor for the construction of the CV&HR, James Mayhew Balls, Richard Hall, John Brasnett Fendick and James Knight all of Castle Hedingham.

21. Census Return 1851: HO 107/
22. Census Return 1861: RG9/
23. Halstead Gazette, 26th September 1861
24. Sale particulars, ERO., B 2570 and Chelmsford Chronicle 8th July 1864.
25. ERO., D/F 6/1/17
26. Chelmsford Chronicle, 13th May 1864
27. Court Books for the Manor of Hedingham Upland, ERO., D/DSm M16
28. A forthcoming book about the history of the Cornish family and their brickworks is in the course of preparation, which will include more information about Orbell Cornish and Alder Hall Brick Works
29. Essex Directories, 1882 and 1886
30. Sale particulars, ERO., D/F 35/7/575 and Chelmsford Chronicle 27th April 1883
31. Sible Hedingham Land Tax Assessment records 1866-1922, ERO., D/Z 2/18/24
32. A Centenary History of Halstead Hospital (1884-1984) by Adrian Corder-Birch, Halstead and District Local History Society 1984 p. 73
33. Sible Hedingham Land Tax Assessment records 1866-1922, ERO., D/Z 2/18/24
34. Census Return 1901: RG13/1721
35. Sible Hedingham Land Tax Assessment records 1866-1922, ERO., D/Z 2/18/24

The author is grateful to Dr. Norman Edwards, Mrs. Enid M. Neville Bird, Steven and Alison Horne for some of the information in this chapter about Hilton House and the Hilton family

Chapter 20 The Sible Hedingham Red Brick Company Limited

1. The Memorandum and Articles of Association of SHRBC dated 22nd December 1919
2. Hunt for Machinery – The Rise, Success and Demise of R. Hunt & Co. Limited of Earls Colne 1825-1988, by P. J. Burton-Hopkins, Halstead and District Local History Society, 1995
3. The Memorandum and Articles of Association of SHRBC dated 22nd December 1919
4. The British Clayworker, February 1920 p. 252
5. Deeds of Alderford Farm, Sible Hedingham courtesy of Norman Page
6. Special Resolutions of SHRBC filed with Registrar of Companies 23rd October 1928
7. Information courtesy of the late Albert Redgewell
8. Account books 1924-1939 of Frederick George Bishop, general, mechanical and electrical engineer. ERO., D/F 115/2
9. NAO., RAIL 798/263
10. Halstead Gazette, 29th March 1929
11. Halstead Gazette, 5th September 1947
12. Harold Henry King, J.P., was Chairman of Halstead RDC from 1946 to 1954. He died in office and was buried in Alphamstone where he had lived since 1936. He joined the Sudan Civil Service in 1906 and retired from the Colonial Office in 1932. He represented Alphamstone and Lamarsh on Halstead RDC from 1942 and as Chairman steered the Council through a difficult post-war period.
13. Halstead Gazette, 14th February 1947
14. Central Land Board form for 'Winning and Working of Minerals and Related Development' under the Town and Country Planning Act 1947 dated 13th March 1950
15. Halstead Gazette, 12th January 1951
16. London Gazette, April 1958
17. Halstead Gazette, 5th March 1920

The author is grateful to the late Stephen Ripper for his kind permission to reproduce five family photographs from, Recollections of an old Woodpecker, by H. T. Ripper, 1947.

Chapter 21 Archaeological excavations on the site of the Langthorne Brick Works

1. Kelly's Directories of Essex, 1926, 1929, 1933 and 1937
2. ERO., D/RH Pb1/283
3. ERO., D/RH Pb1/329

4. Lagoon 2 Flood Alleviation Scheme Wethersfield Road, Sible Hedingham Essex Archaeological Trial Trenching and Excavation, Essex County Council Field Archaeology Unit July 2006.
5. Ibid., p. 22

Appendices

Appendix One

1. The Brick and Pottery Trades Journal, December 1900 p. 76
2. ERO., Reference Library Shelf No. 691.4
3. The British Clayworker, November 1948 p. 215
4. The Clayworker, July 1974 p. 23

Appendix Two

1. The author is grateful to his friend, Andrew Leach, for the history of the Montgomery Worldwide companies

Appendix Three

1. NAO., BT 31/35978/57861

Appendix Four

1 ERO., C/E 1/6/16-26

Appendix Five

1. Proposed Light Railways for North Essex, by Adrian Corder-Birch, Colne Valley Newsline, Number 5, Spring/Summer 1986
2. The British Clayworker, August 1898 p. 150
3. Information courtesy of the late David Possee and Lewis Hamilton Joscelyne, M.B.E., whose firm Joscelyne & Sons, auctioneers and estate agents, were actively involved with plans for this proposed Light Railway or Tramway.
4. Halstead Gazette, 17th January 1919
5. Ibid.,
6. Halstead Gazette, 31st January, 1919
7. Halstead Gazette, 6th June and 1st August 1919
8. Halstead Gazette, 13th and 20th June 1919

Glossary

1. Modern Brickmaking, by Alfred B. Searle, Third Edition, Ernest Benn Limited, 1931 and information kindly supplied by Peter Minter

INDEX